DEC   2004

Emeril!

Inside the Amazing Success of Today's Most Popular Chef

MARCIA LAYTON TURNER

WILEY

John Wiley & Sons, Inc.

Published by John Wiley & Sons, Inc., Hoboken, New Jersey
Published simultaneously in Canada

For general information on our other products and services, or technical support, please contact our Customer Care Department within the United States at 800-762-2974, outside the United States at 317-572-3993 or fax 317-572-4002.

Wiley also publishes its books in a variety of electronic formats. Some content that appears in print may not be available in electronic books.

For more information about Wiley products, visit our web site at *www.wiley.com*.

0-471-65626-7

Printed in the United States of America

10   9   8   7   6   5   4   3   2   1

CONTENTS

TIMELINE

1969: At age 10, gets his first job, as a dishwasher at Carreiro's Bakery, in Fall River, Massachusetts; by age 12, he was working there on the full-time night-shift.

1983: Accepts job (at age 23) as executive chef at Commander's Palace, in New Orleans, succeeding Paul Prudhomme.

1990: Opens his first restaurant, Emeril's Restaurant, in New Orleans.

1992: Opens his second restaurant, NOLA, also in New Orleans.

1993: Publishes his first cookbook, *Emeril's New New Orleans Cooking*.

1993: Asked to do first TV show, *How to Boil Water*.

1994: Second TV show, *The Essence of Emeril*.

1995: Opens his third restaurant, Emeril's New Orleans Fish House, in Las Vegas.

1997: Third TV show, *Emeril Live*.

1998: *Good Morning America* offers him a weekly slot as food correspondent.

1998: Opens his fourth restaurant (his third in New Orleans), through the purchase of the 100-year-old Delmonico's, renovated and renamed Emeril's Delmonico.

1998: Opens his fifth restaurant, in CityWalk at Universal Studios in Orlando, Florida.

1998: Opens his sixth restaurant (his second in Las Vegas), the Delmonico Steakhouse.

2000: Introduces Emerilware All-Clad cookware—100+ pots and pans.

2000: Introduces Emeril food products—sauces and spices, etc.

2001: Opens his seventh restaurant (his second in Orlando), Tchoup Chop, with a Polynesian theme.

2001: *Emeril* half-hour sitcom (*Emeril*), which fails quickly.

2002: Introduces Emeril's Classics wines, from Fetzer Vineyards.

2003: Opens his eighth restaurant, Emeril's Atlanta.

2003: Opens his ninth restaurant, Emeril's Miami Beach.

Emeril's Awards and Other Recognitions

1990: Named Restaurant of the Year by *Esquire*.

1991: Best Southeast Regional Chef by the James Beard Foundation.

1991: Listed as one of *Food and Wine*'s Top 25 New Chefs.

1991 and 1997: James Beard Foundation nominated Emeril for Outstanding Chef and Outstanding Service Award.

Received the *Wine Spectator* Grand Award.

1996: *The Essence of Emeril* had become one of the Food Network's highest-rated shows and *Time* magazine named it one of the 10 best shows on television.

1997: The innovative yet informative approach to *Emeril Live* earned a Cable ACE Award from the National Academy of Cable Programming for best original cable programming.

1998: *Esquire* named him Chef of the Year.

1998: *People* called him one of the Most Intriguing People of the Year.

1998: The National Restaurant Association, the major industry association, awarded him the Salute to Excellence Award.

1998: In Las Vegas, Emeril's New Orleans Fish House was named Best New Restaurant by Zagat's and was awarded Best Seafood Restaurant by *Las Vegas Review Journal*.

Early 2000s: Emeril's Delmonico Steakhouse, also in Las Vegas, won Best Steakhouse in *Las Vegas Life* magazine three times.

2003: Emeril's Delmonico in New Orleans received four stars from AAA and the *Mobil Travel Guide*.

2003: Emeril's Orlando garnered Best Restaurant honors from *Orlando* magazine and DiRoNA awarded an Excellence in Dining Award.

2003: Number 85 on *Forbes* list of 100 biggest celebrities.

INTRODUCTION

He is the spirit of what we can all accomplish if we set out to do it.
— Ella Brennan, owner, Commander's Palace Restaurant[1]

I was devastated. I cried, I really cried," Hilda Lagasse explains.[2] How could her son turn down a full scholarship to study at the famed New England Conservatory of Music?! It was the opportunity of a lifetime for someone so musically gifted. An avid percussionist, he had led his high school's drum squad, played in an orchestra, joined a dance band as well as a local Portuguese band and a symphony, and even played percussion for one of Aerosmith's early backup bands.[3] Clearly, he was passionate about his music.

Surprisingly, there was one thing Emeril Lagasse was even *more* passionate about than music: cooking. So instead of accepting a free ride to college, he opted to work his way through the prestigious culinary arts program at Johnson & Wales in Providence, Rhode Island. Although his parents were initially aghast, his father would eventually tell him, "You go for it."[4]

That was in 1976, at the start of Chef Lagasse's illustrious culinary career. Before training at several European and New England restaurants and being selected to take over as executive chef at the well-known Commander's Palace in New Orleans. Before leaving seven years later to start his own restaurant, Emeril's, and being lauded with awards left and right. Before landing a cookbook deal that would make a television producer take notice of his skills and charisma. Before the plethora of Emeril-branded products hit the market. Before Emeril the chef became Emeril the culinary CEO, he was Emeril the musician, the performer.

The Evolution of Emeril's Success

Today, Emeril Lagasse, at age 44, leads a culinary empire worth more than $70 million[5]—by some accounts, as much as $210 million. He has nine restaurants, eight cookbooks, two television shows, one charitable foundation, and a laundry list of branded products. He is listed 85th on *Forbes* magazine's list of the 100 biggest celebrities in America, and personally earns an estimated $6.7 million from his multifaceted private company. From Emeril's Homebase—his company's official name—in New Orleans, he and his team manage his many business activities.

But as you read about how Emeril rose from student to chef to restaurateur to cookbook author, television star, culinary guru, and head of one of the best-known brands today, you'll also see that aside from the money, little about Emeril has changed through the years. He is still a workaholic with a type A personality who loves what he does, an avid learner who is passionate about food, a mentor who has been mentored throughout his career and now wants to return the favor, and a warm and genuine human being who appreciates everything he has earned and is probably even nicer than the persona viewers see on TV.

Throughout his career, Emeril has had several turning points that paved the way for his step up to the next opportunity. One was his decision early on to focus on cooking rather than music as a career, although it certainly was not the easier road. Then, with a degree under his belt and increasingly responsible positions at several French and New England restaurants, the next turning point was Ella Brennan's offer to come to New Orleans and run the legendary Commander's Palace restaurant. After making a name for himself in New Orleans—which is no small feat—and leaving Commander's to start his own restaurant, the next two turning points were the offer to publish a cookbook, thereby transforming Emeril from a regional to a national chef, and the offer to star in his own television show. Establishing a restaurant off his home turf, in Las Vegas, was the next milestone, and, finally, opportunities to develop commercial product lines bearing his name brought Emeril to an entirely different level of business complexity and opportunity.

There were smaller milestones along the way that helped shape his business empire, which you will learn about, each of which positioned him to take full advantage of the next opportunity that presented itself.

But Emeril's success is less about timing and more about shrewd decision making. Being presented with opportunities is not hard; knowing how to respond is.

What if Emeril had decided that he really did not want to leave New England for Louisiana (his first reaction to the chance to run a restaurant in New Orleans)? What if he had not been able to convince a bank to finance his first restaurant? What if he had not accepted his publisher's offer of media training before his first cookbook tour—would the Food Network producer have found him so magnetic? What if he had decided to take advantage of his growing fame and turn Emeril's restaurant into a national franchisor? Or what if he had partnered with manufacturers who could crank out an inexpensive line of cookware in order to boost profits?

These are all realistic scenarios that were overcome for the better due to smart choices, a long-term vision for his company, and a commitment to his core values. These qualities have guided Emeril to achieve the growth and success of his business. But it has not been easy.

In the process of growing a business, Emeril struggled with finding time for his family. Two of his marriages were dissolved, casualties of the focus and stamina it takes to run a multi-million-dollar venture.

So how did a talented young drummer become a world-renowned celebrity chef? That is the story you are about to read.

The Making of a Megastar

In the following chapters, you will read about the young Emeril who divided his time between music and cooking, playing in several bands and working the night shift at a local Portuguese bakery beginning at age 10. When faced with the choice between pursuing a musical career, which he loved, and attending cooking school, he opted to pay his own way through cooking school, his true passion. His acceptance at Johnson & Wales University, practically around the corner from his Fall River, Massachusetts, home, virtually ensured his ultimate success. His drive and determination were that great, even in his teens.

After receiving his associate's degree in culinary arts, Emeril traveled to France to learn more about French cooking. And even when he was not working, he was studying. In his free time, he visited the best restaurants and took notes about the strengths and weaknesses of the operation. With the few dollars left over from his paycheck, he would buy a bottle of wine on Friday night and carefully appraise its flavor, slowly learning about the varying tastes. When he returned to New England to work, he quickly made his mark at each of the restaurants he was assigned to run. He also impressed Ella Brennan, owner of the Commander's Palace restaurant in New Orleans, who offered him an executive chef position he could not turn down. And he was only 23!

What made Emeril such a success in his new position, where he followed in the footsteps of Paul Prudhomme, was his interest in keeping the traditional New Orleans dishes but adding his own special twist. His style became known as "new New Orleans cooking," not to be confused with old New Orleans cooking, and it drew followers immediately. Unlike most brash young chefs who attempted to make their mark by changing everything, Emeril made modest changes that wowed patrons.

After seven wonderful years at Commander's, where Brennan took him under her wing, Emeril decided to start his own restaurant in an underdeveloped part of New Orleans. His strong following, personal stake, and excellent reputation were what convinced a bank to take a chance on his new enterprise, and Emeril's Restaurant was born.

It was an overnight hit. Industry awards and honors rolled in almost immediately—a testament to Emeril's cooking talent and business savvy. With a strong track record of success under his belt, Emeril decided a couple of years later to try again with a new restaurant, NOLA, which is an acronym for New Orleans, Louisiana. This second restaurant was to be less traditional and more experimental with its cuisine. It, too, was an instant hit.

At this point, the name Emeril Lagasse had spread beyond the borders of Louisiana to a major publisher interested in working with him to develop a cookbook. The book tour he would later go on proved to be an important milestone in his career, introducing him to a television producer who was looking for a charismatic chef to host a new cooking show. Emeril got the job.

Unfortunately, he was overqualified for the show, titled *How to Boil Water*. The stilted script and basic recipes hid Emeril's true gifts, his energy and personality. The producers recognized this and proposed a new concept: his own show. *The Essence of Emeril* was born and became the cornerstone of the Food Network's cooking lineup. Two years later the network added a second show, *Emeril Live*, which would revolutionize cooking shows and transform the way America defined haute cuisine.

Now a national chef, Emeril's notoriety and celebrity grew with each show. In the next few years, he would produce several more cookbooks, open new restaurants in cities outside New Orleans (Las Vegas, Orlando, Atlanta, and Miami), star in his own network sitcom, set up his own charitable organization, and partner with manufacturers to develop his own line of culinary products. Recognizing the importance of his brand, Emeril remains closely involved with every aspect of his business, which is now divided into two entities, Emeril's Homebase and Food of Love Productions. From product testing to recipe development to employee training, Emeril is there.

Secrets of His Success

And that is a big reason for his continued success—control. Many of his decisions have been made to ensure continued control over as many facets of his business as possible. For example, rather than give up an ownership percentage to infuse Emeril's Restaurant with cash at start-up, Emeril opted for debt financing and 100% ownership. To reduce the chance that his best employees might someday decide to work elsewhere, he developed a career path that included stints at new restaurants he would open, as well as the eventual opportunity to become partners in one of the restaurants. In negotiations with potential landlords and partners, Emeril ensures that he retains control over the use of his name and likeness. As his star power and the size of his operations has grown, Emeril has become an industry powerhouse—creating and controlling opportunities for himself and those around him.

He also has broken long-standing barriers and assumptions about cooking and business. Sure, male chefs were typical in the world's best restaurants, but cooking at home was still perceived as mainly women's work until Emeril came along. He made it acceptable for men to enjoy preparing meals at home, breaking new ground along the way and establishing himself as a role model for men with an interest in culinary arts. He proved you can be masculine and a gourmet. In addition, he broke some rules when it came to starting and running a business, choosing right off the bat to locate his flagship restaurant in an out-of-the-way spot rather than on a bustling street corner. Electing to serve as an anchor for an up-and-coming neighborhood is an indication of the confidence and vision Emeril has, as well as his willingness to break with tradition in order to achieve unprecedented success.

Being from New Orleans has certainly been a boost. As Emeril's career has blossomed, so has his adopted hometown. Since opening Emeril's Restaurant in 1990, New Orleans has grown into a popular tourist destination, bringing a constant stream of new customers to sample his entrées. The local economic development, fan base, and culinary prestige have certainly benefited Emeril in many ways through the years.

Partnering has also guided his approach to his business, whether in choosing a location for a restaurant, choosing a supplier for his branded products, or hiring and retaining key employees. Emeril shares the wealth of success with partners, generally in return for greater control.

His name, now so familiar that "Emeril" is enough to identify him, has evolved into a personal brand, and beyond, to a sustainable brand. He has transformed cooking from drudgery to entertainment and opened the doors to include men and children. And he has found love again, with wife, Alden, and son, E.J., now a toddler.

Where Emeril goes from here is anyone's guess, but the opportunities are virtually limitless. He has said he wants to keep a hand in the management of his restaurants, which effectively limits the total number he will open. And he has suggested that after his current contract expires with the Food Network, in 2008, he may retire from TV. But new product development, endorsements, e-commerce, and publishing are wide open. Then again, his real love is cooking in his restaurants, where he can witness firsthand the fruits of his labor and the appreciation of his skills.

Building on Failures

Given his amazing success, you may get the impression that Emeril has never made a mistake, that his track record is unblemished. But that is where you would be wrong.

Emeril has made mistakes—some personal, some business-related—all of which have shaped his approach to managing his organization. After experiencing a failure, such as his inability to land a job in Manhattan after graduation from Johnson & Wales, Emeril devised a new strategy for impressing potential employers: Go to Europe for an internship. Following his stint in France, Emeril came back energized and better positioned for success. He responded similarly when his first two marriages failed and his sitcom was canceled. Rather than viewing these experiences as setbacks, he vowed to learn from them and move on, undeterred.

From the public's perspective, those failures made Emeril human. And they love him even more because of them. Everyone roots for the underdog, even if being an underdog is clearly in Emeril's past. His failures have strengthened his brand and his consumer appeal.

Making Things Happen

Emeril began envisioning his life as a successful chef and restaurateur decades ago, even before he began his culinary training in earnest. Over time, that vision evolved into a strategy—the specific tactics and techniques that would create a restaurant, and a career, to rival all others. Above all, Emeril is a visionary who knows what he wants and puts people and resources in place to ensure he gets there. And that constitutes the first part of this book—the strategies he used to position himself for success.

From studying best practices in the restaurants in which he worked to establishing unofficial mentoring relationships with more experienced chefs and restaurateurs to taking calculated risks with large potential payoffs, Emeril methodically evolved from low man on the totem pole to culinary powerhouse.

The second part of the book is about how Emeril implemented that strategy—how he turned his vision into reality and became one of the world's best-known chefs. Although having a business strategy helps set a company up for success, it is the implementation that makes or breaks a business. Emeril is a prime example, developing human resource strategies to deal with the ongoing challenge restaurant owners face regarding turnover, partnering with leading hotels and resorts to create win-win partnerships, and truly relying on his carefully selected and trained staff to manage the day-to-day activities within his nine restaurants as he jets back and forth from city to city.

Emeril does not just talk about running a different kind of business, he truly does it.

Marching to a Different Drummer

Mention the name "Emeril" and you are likely to hear stories of a superb dining experience at one of his restaurants, a fun anecdote about his appearance at a book signing, or a tale about his impressive memory. The stories are all positive, upbeat, admiring. The essence of Emeril.

Enjoy!

1

SEIZING OPPORTUNITIES

Life just doesn't hand you things. You have to get out there and make things happen . . . that's the exciting part.

—Emeril Lagasse[1]

Smells just like my mom's kitchen," responded Emeril Lagasse to Ella Brennan, who had just asked what the 23-year-old thought of the kitchen of Commander's Palace, the legendary New Orleans restaurant she co-owned.[2] Emeril had been invited to tour the kitchen and restaurant back in 1982 as part of a weekend-long interview process with Brennan and her clan. The Brennans were looking for an executive chef to replace Paul Prudhomme, who had left months before to start his own restaurant, K-Paul's Louisiana Kitchen.

It was that answer, coupled with Emeril's talent and enthusiasm, that may have sold Brennan on hiring him. "The enthusiasm, the integrity, the energy, it was all evident," she says. Soon after, the young chef found himself leading the kitchen of one of the top restaurants in all America.

Now running a company worth, by my calculation, somewhere in the neighborhood of $200 million, consisting of nine restaurants, nine cookbooks, two television shows, and a growing list of culinary products and kitchen accessories, not to mention the Emeril Lagasse Foundation, Emeril has achieved a stratospheric business growth rate. From nothing to $200 million in little more than a decade is quite an accomplishment—and a sign that Emeril is not just a chef who happened to be in the right place at the right time. In fact, he is a visionary who knew what he wanted and pursued it from a very young age. And now instead of pursuing opportunities, they are pursuing him.

A Passion for Cooking

Emeril's quick rise to power in the culinary world is not surprising when you look back at his formative years in Fall River, Massachusetts. Born in 1959 to Hilda and Emeril Lagasse Jr. (a.k.a. Mr. John), Emeril was the middle of three children, which also includes Delores, his older sister, and Mark, his younger brother. His French-Canadian father worked at Duro Finishing, a local textile mill, dyeing suit linings, and his Portuguese mother was a homemaker who took great pride in her cooking.

One of Emeril's earliest culinary memories was of helping his mother add vegetables to a soup pot at around age seven.[3] Said Hilda Lagasse, "He wanted to be right there, put the vegetables in. But I would show him how to do it, slowly with a spoon. But sometimes, believe me, he used to get in my way, right in my way. He was always in front of the stove."[4] Even at an early age, Emeril wanted to be in control when it came to cooking.

"My mom and I spent a lot of time cooking together when I was little," he told Parenting.com. "She was so great about letting me help—and much of what I know, I learned from her. Our family life really revolved around the kitchen and eating and cooking together, and it was then that I learned how happy food can make people."[5] That observation—food can make people happy—would evolve into Emeril's career objective years later.

Emeril did not spend his whole childhood in the kitchen, however. He had his own paper route, played baseball, learned karate, and was a Cub Scout, just like most of the boys his age.[6] But unlike most of them, cooking was his favorite activity. "I was kind of viewed as a weird kid because I liked food," he remembers.[7]

One skill that he would carry forward was his comedic side. "Emeril always knew how to make people laugh in any situation," says former classmate John Ciullo. "He was always kind of a class clown. School was sometimes a tense place and he always knew how to make people relax."[8]

He landed his first job at the ripe old age of 10, by convincing Carreiro's Bakery to hire him as a dishwasher. "One of my chores for my mom was, every day, I would have to go down to the local Portuguese bakery and get bread for the table," he explains. The mouthwatering aromas and congenial atmosphere were appealing to Emeril. That routine led to the opportunity to work with the bakers. For a dollar an hour, four hours after school each day, he would work, washing pans. After a couple of years, he was promoted.

Gradually, the bakers entrusted him with more of the baking duties, and Emeril became skilled at baking breads and cakes. Starting with simple muffins and moving on to sweet breads, Portuguese pastries, custards, and cornmeal breads, Emeril learned quickly.

By age 12 he worked at the bakery at night, attended school by day, and slept in the afternoon. "I worked from like eleven o'clock at night to seven in the morning at this bakery. And then I went to school. Then I'd come home at three o'clock from school and my mom would feed me. Then I'd go to sleep. Then I'd get up and go to work at the bakery." Although it was certainly an unconventional schedule for someone his age, Emeril managed to do well at all his endeavors, while maintaining a B-plus average in school.[9]

His work at the bakery had a formative effect on Emeril, who enjoyed making a difference in customers' lives. "I would just see how happy people were when they came into the bakery," he explained to Molly O'Neill in the *New York Times Magazine*.[10] Seeing the pleasure that he could give customers through food increased Emeril's passion for cooking.

Wanting more instruction, Emeril enrolled in a nighttime continuing education class on cake decorating, where he was the only male, and certainly the youngest, he says. "Every week we whipped up frostings and practiced making buttercream roses and violets." Despite his perfectionist streak, Emeril surprised even himself when he took first prize in the class competition. Wondering if he might truly have a knack for cake decorating, he proceeded to enter a big wedding cake contest and won the grand prize for the Northeast region.[11]

Although baking may have been his first love, music was a close second. And Emeril excelled at that, too, from a young age, playing drums in a local 45-member Portuguese band when he was just eight years old, in addition to playing with several other groups. Never one to limit his learning, Emeril also taught himself how to play several other instruments. "I was a percussion major," he explains in a *January* magazine interview, "but I wrote music and played a lot of instruments besides percussion. I taught myself how to play a lot of wind instruments," including the trumpet, trombone, and flute.[12] Always challenging himself, needing to learn more, Emeril developed skills that would make him successful.

In high school, Emeril opted for vocational training in culinary arts at nearby Diman Regional Vocational High School, where he enrolled in 1973 at the age of 14. Even then Emeril was a standout, according to his former teacher, Chef Edward Kerr. "He was very energetic, a go-getter. He performed his assignments, performed them very well. Even back then he had the signs of being an exceptional student," Kerr reports.[13] Another instructor, Paul Amaral, remembers, "He was a good leader."[14]

But he continued his musical pursuits out of school, playing at dances, weddings, and parties with a Top 40 band. Ultimately, it was his musical skill that would be rewarded—with a full college scholarship to the New England Conservatory. In his parents' mind, it was an opportunity he could not afford to turn down.

But he did.

Bettering His Position

Faced with a free ride to college to study music or having to pay his way somewhere else, Emeril took the hard way, but the right way for him. He chose to pursue a culinary career instead.

Being able to make difficult choices is the sign of an excellent leader. Early on, Emeril demonstrated his ability to weigh his options, factor in the pros and cons of each path, and make a choice that he knew to be the right one, ignoring outside opinions or preferences. That is a rare skill in someone so young.

Researchers have found that many gifted students, as Emeril surely was in music and culinary arts, have a difficult time establishing priorities and setting long-term goals because they have several potential career paths, as Emeril also did. But the existence of a mentor, as the Portuguese bakers were for Emeril, had a maturing effect that helped Emeril "develop a vision of what he could become, find a sense of direction, and focus his efforts"—the sign of a successful mentoring relationship, according to Sandra Berger of the ERIC Clearinghouse on Disabilities and Gifted Education.

Dr. Todd Finkle, who runs the entrepreneurship program at the University of Akron reports that, indeed, Emeril's career planning was remarkable. "Most kids have dreams to be something, but most don't follow through on what it is they want to do. For example, 70 percent of kids that get college degrees don't work in the field in which they got their degree.

"So, at such a young age to have already determined that he wanted to be a restaurateur is unusual," Finkle continues. "There must have been some person who had a significant impact on him . . . a mentor." And, in fact, there was. There were several.

Throughout his career, Emeril has been faced with opportunities to be considered, evaluated, and acted on, but none so important as this first one, which led him on his journey.

Choices Count

Although he loved music, his heart was in cooking. So despite his parents' disapproval, in 1977 Emeril enrolled at Johnson & Wales University, in Providence, Rhode Island. "My mom freaked out," remembers Emeril in an A&E television interview. "I think I might have gotten chased around the neighborhood a few times. She just never thought that the cooking thing would stick."[15]

To earn his college tuition, Emeril worked evenings at the Venus de Milo restaurant in nearby Swansee, Massachusetts, where he started as a prep cook and worked his way up to chef de cuisine by graduation.[16]

Although serious about his studies, Emeril still had his own sense of how things should be done, observed one of his friends, Michael Medeiros. Says Medeiros, "He would try to create his own type of recipe. When it was all spelled out for him on paper exactly how much to put in, he would always try to add in an extra spice, or cut back on the water, or add more spices."[17] Even in college, Emeril would try to kick things up a notch. Despite always experimenting, always trying to put his own special twist on a dish, Emeril earned his associate's degree in culinary arts in 1978. Later, in 1990, he would be awarded an honorary doctorate from his alma mater for his contributions to the field of cooking.

The fact that Emeril was able at such a young age to make such a life choice—between two potential career paths he would likely have enjoyed—is unusual. Many teenagers might have been caught up in the prestige of a scholarship and the possibility of a flashy life in a successful band. But Emeril was much more of a realist who knew what would make him happiest long-term—cooking. Such self-knowledge is rare—even rarer at the age of 17. Coupled with the reality that he would be letting his parents down by refusing the music scholarship, Emeril showed great courage and maturity by making the harder choice, the less popular choice. But it was the one he knew would ultimately be right for him.

It is clear that Emeril had a vision, even then, for what he wanted his life to be like. Or at least what he wanted it to include—cooking. Knowing what would be most fulfilling for him careerwise was a critical first step on his way to becoming a world-renowned chef.

Fortunately, his parents eventually calmed down. Emeril's father was the first to concede that his son's choice was probably a good one. He told him, "Listen, Emeril, if you think that this is something you love, which obviously you do, and if you think this is a way you can get a ticket out of here, then you go for it."[18] Getting out of Fall River typically meant getting a college degree and settling in Boston.

After two years in Providence, Emeril headed farther from home, into restaurants and hotels in the northeastern United States, as well as to France, where his real training as a chef began.

A Student of Food

Emeril's first position out of college was in the kitchen of the Sheraton Hotel in Philadelphia.[19] He then headed to New York City but had trouble getting a job because he lacked the right pedigree. "I went to New York City to cook but had trouble there because I was American," explains Emeril. "Americans weren't supposed to know anything about food. . . . At the time, in the mid-seventies, the good New York kitchens were run by French and German and Swiss cooks. It was difficult to get a job."[20]

His solution? Get firsthand training abroad. That led to a three-month apprenticeship in France—in Paris and Lyon—where he started at the bottom again.

Such a decision is classic Emeril. Undaunted by his inability to land a cooking job, he looked for ways to improve his skills, rather than return to his last job and take a step back. Maybe it is ego, maybe it is a well-developed problem-solving ability. Either way, Emeril always manages to find a way around a temporary setback or roadblock. He is always moving forward, and if he cannot move forward, he takes a lateral move in order to make a move up possible later. Unafraid of hard work, Emeril never limits his opportunities initially.

Lacking opportunities to learn in New York, Emeril created a new opportunity in Europe and vowed to make the most of it.

Taking His Education Abroad

His goal for his time in France was to learn everything possible about classic French cuisine, so revered in the top American restaurants. Although he could not change the fact that he was American, to appease the European chefs making the hiring decisions back in the United States he could beef up his resume with European training.

Unfortunately, the French approach to training was rough—rougher than in America. "You got laughed at, you got yelled at, you got treated wrong," describes Emeril. It is "a very European way of operating," he contends. Despite his culinary degree, his French bosses viewed him as inexperienced. "I was beat up and pushed around and shoved and made to do all the grunt work. But that was OK. That was part of it. I didn't speak the language. Didn't make any money,"[21] which was also okay, since he was there not to make a lot of money, but to learn.

The commonly held belief abroad, Emeril discovered, was that "Americans are stupid, we only know about cheeseburgers and

French fries and fried chicken, and we know nothing about real cuisine." Despite the negative stereotype, Emeril persevered, knocking on a lot of doors and getting "kicked in the you-know-what a lot of times," he says about his experience.[22] He took this in stride, recognizing that once he had European cooking experience under his belt, new opportunities would become available back home.

Being American was not his only disadvantage, however. His Portuguese heritage was also seen as a black mark. Explains Emeril in a *Playboy* interview, "In a lot of the fine-dining restaurants the dish washers were Portuguese; they were the inexpensive labor. So I had to cross that road also. 'Oh, you're just a Portugee? You're lucky to be shucking oysters. You should be washing pots.' Fine, I'll wash pots. I just sucked in every piece of knowledge I could," he says.[23]

Emeril never resented having to take on some of the kitchen's more menial tasks; no matter what the role he was expected to play or the unpleasant duty that was assigned him, he resolved to learn everything he could from that experience. Even if it was a better way to clean out a grease trap, Emeril would take away something useful.

His biggest breakthrough, however, was not about the food. It was about connecting with patrons. "The biggest lesson I learned was that it wasn't the foam of a sauce, or the aeration of ice cream, or the glossiness of a sauce," he says. "Those things were great. The lessons coming back for me, which changed the curve, was that we all put our pants on the same way."[24] Emeril says he learned more about "just being a person. . . . That it doesn't matter if you're American, Canadian, Swiss, French, German. . . . I mean, if you love what you do—whether you're an auto mechanic or you sew clothes or you cook—it's all about personal passion and love that really makes the thrust to the level that you want to get it to."[25] At that point, Emeril had decided that cooking was what he *had* to do, what he was meant to do.

Emeril says he also learned "that it's not just food. Food is an equal part of a little formula that encompasses ambiance, service, and a wine program. Food is only one of the four parts, and no one of those parts is greater than the other parts. In Europe, I saw the attention paid to all these little things and I realized there was so much more."[26] This realization would shape how Emeril approached his career and his vision for his first restaurant.

On his return to the States, Emeril spent the next four years continuing his training, quickly moving up the career ladder as he demonstrated his cooking prowess.

Stepping-Stones

He first went to work for a small hotel company, Dunfey Hotels, which owned several properties in New England. There he met one of his mentors, a German chef named Andreas Soltner. "Dunfey ended up buying a hotel that later became one of the original Four Seasons Hotels. I went there as a sous-chef," Emeril explains, and "he became the director of food and beverage, and I ended up taking over the chef's job."[27] Under the tutelage of Andreas, Emeril was groomed to move up the ladder at the company.

Next, he moved to the Parker House in Boston—birthplace of the Boston cream pie, Boston scrod, and Parker House rolls—where he turned his focus to learning about wine and began keeping his own wine journal. "Every week, or whenever my 'Friday' was, I would go buy a bottle of wine for $10 or less. Smell it, taste it, make notes, read about it," says Emeril.[28] In addition to educating him about the many varieties of wine, this self-education process served to increase his enjoyment of them. His appetite for knowledge was unlimited it seemed, as he studied every aspect of what makes a fine meal— including the food, the wine, the atmosphere, and the service.

He then accepted a position working for Wolfgang Puck at the Berkshire Palace Hotel in New York City, where he learned how to work in a high-pressure environment. Although he says they are great friends now, back then "Wolf was very hard on me. I was no one. He was a perfectionist and very talented. But he worked me hard."[29] That perfectionist bent also rubbed off on Emeril.

While working in Manhattan, Emeril used top chefs, such as Alice

Waters, as his role models, studying Chez Panisse and An American Place, among others, and analyzing every facet of each restaurant's success. He made notes on everything from the flatware to the cleanliness of the bathrooms—anything that would impact a guest's dining experience. These notes would later serve as a guide for his own restaurant, which he was already planning, even in the early 1980s.

Mentors, or role models, have played a significant role in Emeril's life, from his mother to the Portuguese bakers in Fall River to Andreas Soltner, who taught him and positioned him for success, to Wolfgang Puck, who showed him what it took to run his own successful restaurant, to Ella Brennan, the major influence in his career. Those relationships were possible only because Emeril was always looking to learn from everyone he met. "Exposure to a mentor who is willing to share personal values, a particular interest, time, talents, and skills . . . can provide both mentor and student with encouragement, inspiration, new insights, and other personal rewards," reports Sandra Berger.[30]

The individuals involved in mentoring Emeril received the satisfaction and fulfillment of making an impact in a young person's life, of influencing what Emeril envisioned for himself. And even so early in his career it was becoming clear that he was exceptional.

Fortunately, Emeril was patient and did not rush to tackle a head chef position right out of Johnson & Wales, or even on his return from France. His focus on learning as much as he could about being a top chef is what prepared him to be one later.

Emeril took his time absorbing every bit of knowledge about the many facets of cooking and running a restaurant, never in such a hurry that he missed an experience, and never skipping ahead to a position he was not ready for. Confident that he would ultimately get there, Emeril appreciated the process of becoming a chef.

Emeril's Big Break

Emeril's next position was as head chef at the struggling Seasons restaurant in Portland, Maine, which was owned by Dunfey Hotels.

In short order, Emeril's cooking and management know-how turned the restaurant around. Impressing his superiors, he was offered a position at another Dunfey property on Cape Cod—Clancy's, where he was given the same marching orders.[31]

It was there, on Cape Cod, that all of Emeril's hard work would pay off. A restaurant recruiter on vacation happened to sample some of Emeril's cuisine and reported back to Ella and Dick Brennan of Commander's Palace in New Orleans that they should take a look at this innovative young chef. Commander's had recently lost its well-known executive chef, Paul Prudhomme, when he elected to open his own eatery. An interim chef was in place for the short term, but the Brennans knew they had to find a permanent replacement. The recruiter thought he had found him. But when approached about considering a job in New Orleans, Emeril was initially resistant, not wanting to leave New England.

Until he learned who was hiring.

By the same token, Brennan was skeptical that Emeril was right for Commander's. "He was young and, in my opinion, inexperienced, and here we had this restaurant that was 'going and blowing,' and doing very well, and oh my Lord, we're going to let this child come in here?"[32] There was plenty of competition for the opening, with many of America's finest chefs applying for the job. But something about Emeril stood out. So she called him to learn more.

Thus began the four-month job interview. "Every week we would talk," says Emeril. "She would say, 'Today I want to talk about what inspires you. Is bread inspiring you? Is a book inspiring you?' Ella is a genius with people. We would talk for a half hour, 40 minutes. The next Wednesday, the phone would ring: 'Today I want to talk about your philosophies about people. How do you motivate people?' "[33] During these phone calls, Emeril would learn about Brennan almost as much as she learned about him. The mutual respect grew.

After grilling him for about 16 weeks, Ella was ready to meet her chef candidate in person. Says Emeril, "The last week she called three times. 'OK, I guess now I'm convinced you deserve a trip down here, but I want you to know, you have to give me a long weekend—not just Saturday and Sunday. I have to have Thursday, Friday, Saturday, Sunday, and Monday, because my family is so big." The Brennan family is a well-known institution in New Orleans, revered for their culinary and management savvy. Many family members are involved with managing the restaurant.

And so began the interview that would change his life. Emeril spent all weekend with the Brennans, culminating in dinner with Ella and her brother, Dick. Recalls Ella, "My brother, Dick, and I sat down and had Sunday dinner with him. And I promise you, we weren't sitting there 15 or 20 minutes when my brother left the table. Next thing you know, I have a phone call—it's my brother calling from the next room, and he said, 'I think he's our man.' I said, 'I do, too.' "[34]

Emeril was hired.

His Own Style

"The enthusiasm, the integrity, the energy, it was all evident," claims Brennan, who is not at all surprised by Emeril's success following his stint at Commander's. "Emeril can do anything he wants to. He has great talent and great energy."[35]

Nonetheless, his first few months on the job as executive chef at Commander's Palace were not easy ones, as he tried to put his own imprint on the operations. So perhaps drawing on his own training in France, where standards are high and chefs volatile, Emeril's early days reflected those experiences. It was not pretty.

"I was a young 26," he says, although when he started at Commander's he was actually 24. "I came in with guns drawn. I lost a lot of people real quick because I was young, but I wasn't stupid. I wasn't going to put up with mediocrity. I began right out of the gate setting standards: No, we weren't going to use canned this. We weren't going to use frozen that. We were going to cook from scratch. I brought in a young sous-chef from France."[36] Whatever it took to make Commander's even better was what Emeril was willing to do, and what he expected everyone around him to commit to. But some of them hadn't banked on the upheaval and change in leadership style that Emeril represented.

Fortunately, he realized that he had a lot to learn and saw that his tactics were not getting the results he wanted. So he turned to Ella Brennan, who became his mentor, for help in managing his staff.

"Miss Ella really influenced me to change my style," admits Emeril. "I had everything going for me, but I was harsh." Unintentionally, Emeril was modeling behavior he had witnessed in Europe, in the French restaurants where he had apprenticed. Instead of attempting to hide his frustrations or anger with his staff, his temper showed his inexperience.

"He did some dumb things," allows Brennan. "Every now and then the adrenaline would be pumping and he would do a little screaming and yelling. I had a yellow legal pad and I would write a note on it, 'You are too damn smart to be so damn dumb,' and I'd tear it off and hand it to him. And he'd look up at me like, 'Why did I do that?'"[37]

Today, however, he says he has "calmed way, way down." He explains, "I didn't know any better because that's how I was trained. She really sort of turned the world around for me—you know, you don't have to be an asshole to people. If you respect people and treat them the way you want to be treated and do it with intelligence and finesse, you could walk into the room wearing a T-shirt and they'll know you're the chef." (Perhaps to test his own clout, Emeril routinely wore T-shirts on the set of *The Essence of Emeril*.) Nowadays, instead of screaming and yelling in public, Emeril is more apt to take someone aside for a chat privately. "I have my sessions where I have to get my point across, but I never do it in public anymore. It's always closed-door."[38]

That does not mean he never has bad days, however. *Cigar Aficionado* reports that a fishmonger who repeatedly tried to sell Emeril fish that did not meet his standards found his entire bale of seafood thrown onto the sidewalk. And a customer who insisted that one of Emeril's waitstaff had misidentified that night's salmon suddenly found Emeril himself standing before him, "brandishing a 15-pound whole salmon, none-too-subtly asking the customer to please enlighten everyone."[39]

High standards were at the root of his temper. "I'm not saying I was a tough guy," explains Emeril. "I just, I would not compromise. I refused to compromise quality, respect, tradition. So it was like, 'Don't bring me bad fish,' 'cause if you brought me bad fish, I would throw it in the middle of the street. . . . I would fire seven or eight or nine cooks, doesn't matter, one shot. Whatever I had to do, whatever it took"[40]—that is what Emeril was ready for.

"Emeril was the type of boss that you gave your all, and if you didn't, you didn't fit into his world," says Eric Linquest, now vice president and general manager of Emeril's Homebase. "Giving your all" was the least he expected. Fortunately, he also gave plenty of recognition for the job well done.

His perception of the type of chef he wanted to become and the type of establishment he wanted to run was clear from the very beginning of his tenure at Commander's. Although his methods may have been rough at the outset, the prestige of working at Commander's and the excitement of witnessing a new chef take over may have convinced some employees to stay. Those who did certainly were privy to an important time in Emeril's development as a chef.

Rather than overhauling the menu at Commander's Palace, Emeril sought to update it, fusing Cajun and Creole cooking with some of the seasonings and techniques from his Portuguese background. Although guests will still find traditional dishes on the menu, such as Louisiana Seafood Courtbouillon filled with wild fish, shrimp, and oysters in a Cajun, or Acadian, sauce, there are more sauceless dishes now, such as Pecan Crusted Gulf Fish, Muscadine and Chicory Coffee Lacquered Quail, and Grilled Veal Chop. Typical New Orleans desserts like Bread Pudding Soufflé are featured, in addition to Lemon Flan, Chocolate Fudge Sheba, or a less sugary cheese plate.

Not wanting to scare away Commander's loyal following with his arrival, Emeril tweaked a recipe here, modified another there, adding his own touch to a top-notch selection, making it even better.

A Valuable Lesson: Recognizing Opportunity

Most critics agree that Emeril the chef is quite talented—his numerous awards attest to that. But Emeril the businessman has received far less press. And, in fact, his abilities as a businessman have fueled that reputation as a chef.

As mentioned, even as a child, Emeril had a unique ability to sense important opportunities and pursue them. After all, how many 10-year-old children do you know who would have the willingness and confidence to persuade the owners of a bakery to hire them? Very few. Even when that job entailed working unconventional hours—overnight—Emeril negotiated an agreement with his mother that as long as he kept up his grades, he could continue his employment.

It may be that his music career, which had him touring with a local band as early as age eight, also fostered his foray into cooking. The experience of working with adults on a regular basis, hearing the applause and appreciation the audience provided, may have led him to understand that he was capable of much more—and gave him the self-confidence to ask for opportunities he wanted.

But again, when it came to choosing a career path, Emeril realized he could not do both music and cooking. So even when he was offered that full scholarship to study music, he recognized that was not an opportunity that was right for him, and he turned it down.

That in itself is unusual, but his decision also taught Emeril a lesson: that sometimes you need to turn down good opportunities in order to pursue great ones. As his career has flourished, Emeril has increasingly had to sort through the good opportunities in order to identify and pursue the extraordinary ones. Many restaurant deals have been rejected and licensing opportunities declined as Emeril has refined his vision for his company, clarifying what it will and will not be, just as he has defined his brand name.

But Emeril has had help in this regard, from his current staff and advisors, all the way back to his early influencers, his mentors.

Benefiting from Mentors

Emeril has had several mentors, most of whom evolved into that role, assuming it informally rather than officially. Either way, the impact of a mentor can be profound, says Rene Petrin, president of Management Mentors, Inc.[41]

The impact of a mentor is twofold, explains Petrin, helping the mentee learn both interpersonal skills and specific tasks and responsibilities. Through a close relationship with a mentor, individuals can build their self-confidence and foster a belief in themselves. "A mentor also provides a vision [the mentee] may not have thought of," says Petrin. The mentor might also share the vision the mentee has already developed. Like the Army motto, a mentor can help someone "be all they can be," says Petrin. Emeril clearly exudes the self-assurance and poise of someone who grew up surrounded by mentors who believed in him.

On top of building interpersonal abilities, a mentor can also teach his or her charge valuable skills, sharing the secrets of success that outsiders do not have access to, explains Petrin. "Mentees learn about the inner workings [of a company or industry] not usually available to the average person." The mentors who most likely did the most to improve Emeril's insider knowledge were the Portuguese bakers and Ella Brennan, both of whom tutored him in the art of running a kitchen, but at different professional levels.

Although not the case with every mentor-mentee relationship, mentors can also move an individual's career along. "Even the most talented individual may not be the most successful," says Petrin, "but most [successful people] have support, such as from a mentor." By virtue of the mentor's access to powerful people, the mentee can be presented with opportunities that would have been out of reach. Such a mentor can be a career champion of sorts, providing encouragement and opening doors.

Interestingly, the most successful mentor relationships are built on chemistry, which is hard to predict and sometimes hard to find. And if chemistry becomes the top criterion for identifying a potential mentor, mentees may limit themselves too narrowly, says Petrin. Looking for compatibility, rather than chemistry, may be more realistic.

His mother was Emeril's first mentor, teaching him the basics of cooking, allowing him to gradually take on more responsibility as she felt he was able, and teaching him basic skills. Much of his family life revolved around cooking and sharing meals, which also served to communicate the value of the art.

His mother encouraged his interest in cooking, allowing him to work in the local bakery from a young age. Rather than stifling his interests, Hilda Lagasse was a role model. She also gave Emeril support and encouragement early on, which helped him become more self-confident and poised.

Building on his cooking experiences at home, Emeril expanded his baking repertoire with the help of the male bakers he worked with. Although at first they may have viewed him simply as a nice neighborhood boy, over time he demonstrated his true interest in their vocation. And they slowly tutored him in how to make various baked goods. His confidence and his knowledge base grew as he did, as he faced a serious choice between his two loves, music and cooking. In this, his mentors certainly played a significant role.

Having worked in a bakery for several years, Emeril's perception of what it took to run such a business was realistic. And he wanted that type of life—a life filled with cooking and food and enjoyment. The baking skills he had learned from his mentors there provided a strong foundation for a career, but their friendship and confidence in him may have actually meant more in the long run.

Once back from his training in France, his boss at Dunfey Hotels mentored him more in the management side of cooking: how to run a successful business. With his support, Emeril was promoted through the organization.

Learning from Culinary Leaders: Wolfgang Puck

Wolfgang Puck was also undoubtedly a role model for Emeril— someone he aspired to be like—and helped shape his concept of what a successful chef looked and acted like. By working Emeril to the bone, he also conveyed the importance of hard work— something Emeril was by now quite used to. But Puck demonstrated to Emeril that it was acceptable to expect that same level of energy and commitment from your staff.

Like Emeril, Wolfgang Puck began his culinary career early in life, inspired by his mother, Maria, who was a hotel chef in his native Austria. He began his formal culinary training at age 14, working in such famous three-star French restaurants as the Hotel de Paris in Monaco, Maxim's in Paris, and L'Oustau de Baumaniere in Provence.

But Puck left Europe in 1973 at the age of 24, taking a job as chef at La Tour in Indianapolis, and moving on two years later to Los Angeles, to become the chef and part owner of Ma Maison. As Emeril was to Commander's Palace and is now to his own nine restaurants, Puck was the star attraction. Melding French, Asian, and California techniques and ingredients, Puck created a signature style that is world-renowned.

In 1981, Puck published the first of his five cookbooks, *Modern*

French Cooking for the American Kitchen (Houghton-Mifflin), which led to the 1982 opening of Spago in West Hollywood, in partnership with his wife, designer Barbara Lazaroff. Immediately successful because of its casual, sophisticated style and cuisine, Spago won rave reviews.

Puck quickly became involved with branded products, commissioning well-known contemporary artists such as Andy Warhol and Richard Meier to design wine labels for the restaurant's own chardonnay and cabernet. However, he didn't really jump in with both feet until 1986, when he released his first video, *Spago Cooking with Wolfgang Puck*. That would be followed by other cookbooks and a line of frozen foods in 1987, through the Wolfgang Puck Food Company. In addition to his food company, Puck also formed WP Productions for the licensing and product-related marketing activities, including his line of cookware sold on the Home Shopping Network. Puck separates his other culinary activities from the restaurant side of his company, and Emeril did the same in his own.

While extending his brand beyond restaurants, Puck was simultaneously growing his restaurant empire. In response to customer demand, Puck opened other Spago branches in Beverly Hills, Palo Alto, Chicago, Las Vegas, and Maui, although the original Spago closed in 2000. Other restaurants include Postrio, Granita, Trattoria del Lupo, and Vert, as well as a chain of Wolfgang Puck Café casual dining restaurants and Wolfgang Puck Express fast-food-oriented eateries. He also moved his catering company, Wolfgang Puck Catering and Events to a larger complex in 2001, positioning it to handle Hollywood's largest special events, and established a base of operations in Chicago, where the company handles events for the Museum of Contemporary Art, among others.

In 2000, Puck developed his own TV show, *Wolfgang Puck*, which airs on the Food Network and won a Daytime Emmy for Outstanding Service Show in 2002. In 2003, later, Puck broke into print media when he originated his own syndicated column, Wolfgang

Puck's Kitchen, through Tribune Media Services in which he shares cooking tips and easy recipes.

Not satisfied to grow his own restaurants, Puck acquired other restaurants as well, including Cucina! Cucina! in the Pacific Northwest.

In many ways a role model for Emeril, whose revenues are dwarfed by Puck's sales of more than $375 million a year, Puck is a hardworking innovator who relies on partnerships and high standards of quality to maintain his brand image. Although he had not yet reached this level of success back in the early 1980s when Emeril and he crossed paths, the similarities in their business strategies suggests Puck surely made an impact.

2

NEW FRONTIERS:
STRIKING OUT ON HIS OWN

We got Emeril when he was 25. He was very talented, but we also Creolized him.
—Ella Brennan, co-owner, Commander's Palace restaurant, New Orleans[1]

I lived across the street from this burned-out building in the Warehouse District and had this burning desire to turn it into my own restaurant," says Emeril. "As a resident, I was frustrated with not having anywhere to go. At the time, there was only one restaurant in the area, a place called Gus', open for breakfast and lunch. So I started thinking it would be great to have a fine dining restaurant in the neighborhood, along with the galleries and other places that have opened up."[2] Converting that warehouse into his own restaurant became Emeril's dream.

At the time, however, he was already employed as head chef at the best restaurant in town—in the nation perhaps—Commander's Palace, and was not sure he was ready to go it alone. So he approached the Brennans about partnering on a new restaurant. Ella Brennan loved the idea but was not as enamored with Emeril's first-choice location as he was; she was set on the more bustling and popular French Quarter. Unwilling to give up his dream, they parted ways amicably and he took a leap of faith, which he named Emeril's Restaurant.

Emeril's arrival at Commander's Palace, in 1982, was the beginning of the next phase of his career and heralded an important shift for the landmark restaurant. Placing the restaurant's success in the hands of a twenty-something talent took guts, but once Emeril arrived on the scene, few observers had doubts that he was the right choice. Reports CNN.com, "He was an immediate hit with the customers and staff of Commander's Palace," minus, of course, those employees he had scared off during his first few months in charge.

Tom Fitzmorris, a long-time New Orleans restaurant critic, remembers, "He was really coming up with fantastic ideas," and he quickly gained a reputation for his unique approach. Says Fitzmorris, "He was hell-bent on making everything from scratch. In New Orleans, he was also the only one doing it." Locals took note of this intriguing new chef they were hearing so much about, and he became a frequent topic of conversation in the area. In New Orleans, notes Fitzmorris, no one talks about sports or the weather; it's the city's restaurants and chefs that provide the entertainment and drama. Consequently, Commander's Palace was on the tip of everyone's tongue back in the 1980s, thanks to Emeril.

Unfortunately, as Commander's star was rising, Emeril's personal life was falling apart. His first wife, Elizabeth, and two daughters, Jessica and Jillian, returned to Massachusetts soon after arriving in New Orleans. The Lagasses divorced in 1983. During that difficult time, Emeril threw himself into his work, focusing even more time and attention on his career and the restaurant.

The result was that Zagat's, one of the nation's leading restaurant guides, named Commander's Palace the most popular restaurant in New Orleans in 1988—the first time the restaurant was so honored. Interestingly, by then Emeril had met and married his second wife, Tari Hohn. Since then, Commander's has earned the "most popular" title every year through 2002, based on input from volunteer diners nationwide.

Having led Commander's for six years, Emeril began to consider opening his own restaurant, weighing the pros and cons. He had seen his predecessor, Paul Prudhomme, leverage his success at Commander's into a popular restaurant of his own and began to wonder whether he could do it as well. Brennan recalls, "He had that urge to go on his own. I'm sure that took many hours of thought. Should I do [it]—give up what I have, take this chance?"[3] He considered the idea for a couple years and, in 1989, decided it was time.

After more than seven years at Commander's Palace, where Emeril learned about running both a kitchen and a restaurant, he was ready to strike out on his own. With Brennan's blessing, he left Commander's in the hopes of starting his own restaurant. According to Emeril, "I wanted to kind of do my own shingle. It was time to do Emeril's philosophy, not just Emeril's food, but Emeril's philosophy. Whether it was 'How are we going to answer the telephone, how are we going to park the valet, how the valet tickets were, what the lighting was . . .' "[4] Emeril's vision for his own restaurant had taken shape, and despite skepticism from those around him, he was sure of what he was doing.

He had been discussing the opportunity to own his own restaurant with Henry Lambert of RCB Builders, which had purchased and renovated a pharmaceutical storage facility in the Warehouse District. The top floors had been converted into apartments, leaving the first floor for a commercial operation. The space, still in need of renovating, was available. It would be a perfect site for a restaurant, suggested Lambert.

Easier said than done, Emeril discovered. Emeril's in the Warehouse District was a hard sell, and he was turned down by nearly every bank in town. But he could hardly blame them, given the neighborhood at the time. "There wasn't even a streetlight back then," says Emeril. "Bums sleeping out, one art gallery. You could shoot a cannon down Tchoupitoulas Street and not hit anybody.

[Skeptics would ask] 'Why is he trading in his Porsche and giving up one of the top-five paying chefs jobs in America? Is he out of his fucking mind?' "[5] Emeril did not think so.

Emeril's commitment to his vision for a restaurant bearing his name eventually paid off when the Whitney National Bank agreed to lend him start-up funds. But not before thoroughly checking out his reputation and prospects for success, going so far as to ask for an assessment from Fitzmorris, the long-time New Orleans food critic, who told the bank, "If there's any chef in this city who's going to be successful, it's him."[6] Soon after, Emeril's loan was approved.

"We started construction on Emeril's in New Orleans in 1989," Tony Cruz, director of finance for Emeril's Homebase tells the *Treasure Coast Palm*. "Emeril basically started out with a small line of credit, about $150,000."[7]

Once he landed the funds he needed to proceed, Emeril invested heart and soul to make the restaurant a reality, working night and day on his plans. From the interior design, which his then-wife Tari created, to the budget, to the kitchen layout, wine list, and customer demographics, Emeril nailed down every detail.

Emeril's life has always been filled with gusto and passion. That passion was reflected in his first restaurant. As his friend Eric Linquest describes the event in an A&E television interview, "He was psyched, he was just psyched. He was energized, we were excited. It was like doing a play. It was, we rushed to the finish, you know, for opening curtain, got all the last details in place just in the last minute, and opened up, and it was exhilarating."[8]

A Valuable Lesson: Be a Trailblazer

Having watched the slow rejuvenation of the post–World's Fair neighborhood in the Warehouse District, Emeril was confident of his location. He lived in the area and recognized its pluses and minuses. The fact that he seemed to be the only person ready to set up shop in a seedier part of town did not bother him either. As we have seen, Emeril was used to breaking new ground and had already distinguished himself in a number of ways.

For one, Emeril was young. He had decided years before that cooking gave him the greatest pleasure—an important career realization to have in one's teens. But he was mature in that respect. From a young age he had traveled, playing in popular adult bands while in grammar school, convincing local bakers to hire him at age 10, and showing his dedication and commitment to his job by working at the bakery until he was in high school. Following culinary training in high school, he went on to earn an associate's degree in culinary arts from a well-respected school. From there he went to work at several East Coast and European restaurants.

In his 20s, he was offered the top job at one of the most prestigious restaurants in the United States. Although Brennan was initially doubtful that someone so young could be talented or experienced enough to follow in the footsteps of the great chef Paul Prudhomme, Emeril convinced her otherwise. By hiring Emeril, Commander's Palace also broke new ground, allowing a relative unknown chef to rule their traditional New Orleans kitchen. It turned out to be an excellent match.

Only a few years later, at age 30, Emeril was ready to move beyond Commander's and put his name on a restaurant. The Small Business Administration says that the average age of most entrepreneurs has traditionally been between 30 and 50, so Emeril was breaking new ground again.

A Different Type of Chef

A big part of Emeril's appeal is his appearance. "He looks like Everyman," explains Samantha Ettus, brand expert and president of Ettus Media Management. "A lot of different groups associate with him."

His dark features look both European and Latin American, although his true roots are French-Canadian and Portuguese. Just as in his cooking, which is an amalgamation of several styles, his own background is a blend.

He does not, however, look like a typical celebrity. And that is part of what makes him so popular. He defies stereotyping or pigeonholing.

Even beyond Emeril the person, Emeril's business ventures also reflect a diverse ethnicity. On his television show, *Emeril Live*, for example, the audience consists of a diverse mix of ages, genders, income levels, and cultures. The band, which consists mostly of African-American musicians, echoes that appreciation for different backgrounds.

In virtually everything he does, Emeril is able to connect with consumers. His ethnicity and respect for other cultures strengthens that connection. He has also made a connection with men that has eluded previous TV chefs.

Before Emeril, the best-known chef in the world was an older white woman, Julia Child, says Ettus. However, traditionally, chefs in fine dining restaurants and high-class hotels have been men. On a professional level, men ruled the kitchens, whereas women did the cooking at home. Despite male domination of fine dining, men who enjoyed working in the kitchen at home were an anomaly. Not anymore.

Emeril's rugged appearance and masculine style have reassured men that it is okay to cook, as well as to enjoy it. In fact, a large percentage of his television viewers are men, which certainly was not the case when Julia Child was on the air years ago.

Emeril has made it acceptable—even stylish—for men to develop their culinary skills. He has bridged the gap between professional chefs and cooks.

He has also bridged the gap between men and women, finding a happy medium that allows him to appeal to both sexes simultaneously.

He exudes machismo for the benefit of men—and women, too, per-haps—and is able to instruct and encourage both genders without offending or patronizing. That is a skill few chefs have.

In addition to being a young man, Emeril's New England roots differentiate him from his born-and-bred colleagues in Louisiana. Even if his looks do not tie him to a particular area or country, his dialect does—that Boston accent comes through whenever he opens his mouth. Just listen when he says "gahlic." So even if he wanted to try to pretend to be a New Orleans native, he could not.

Initially, that may have put some Commander's patrons off—a Yankee heading the kitchen in a traditional New Orleans fine dining establishment? But his cooking quickly eliminated any doubts they may have had about his place in their town.

Despite his Northern roots, Emeril has the charm and manners of a Southern gentleman, says *Esquire* food and restaurant correspon-dent John Mariani, which allowed him to settle in more quickly than most.

Evolving the Traditional New Orleans Cuisine

In a city proud of its culinary prowess, steeped in traditional dishes and resistant to change, it is almost a miracle that a young, innova-tive chef like Emeril succeeded. But his approach was wise beyond his years: evolution, not revolution. He won over the local palates slowly, by tweaking their beloved dishes rather than giving menu items an extreme makeover.

As Ella Brennan's daughter, Ti Martin, explains in her book *Com-mander's Kitchen* (Broadway Books, 2000, written with Jamie Shan-non), "Radical change is simply not what New Orleanians want in their restaurants." Emeril quickly learned this, and applied it to his own culinary repertoire.

Under Brennan's tutelage, Emeril learned about Creole and Aca-dian, or Cajun, cuisine, and how to marry that with his own

Portuguese heritage and cooking preferences. As Emeril explains it, "Fusion is what made me what I am now."[9]

In his cookbook *Emeril's New New Orleans Cooking* (Morrow, 1993), Emeril describes that evolution from traditional to fusion cuisine: "When I first arrived in New Orleans in 1983, everyone was eating Old New Orleans food, meaning wonderful but heavy Creole and Cajun delicacies such as baked, smothered oysters, shrimp remoulade, crabmeat ravigote, stuffed artichokes, thickly rouxed gumbos . . . and bananas Foster. I was the chef at Commander's Palace and my customers loved eating Old New Orleans. I did, too, but I soon grew bored and started experimenting with both the local palate and with the fresh local food products. Gradually I developed a repertoire of what I call new New Orleans dishes: food whose roots are planted in a solid foundation of Creole heritage, but which has grown through exposure to other exotic cultures; Creole reinvented with an Oriental, Portuguese, or New Mexican flourish." Emeril succeeded in melding them into a delicious combination that locals gobbled up.

Cooking from scratch also distinguished Emeril from many of his colleagues, who were willing to take a shortcut here and there in the kitchen. Using fresh ingredients, rather than canned or frozen, set him apart as well. Having grown up with a family vegetable garden, Emeril was used to having access to the freshest produce. Once at Commander's, that became the restaurant's new standard.

Emeril's fame served to boost New Orleans's reputation as a culinary hot spot. Formerly thought of as very traditional, even "stultified," as John Mariani put it, New Orleans garnered new attention with Emeril's debut of his new New Orleans cooking. Paul Prudhomme had tried, unsuccessfully, to transform the Commander's menu with his Cajun recipes, but most locals did not go for it, says Mariani. Conversely, Emeril's fusion of tradition with Creole and Cajun was a hit.

Once on his own, Emeril renewed his commitment to fresh, made-from-scratch dishes and condiments, going so far as to prepare his own Worcestershire sauce and sun-dried tomatoes. He said,

"When I created my own restaurant in New Orleans, I made a vow. I promised myself I would use only the freshest, top-quality products at all times in every dish served at Emeril's, or close the doors. I've never broken this vow."[10]

Building a Reputation for Great Wines and a Modern Ambiance

When it comes to running a fine restaurant, most owners focus initially on the food and service. But Emeril—always up for a challenge—wanted to position his restaurant at the top from the outset. Which meant adding two of the other four linchpins to the mix—wine and ambiance, starting with wine.

On the day it opened, Emeril's had a one-page list of 75 different wines available—a sizeable selection for a brand new restaurant. Within the next three years, that figure doubled, reached 500 by 1995, and 1,200 by 1999. To be sure the restaurant never ran out of a particular selection, those 1,200 different wines were backed by an inventory of 17,000 bottles.

"I was always determined to have a serious [wine] list," says Lagasse. "For years, I put all the profits right into the cellar. I begged the bank for money to buy wine." Boasting that his staff discovers wines that no one in the area has even heard of, Emeril explains, "It's a turn-on and I love it."[11]

Each of Emeril's nine restaurants has selections ranging anywhere from around 700 to 1,000 different wines, overseen by its own sommelier. Emeril also challenges his sommeliers to best each other with their selections and sales. "All the guys are dying to outdo each other," he says. "They all ask me, 'Chef, how much money can I have?' They find what they can, and then they barter with each other for what they want. It keeps them on their toes."[12] It also provides a means of distinguishing each of the restaurants.

Even with just six restaurants, back in 1999, wine revenue alone amounted to more than $8 million a year.[13]

In addition to breaking with tradition on his menu, Emeril opted for an unconventional restaurant design as he worked to master the fourth aspect of a successful restaurant—the ambiance. Says John Mariani, "Emeril's was strikingly modern in a city with very traditional architecture." Never one to play it safe, Emeril had broken new ground with his new business in more ways than one.

Says Tom Fitzmorris, "When Emeril left Commander's Palace, everyone knew he would open his own restaurant." Its opening was the "most eagerly awaited event" for local foodies.

In short order, Emeril's Restaurant was a major success. Although the restaurant's opening night had not been formally announced, there was a line around the block by the dinner hour. Fans from Commander's showed up in droves to sample Emeril's cuisine, capturing the attention of food critics nationwide. One such critic was Mariani, who named Emeril's "Restaurant of the Year" in 1990, just months after it opened. Some restaurants try for years to earn the coveted honor of being named the best restaurant in all of America. It took Emeril only a few short months.

Early Indicators of Entrepreneurial Success

Becoming a business owner was actually a natural evolution for Emeril, who had been training to be a restaurateur since he was a young boy. Although many of the lessons he learned early in life were probably absorbed unconsciously, says Randy Herz, senior vice president of Herz Financial, which specializes in advising America's wealthiest entrepreneurs on their personal financial strategies, Emeril was gaining experiences that would fuel his success later in life.

Several experiences that successful entrepreneurs, such as Emeril, have as youth include the following, according to Herz:

- Future entrepreneurs typically enjoy being in a particular type of environment, whether on a sports field or in a bakery. The things they enjoy being around have an impact on their life later on.
- Future entrepreneurs learn a work ethic that is different from the average person. They learn to work hard to get ahead. No matter what they work on, they work hard to succeed at it, even as children.
- Future entrepreneurs are also very focused and have the mental stick-to-itiveness that allows them to concentrate for extended periods of time on one activity or project.
- Future entrepreneurs are known for juggling many tasks well, which is an extension of their ability to focus.
- Future entrepreneurs have a need to be constantly challenged, to be continuously learning new things.
- Future entrepreneurs learn to face their fears—fear of failure and fear of success—early in life, enabling them to take risks and envision grand success, albeit on a smaller scale at first.

A starting point for this type of learning, says Herz, is having someone the child looks up to and admires—perhaps someone they want to be like, or someone whose lifestyle they aspire to have. "Successful entrepreneurs had someone they look at as a role model," according to Herz. In Emeril's case, it was his mentors—his mother and the Portuguese bakers initially, and, later, teachers at Diman Regional Vocational High School.

As mentioned, one of Emeril's earliest experiences was hanging out at the local bakery. The amount of time he spent at the bakery was significant, as, apparently, was the impact his fellow workers and supervisors had on him. At this stage, although he may not have been thinking that he might want to be a baker or chef, the fact that he associated a bakery with pleasure was a strong foundation for a later business career involving food, comments Herz.

Hard Work

Everyone around Emeril, from his staff to his former employer to his current wife and children, has commented on Emeril's willingness to work hard. His daughter Jessica went so far as to say that he "is your quintessential workaholic; he was always busy. He would go-go-go."[14] Emeril would be unlikely to dispute that observation.

But that work ethic did not kick in suddenly when he started his own restaurant or when he was just getting started in his career. It began during his childhood, when he was learning to play the drums, manage his newspaper route, play sports, and cook. It was that work ethic and energy level that made it possible for him to work several hours a day at the bakery, play in bands on the weekends, and still earn above-average grades in school. Emeril has always been a hard worker.

After leaving Commander's to set up his own restaurant, it took 3½ months, 16 to 18 hours a day, to get ready, during which he did "everything from painting to you-name-it."[15] And he knew that once the restaurant opened, the work required would only increase. He was ready.

Emeril's vision for his restaurant, his plan for his career, did not appear out of thin air. Since his teens, Emeril has been piecing together a visualization of what he wanted his life to be like. And his ability to remain true to that goal, unwavering through the years, is almost the definition of focus.

"Entrepreneurs have the mental focus to work at something for a long time," observes Herz, which seems to summarize Emeril's career history. He has been working at being a chef since around age seven.

It is that focus that has kept him on course for success, rather than being sidetracked by other interests. Focus has also aided his decision making, simplifying the issues to be weighed when considering a move to New Orleans or a jump to his own restaurant. When laid next to his goal of being a chef-restaurateur, his next career move becomes obvious.

On top of the ability to focus on one task until it is completed, successful entrepreneurs are also able to focus on more than one project or activity at a time. This skill does not come naturally, however; it is learned at a young age, says Herz. Over time, children who can focus intently learn to extend that degree of focus to two activities, then three, then more. The same level of attention is given to each endeavor, allowing the entrepreneur to make progress toward his or her goals more rapidly than the average worker, who can concentrate on only one activity at a time.

In Emeril's case, not only does he juggle several profit centers within his business—which includes nine restaurants, two television shows, eight cookbooks, and four major lines of merchandise—he also stays involved in his charity, the Emeril Lagasse Foundation, a nonprofit organization that supports and encourages programs that create developmental and educational opportunities for children.

Emeril oversees several business units while traveling approximately 30 weeks a year, spending 1 week a month in New York to tape his Food Network shows, 1 week in New Orleans, and the remainder in either Las Vegas, Orlando, Atlanta, or Miami, where his other restaurants are.[16] Once in a while, he even finds time to golf, although those opportunities are rare, he admits.[17]

The key to his success in managing his time is being able to quickly jump from one topic to the next without much preparation. Emeril can move from taping a show to conducting a magazine article interview in minutes, without added prep time. He can also monitor the appearance of the salads that come out of one of his restaurants' kitchens while simultaneously instructing new employees or reviewing notes regarding the day's sales. Emeril's energy level and intelligence require constant challenge, which can make it tough for his staff to keep up with him.

In Constant Search of New Challenges

As a by-product of constantly needing to be challenged, entrepreneurs like Emeril may suddenly shift course or commit to a venture or strategy that seems crazy to outside observers. This is typical, says Herz. Once an entrepreneur can envision the next move career-wise or businesswise, it is no longer challenging, he explains. This may be why Emeril elected not to attend the New England Conservatory: Getting in was the biggest challenge; what lay ahead would be less so, suggests Herz. Cooking—now that was a challenge!

Evidence of this need for a challenge crops up repeatedly throughout his career, such as when he decided to head to Europe for a brief apprenticeship—he had already received basic training in the United States and wanted to kick it up a notch, so he went to France. Once there, he was challenged to win over his bosses, who showed no glint of respect for his training thus far. Then he relished the opportunity to lead Commander's Palace so early in his career—a fantastic challenge for a chef.

The need for a new personal test may also explain why he left Commander's after 7½ years. Outsiders might have thought him nuts for leaving a prestigious, well-paying job for the chance to be his own boss, but for Emeril it was breaking new ground. He knew at that point that he could successfully lead Commander's, but could he convince his loyal patrons to follow him to a new restaurant? Could he make his vision a reality and have it succeed? That, he did not know.

True to his need for ongoing challenges, once he was ready to strike out on his own, Emeril did not choose a high-traffic, well-established spot on which to locate his restaurant—a sure thing—he went with the location no one else liked. The questionable, up-and-coming neighborhood that needed a boost was where he most wanted to be. It was a winning decision.

After Emeril's became a success, it was time to expand, to find a new challenge.

No Fear

Emeril's musical talent early in life likely helped him face both his fear of failure and his fear of success. He may have had to get over stage fright or performance anxiety, which many popular musicians have to deal with (and some, like Barbra Streisand still struggle with) as he wrestled a fear of failure.

As he began to succeed, such as when he landed a full college scholarship, he had to decide for himself how to face that success—where to go from there. He had to become comfortable with uncertainty and with choosing from the range of new opportunities that accompany achievement.

Stating that the most important lesson an entrepreneur can learn is the ability to deal with your fears, Herz explains that "you can't, at age 35, suddenly say 'I'm not afraid anymore.' It's not how you're mentally made at that point. All people experience degrees of fear. Successful entrepreneurs face their fear of failure and embrace their fear of success as kids. Success is built on recognizing your fears and managing them to your advantage." In effect, they feel the fear and do it anyway, getting beyond the fear that holds them back.

Clearly, Emeril's childhood experiences readied him for his eventual entrepreneurial success.

Business Skills

Set up for entrepreneurial success early in life, through his role models and personal experiences, once Emeril began pursuing his dream career, he also began learning the skills needed to run a business, says Herz. These include the following:

- Weighing risk and reward
- Gaining independence
- Learning how to use money
- Getting along with people in the business
- Deal making

Weighing Risk and Reward

Average workers may grasp the concept of risk, but fail to see the upside potential. In many corporate environments, risk is to be mitigated or avoided, not pursued or leveraged. Entrepreneurs, on the other hand, deal with risk day in and day out, learning how to use it to their advantage.

This is not to say they are risk takers, but, rather, that entrepreneurs are generally more comfortable with risk. They understand that with risk comes the possibility of reward. Thus, they may weigh outcomes before deciding how to proceed, rather than dismissing risky situations out of hand.

Emeril's decision to leave his full-time position in order to start his own restaurant was risky, and yet he probably could not have envisioned anything else. Most entrepreneurs cannot imagine working for someone else any longer than they have to; as soon as they stop learning, stop being challenged, they are ready to move on. Such was Emeril's situation after more than seven years at Commander's Palace.

Yes, leaving a regular paycheck was risky, but the possibility of independence, total creative freedom, and an even larger paycheck were, in his mind, worth considerable risk. Entrepreneurs simply see opportunities differently.

Gaining Independence

As a group, entrepreneurs are more independent. This is reflected in a number of ways, from disliking the role of employee, to needing a greater degree of control over their life, to making decisions without a committee. Entrepreneurs are confident in their own ability to get things done, which feeds their preference for work that is challenging and self-defined.

Emeril's independence was fostered from an early age, when his interests did not always match those of his classmates, and when his thirst for learning outweighed any need he had to be part of a crowd. Emeril certainly had friends, but he did not follow the pack. That is typical of entrepreneurs.

By the time he landed at Commander's, Emeril was self-confident and independent enough to try to carve out his own niche, his own reputation, rather than simply following the tried-and-true recipes the successful restaurant had always used. He was eager to create his own reputation separate and distinct from the reputations of the chefs who preceded him at the restaurant, and he did that by infusing the cooking with spices from his childhood, as well as introducing new flavors from Asia and South America. The fact that no one else was cooking quite the same way was a plus.

As the challenge of being head chef began to wear off after a few years, Emeril was ready for more independence—his own restaurant. Even in this regard, as he encountered unfamiliar decisions and situations, Emeril remained self-reliant and confident. His colleagues and friends questioned his location choice, and he could have cared less; other, less independent individuals, would have begun second-guessing and questioning their decision. But not Emeril.

Learning How to Use Money

Having spent many hours behind the counter at the Portuguese bakery, Emeril watched firsthand how money was made. He got an early look at business ownership, which may have improved his understanding of how to make a business financially viable. Although he probably did not take notes on the company's profit margins, cost of goods sold, and overhead, watching customer transactions invariably helped him absorb the relationship between profits and expenses.

Later, when he applied for a loan to renovate the bare Warehouse District building that he wanted to house his first restaurant, he was ultimately successful because he could demonstrate why his eatery would do well. Beyond recipes, furniture, and food, Emeril also had very detailed budgets that he used to prove to bank officials that he knew what he was doing. His floor plans, designs, and careful calculations proved his seriousness and his expertise.

He also had determined what was going to distinguish his fine dining establishment from equally good alternatives. One of those aspects was an amazing wine selection. Having studied wine intensely after returning from Europe, Emeril was ready to invest in a product inventory that would make area sommeliers jealous. Here again, he knew that in order to make money, he had to invest money up front to properly stock his restaurant—another risk, but with serious potential reward.

Whereas many individuals view money as a goal, something to strive for, entrepreneurs often see money as a tool to be used to achieve other goals.

Getting Along with Others

Known far and wide for his charm and self-effacing manner, Emeril has the personality of an entrepreneur. He recognizes the importance of personal relationships—and that applies equally to customers, employees, suppliers, fans, and reporters—and works hard to create and strengthen those bonds whenever he can.

Explaining that he tries to treat others the way he prefers to be treated, Emeril seems equally comfortable talking with schoolchildren, his waitstaff, or corporate executives dining in his restaurant. The interpersonal skills gained through his many mentors have helped him charm his way into getting what he wants, whether that is a job at Commander's or a bank loan to start his own business.

Deal Making

Finally, childhood entrepreneurs have an easier time participating in business negotiations, having understood long ago that wheeling and dealing is part of every business relationship.

Emeril applied his familiarity with negotiating when he settled on his salary at Commander's; when he arranged with local suppliers to bring him the freshest meats and produce; when he secured Brennan's blessing to leave Commander's and open his own, competing, restaurant; as well as when he got down to the nitty-gritty in getting his restaurant constructed and staffed within an agreed-upon timetable and budget. Later those deal-making skills were tested as he branched out into licensing agreements, cobranded locations in hotels, and renewed his contracts at the Food Network.

The less comfortable business owners are with bargaining, deal making, and negotiating—whatever term you use—the less control they are exercising over their venture, and the less successful they are likely to be long term.

Without question, Emeril possesses all of these skills that are typical of adult entrepreneurs. Built on experiences he had as a child, Emeril the chef took every opportunity to add to his knowledge base in preparation for that one day when he would have the chance to run his own place. When that day did come, he was ready.

In addition to characteristics typical of a successful entrepreneur, which he clearly is, Emeril possesses traits that have enabled him to break barriers and succeed when others would have failed.

Another Mentor: Ella Brennan's Influence

There are people who enter our lives and change them forever. Ella Brennan was that person for Emeril Lagasse. "With Ella and me, it was love at first sight," he gushes in *Emeril's New New Orleans Cooking*. Where his mother and the Portuguese bakers were culinary mentors, Ella was a business mentor, teaching him the ins and outs of running a fine dining establishment. The two obviously had chemistry, as even Brennan has described it, which explains the major impact she had as his mentor.

Emeril's most significant mentor, Ella Brennan, the "Queen of Creole Cuisine," is different from Emeril's other teachers and role models in that she is not a chef. Famed restaurateur, yes. Culinary pioneer, yes. Cook, no. Claiming that her administrative duties have kept her so busy she has not had time to learn how to prepare haute cuisine,[18] Brennan relies on the talents of an executive chef to lead the kitchen at Commander's Palace. During the 1980s, that chef was

Emeril. Today it is another young talent, Tory McPhail, who succeeded Emeril's protege, Jamie Shannon, after his untimely death.

Brennan started in the restaurant business at age 19 and was
mentored by Roy Alciatore of Antoine's and Max Kreindler of 21.
She actually became involved in food service as a means of helping her younger brother, Owen, who was trying to get started in
business. He had bought a bar, the Old Absinthe House, in New
Orleans, and after noticing that there was a restaurant available
across the street, Owen quickly decided to buy it and run it. He
clearly needed help, and Brennan and the rest of the clan pitched in,
beginning a rich history of family involvement with the New
Orleans restaurant scene.

In 1974, Brennan, along with siblings Dottie, Dick, and John,
purchased the nearly century-old Commander's Palace and devoted
themselves to restoring it and returning its reputation to that of a
stately fine dining restaurant. The interior was renovated and the
dishes updated, offering a blend of Creole and American cuisine.

Of course, Commander's is perhaps best known for its service.
Brennan is credited with setting the bar so high that few other establishments can compete with the warm, gracious, and efficient service the restaurant is known for. Commander's regularly wins
awards, including those proffered by Zagat's, the James Beard Foundation, and *Food and Wine* magazine, among many others. "Trying to
retire," Brennan can still be found pitching in at Commander's on a
regular basis.

3

BANKING ON HIS POPULARITY

For me, it all stems from the food.

—Emeril Lagasse[1]

The opportunity came in the French Quarter, which was basically eight blocks away [from Emeril's Restaurant]. That's when I decided to do NOLA," says Emeril.[2] Of course, he had opened his first restaurant, Emeril's, just two years earlier in the Warehouse District and could barely keep up with demand for his food. Hundreds of guests dined daily at Emeril's,[3] which had been made even more popular by enthusiastic food critics. "It did well and got lots of attention and we were turning people away every night," says Emeril.[4] With Emeril's being named Restaurant of the Year by *Esquire* in 1990 and Emeril himself cited as Best Southeast Regional Chef by the James Beard Foundation the following year, in addition to being listed as one of *Food and Wine*'s Top 25 New Chefs[5] and garnering the *Wine Spectator* Grand Award, Emeril was on a roll.

Restaurant number two, NOLA, which is an acronym for New

Orleans, Louisiana, was an attempt to satisfy his fans' hunger for his food and his employees' need for professional growth. Although still a fine dining establishment, the atmosphere and dress code were more relaxed at NOLA than at Emeril's, and lighter, healthier cuisine prevailed. The quality of cooking was the same—it was the bistro-style, two-story design[6] that was a little different from Emeril's. As one food critic points out, "Emeril doesn't open cookie-cutter eateries";[7] each of his restaurants has its own distinctive style, menu, and ambiance.

Since the two places were within a mile of each other, making sure they were different was a smart move, so as not to cannibalize Emeril's. However, by not copying the formula that made his first restaurant a success, once again Emeril was taking a risk. Would guests come? Would they like it as much as Emeril's? Questions like these must have been spinning in Emeril's head as he prepared to open NOLA's doors.

Innovations in the Dining Experience

In just a few years the Warehouse District was transformed, in good measure because of Emeril's Restaurant. The new eatery spurred more art galleries, other casual restaurants, and increasing renovations of area lofts. In fact, says Patricia Gay, executive director of the Preservation Resource Center in New Orleans, it was subsequent residential development that had the biggest impact on the district's turnaround: "It is actually the residential development that gives the area substance and attracts additional interesting development."[8] Where there were bums before, now there is a bustling neighborhood strong enough to support a thriving fine dining establishment.

On top of rejuvenating an ailing locale outside the walls of the eatery, Emeril also introduced several new concepts designed to enhance his guests' experience inside the restaurant.

One of the innovations at Emeril's was the construction of a chef's food bar, where dinner guests could sit and watch food being prepared in the kitchen, just a few feet away. Planned as a place where single diners could enjoy their meal, the food bar quickly became one of the most popular seats in the house,[9] a seat providing built-in entertainment. At one point, reservations had to be made two or three months in advance to land one of the coveted 10 spots at the counter.[10]

He also went against the grain when it came to smoking. Although cigars were still forbidden in most restaurants in the early 1990s, Emeril decided that they "would help complete a fine dining experience." A cigar fan himself, Emeril began to allow cigar smoking in his restaurant. "What started for local, special customers, long before it was cool to smoke cigars, has evolved into a great part of our dining experience," reports Emeril in a *Cigar Aficionado* interview. "People know when to come if they want to smoke—which means they don't make reservations for 6 o'clock, they come at 10 o'clock, or there's always the bar option."[11] Later, those rules were amended to allow for cigars after the lunch crowd left, around 1:30, and after the dinner crowd simmered down around 10:30.

As cigars became more popular in the 1990s, Emeril's began a special smoker's night, which was frequently sold out even before it was publicly announced. The special event consisted of food and wine pairings selected to complement the selection of cigars,[12] similar to smokers held in other fine restaurants nationwide.

Monitoring dining trends helps Emeril keep his restaurants on the leading edge, providing top-notch food and service, with subtle shifts that mirror new interests on the part of his customers. Whether it is kitchen entertainment, cigars, or a new ingredient that is on everyone's lips, Emeril tries to incorporate it into his restaurants' repertoire.

Even in the earliest days of his career as a restaurateur, Emeril understood what makes a great dining experience for his guests. Although delicious food is at the heart of why people dine out, the entire event consists of much more than just eating. Consequently, Emeril has made sure his restaurants have some of the most extensive wine inventories around (as discussed in Chapter 2), the most accommodating service possible, and the most comfortable seat from which to enjoy the evening's festivities—whether that is at a cozy table in front or an elevated chair at the food bar. Entertainment is part of the package.

Building a seat where customers could watch him in action is also a sign that Emeril was beginning to recognize the power of his popularity. Not only did customers want more of his food, they wanted more of him, personally. And he wanted to accommodate them as best he could.

It was that popularity that pushed him to once again take a risk by opening a new restaurant. Taking a gamble that his fans would want to eat with him even more frequently than they already did, Emeril opened NOLA a few blocks away from Emeril's. Unlike the first restaurant, which was a risk because he didn't know whether fans would follow him from Commander's Palace, NOLA was a risk because he was essentially competing with himself. Would a new restaurant draw guests away from Emeril's and weaken his revenues?

Emeril was sure it would not and, once again, he was right.

Bringing Back Traditional Cajun-Creole Cooking

Where Emeril's featured innovative interior design elements and services to kick the entire dining experience up a notch, NOLA relied on the kitchen for its innovations. Going against the grain of the new and trendy, Emeril elected to feature traditional Creole and Cajun cooking at his newest restaurant. Critics found it refreshing.

Explaining his new concept, Emeril said, "I'm tired of city cooking bastardizing Creole cooking by blackening everything."[13] Perhaps a misinterpretation, or "bastardization," of Paul Prudhomme's Cajun approach, "people who never really experienced New Orleans cooking, who never experienced the ingredients and techniques that have made it one of the true American cuisines for hundreds of years, made up their own ridiculous versions . . ."[14]

In response, Emeril contends that he was "trying to bring back honest Cajun-Creole cooking,"[15] using authentic local ingredients. However, his new New Orleans cooking, as he dubbed his version of the traditional local fare, was also lighter. "Moderation is everything," he explains. "I take health into consideration in my cooking."[16] While other local eateries were piling on the heavy cream sauces and cholesterol-laden entrées that New Orleans is famous for, at NOLA Emeril was creating healthier variations with all the flavor and less fat.

Where more traditional New Orleans entrées might feature a cream sauce or heavy marinade, NOLA's menu items include roasted fish and meats, such as Cedar Plank Roasted Fish of the Day and hickory-roasted duck, as well as NOLA Shellfish Stew, which is Emeril's take on the traditional seafood entrée. Accompaniments are often stir-fried, such as the Black Bean-Bok Choy Stir Fry, or grilled, such as the lemon-grilled vegetables. Nuts are frequently used ingredients, both in salads and as a coating for meats and fishes. The textures and the flavors are rich without being overbearing, always relying on organically grown fresh vegetables.

To ensure access to fresh, organically grown foods, Emeril established a network of more than a dozen farmers, ranchers, and fishermen to supply his restaurants.[17] He even went so far as to raise his own hogs to ensure fresh andouille sausage. Explaining the importance of these relationships, Emeril says, "To have great cuisine, you have to have great products. I spend a lot of time seeking great products and great people."[18]

Once he has discovered those gems, he does everything he can to hold onto them.

An Emphasis on American Foods—Learned from American Mentors

Although Emeril may have been the first chef in New Orleans to rely solely on local suppliers for ingredients, it was Larry Forgione who showed him the way.

Described by Emeril as someone who influenced him considerably, Larry Forgione is perhaps best known for bringing back an appreciation of farm-fresh American foods. His restaurant, An American Place, in New York, served as a role model in many respects for Emeril's own restaurant.

But Forgione did not start out with a passion for cooking, as Emeril did. In fact, he connected with cooking almost by accident. After contracting pneumonia and having to take a semester off from college, Forgione began working at a catering company. It was there that he found his true calling. He then enrolled in and graduated from the Culinary Institute of America in 1974 before heading off to Europe for training in some of the best hotels around. During his two years there, he identified a key weakness of American restaurants: lack of access to the finest ingredients. He wondered, "How come they have everything and we have nothing? Why don't we have chanterelles in the United States? We have oak trees, don't we?"[19]

On his return to the United States, he worked at Regine's before landing the head chef position at the River Café in Brooklyn. It was there that Forgione began cultivating relationships with farmers nationwide in order to gain access to such delicacies as free-range chickens, native buffalo, and native fruits and vegetables. In fact, he guaranteed his network of farmers, producers, and foragers that if they raised the produce and meats he needed, he would buy them.[20] Creating a cottage industry that supplied everything from goat cheese to wild berries to field lettuces, Forgione reintroduced the concept of using only the freshest ingredients for cooking. Through Forgione's concerted efforts, Americans now find homegrown ingredients such as black walnuts, monkfish, American oysters, wild rice, and morels on the menu at white-tablecloth establishments nationwide.

Forgione even started the first free-range chicken farm in 1980 in Warwick, New York, to be sure he would have an ample supply of succulent poultry, coining the phrase to describe the lack of coops to box the chickens in.

It was in 1983 that he opened his signature restaurant, An American Place, on Manhattan's Upper East Side. Its success spawned a cookbook by the same name, published in 1996, that was praised for revitalizing traditional American fare.

Several years later he started American Spoon Foods, which produced jams, sauces, and dried fruits. He also subsequently opened The Beekman 1766 Tavern in Rhinebeck, New York, and The Grill Room on Wall Street. He's been feted with a James Beard Chef of the Year Award as well as an Ivy Award, essentially an award for being best chef as determined by his peers.

Hailed as "the godfather of American cooking," Forgione certainly influenced Emeril's approach to cuisine, inspiring him to establish his own network of local suppliers and to set freshness standards never before seen in New Orleans.

Likewise, Alice Waters, the owner and founder of Chez Panisse, in Berkeley, California, also shaped Emeril's devotion to organic foods and seasonal menus. Her reliance on only fresh ingredients of the highest quality from a network of small suppliers served as another model for Emeril's own approach in New Orleans.

As San Francisco food critic Patricia Unterman observed, "Julia [Child] set the stage for the culinary boom in America by teaching people how to cook, and then Alice Waters took everyone to the next step by teaching about ingredients."[21]

Waters graduated from the University of California in 1967 with a degree in French cultural studies, followed by a stint training at the Montessori School in London and a year traveling in France. On her return, she began teaching children at a Montessori school and cooked for her friends each night for fun. But soon she realized that she enjoyed the cooking so much more that she gave up the teaching and, with a friend, opened Chez Panisse.

Robert Wilson and Stanley Marcus, authors of *American Greats* (Public Affairs, 2000), describe Waters's vision for the restaurant: "Having been to France, she had seen the way a good bistro could become the heart of a neighborhood, a place where people went for comfort and sustenance. She was not a professional cook, but she enjoyed feeding people, and she envisioned a cozy little café, which would be open every day for breakfast, lunch, and dinner, a place where everyone from the dishwashers to the cooks would be well-paid, a sort of endless party where everyone would have fun."

It took her father mortgaging his house and loans from friends, but eight years later, Chez Panisse finally earned a profit and has been doing well ever since. Members of her staff now own shares in the company as well.

From day one, Chez Panisse has served a multiple-course fixed-price menu that changes daily. Two seatings for dinner, which may be reserved up to a month in advance, are available. The café upstairs, which opened in 1980, offers an à la carte menu prepared in an open kitchen, which features a wood-burning pizza oven.

The restaurant has evolved from struggling to extremely successful, from amateur to industry leading—ecologically sound agriculture—with the support of customers and more than 60 local suppliers.

Waters is also the author of several cookbooks, including *The Chez Panisse Menu Cookbook* (Random House, 1982) and *Chez Panisse Vegetables* (HarperCollins, 1996). Like her peers, she has also received numerous culinary awards, most notably being named one of the 10 best chefs in the world by the magazine *Cuisine et Vins du France*, as well as the Best Chef in America, and her establishment was hailed as the "Best Restaurant in America."

Beyond her insistence on fresh ingredients, several of Waters's operating principles seemed to have been adopted by Emeril as well. Her willingness to share the financial benefits that her restaurant provides with her loyal staff is an approach likewise taken by Emeril. He also employs the open kitchen design and seasonal menu variations that are dictated by what is available.

Remaining true to her vision for her restaurant was a key to success for Waters. The same may be said for Emeril.

Creating New Opportunities for His Employees

Although Emeril has been praised for his seemingly innate ability to attract and leverage business opportunities for himself and his company, he is also a master of creating opportunities for the people who work with him. More than just a mouthpiece who talks about the importance of continuous learning, Emeril lives that philosophy. Evidence of that is his willingness to reorganize and reshape his business in order to provide additional training and professional development opportunities for his employees. In fact, one of the main drivers behind NOLA's opening was a need to provide advancement opportunities for key employees.

With extremely low turnover at Emeril's during its two-year run, the lack of openings meant stagnant professional growth for his staff looking to move up in the restaurant's hierarchy. "Most of these people have been with me a long time, and a lot of them have been here from day one," reports Emeril.[22]

Despite the benefits of low turnover, such as lower administrative and training costs, it also has a downside: little upward mobility. "If you're not growing as a business, then your human capital isn't growing," says Marty Kotis, president and CEO of Kotis Properties, a restaurant and real estate development firm. He cites the example of a general manager and assistant manager who have been in place for a few years at a restaurant. Once the assistant manager is capable of tackling the general manager's job, the owner needs to find an opening for the assistant to move into, explains Kotis. "Unless you have other options for them, they'll leave," he says.[23] This is a situation successful business owners commonly face at some point. For Emeril, it took only a couple of years.

His response was to expand his company by opening his second restaurant. As mentioned at the beginning of this chapter, Emeril and his co-owner wife, Tari, decided to expand into space in the French Quarter, which had recently opened up. The building owner was looking for a tenant and made Emeril a deal he could not refuse, forming a partnership that would benefit both. With the landlord's financial help and Tari's interior design expertise, the concept for the 170-seat restaurant was born—and 90 new jobs were immediately created.

"Once you have a successful restaurant," observes Kotis, "you breed your staff," using the existing experienced workers to populate and train new employees at the next restaurant. In addition to being less expensive to have existing employees training new ones, this approach also ensures that the restaurant's policies and procedures are spread throughout all of the restaurants.

"The reason we have more than one restaurant is because I didn't want to put a revolving door by the front door and just become an educational center," explains Emeril. "These people wanted to stay with me. They wanted to be loyal. They wanted to grow. They wanted to make more money. They wanted to go up in position."[24] And he wanted them to have those opportunities.

But perhaps more important than the additional jobs were the new managerial posts, which gave existing and aspiring supervisors the chance to move up within Emeril's organization—some even to the level of partner. "I want people to feel that pride in ownership," he says.[25]

Offering part ownership to key employees is a smart strategy, says Kotis. By giving staff the chance to buy into a restaurant, Emeril was essentially buying their loyalty. In addition to giving these top employees an incentive to stay and benefit from the company's long-term success, the buy-in required to become a partner becomes an added reason not to leave; most agreements stipulate that partners lose some or all of their equity if they leave within a certain amount of time. Such partnership agreements can become golden handcuffs for employees, making it almost unaffordable to leave or, at the minimum, a major disincentive.

Maintaining Success

Shortly after launching NOLA, however, Emeril wisely upgraded the interior at his first restaurant. So as not to lose his regulars to his newest competitor down the street—his own restaurant—Emeril strengthened its appeal. As part of this renovation, he expanded the restaurant, taking over an additional 2,400 square feet that became available next door and redecorating the existing 120-seat main dining room. He divided the added space into a new private dining room that seated 30 guests, a new wine room that seated 12, and more space for the kitchen, which he doubled in size and furnished with new equipment.[26]

Although he was banking on the popularity of Emeril's to make NOLA a success, he hedged his bet by sprucing up his biggest asset. Fully aware of the risk he faced, Emeril approached the situation like the savvy businessperson that he is and managed to win new customers while increasing the amount of business he did with his loyal clientele. In terms of growing his business, he truly covered all his bases.

Experts point out that the three main ways to expand a company are to sell to more (new) customers, increase the value of the sales you do make, or convince your customers to buy from you more often. Emeril managed to combine two of these strategies—selling to more customers and convincing customers to buy from you more often—with NOLA's opening.

On top of that, NOLA began winning industry recognition for its dining experience almost immediately. In its first year of operation, in 1992, John Mariani again bestowed on one of Emeril's restaurants one of *Esquire's* highest honors—Best New Restaurant.

Emeril's capabilities and flexibility as a chef are apparent in his two disparate restaurants. Despite the fact that the locations are a stone's throw away from each other, the two eateries are on opposite ends of the fine dining spectrum.

Emeril's, well-known for its upscale, white-tablecloth atmosphere, serves traditional New Orleans cuisine out of a chic space in the now trendy Warehouse District. NOLA, better known as a more casual bistro, is where more experimental dishes are prepared. And yet both are classic Emeril—serving the best-quality cooking supported by fresh local ingredients, impressive wine lists, and well-trained waitstaff.

Although Emeril initially gained a reputation as an innovative chef during his stint at Commander's Palace, the range of cooking techniques and dishes he displayed at his two restaurants were a hint that Emeril had much more to show his fans.

A Springboard into Cookbooks

Unbeknownst to him at the time, John Mariani would play a pivotal role in Emeril's ultimate success. Yes, he named Emeril's the Restaurant of the Year within a year of its opening, but, perhaps more important, he helped Emeril land his breakout cookbook deal[27] in 1993, just a year after NOLA opened.

Because Mariani bestowed on Emeril the honor of best restaurant in the nation, people outside of New Orleans had now heard of the young chef. His newfound prominence had also caught the attention of the acquisitions editor at William Morrow who had published Mariani's work. At a culinary industry convention in 1992, the editor took the opportunity to be introduced to Emeril and begin to court him as a client. "[Emeril] was in the right place at the right time," says Mariani.[28]

Of course, the fact that hundreds of thousands of *Esquire's* readers had already heard about the phenomenal New Orleans restaurant didn't hurt. Morrow recognized this and quickly signed Emeril to create a cookbook that captured his unique approach to Creole cuisine, titled *Emeril's New New Orleans Cooking*, which was released in April 1993.

To help Emeril get face time with as many of his fans as possible, his publisher planned a three-month, 18-city tour to promote his first cookbook. With Emeril's personality and charisma, his chances of being a success were good. But to be sure, Morrow hired Lisa Ekus Public Relations Co., which specializes in serving the culinary industry, to give Emeril some media training in preparation for the numerous television, radio, and phone interviews he would be asked to conduct.

"I got involved six months before the first cookbook was published," says Ekus, "and was hired to handle the national publicity and launch of *Emeril's New New Orleans Cooking*."[29] That promotional campaign included creating press materials for the book as well as scheduling a large number of TV, radio, and print media interviews, as well as special restaurant events in cities across the country. Essentially, Ekus set up publicity opportunities and media, and then made sure that Emeril was well prepared for all his interviews and appearances.

During his two days of training, Emeril worked to develop skills he would need in order to successfully go in front of the camera—at this stage in his career, he had never been on TV, reports Ekus.[30] The two main areas they focused on during that time were defining his message points and getting him to play to the camera and his audience, which meant getting rid of his "chef's hunch," says Ekus.

Message points, explains Ekus, are like key ingredients. They define in two to three sentences who you are, your credentials, and what your book is all about. Clarifying those message points and practicing how to incorporate them into every interview were two of the main objectives of the media training on which Ekus worked with Emeril.

Getting rid of Emeril's chef's hunch, which is the tendency of most chefs to lean over the stove while cooking, rather than standing up straight and talking to their host, was harder. "Looking up to the host and camera was a big challenge for him," she recalls. "First and foremost, he's a restaurant chef." Today, she observes, he goes back and forth between the dishes he's preparing and playing to his audience,[31] having learned how to balance his rapport with viewers and his need to be involved with the cooking process.

Other issues they worked on included maintaining his energy level while on camera, playing to the camera, and being clear about his message, which was and is, that cooking is more than just the food. It should be fun and it should teach the viewers something.

In the end, Emeril's ability to make a personal connection with virtually anyone who comes into contact with him—on camera or off—created even more opportunities for him. Feeling more confident about his interviewing skills, Emeril was ready and willing to promote his book and his restaurants to audiences everywhere.

Bringing in Reinforcements

With two burgeoning restaurants and a new cookbook, Emeril must have sensed he was onto something big. To make sure he could handle whatever new opportunity was headed his way, he decided to try to bring his biggest fans—his parents—on board as well. So his father and mother gave up their Massachusetts home and moved in, initially, with Emeril[32] in New Orleans to support him in managing his two restaurants; they later got their own place. His then-wife, Tari, was already heavily involved in the daily operations of both locations after having developed and overseen the interior design.

And her parents, the Hohns, had also recently moved to New Orleans, settling in a home about a block away from the senior Lagasses.

Although it was Emeril's mother who long ago inspired him to pursue cooking as a career, it was his father who was assigned the role of chief problem solver at Emeril's and NOLA, assuming the mantra "Whatever It Takes."[33] Mr. John, his dad, now opens up the restaurant each morning and helps keep the operation running smoothly.

A Stepping-Stone to National Exposure

The combination of Emeril's recipes with photos of local dining landmarks and his own perspective on New Orleans culture and cooking was a hit. And Emeril himself was designated unofficial ambassador of New Orleans. As such, it was his responsibility to educate the rest of America regarding Southern cooking. "Folks from other parts of the country believe all New Orleans cooking is heavily fried or blackened,"[34] laments Emeril. His mission is to correct that misconception, replacing it with his own take on New Orleans cuisine.

With an estimated 600 cookbooks hitting the market each year, lesser-known chefs face a significant challenge to build sales. Literary agent Doe Coover explains in a *Publishing Trends* report, "In the nonfiction world, what we've seen for years is that publishers want authors who have a platform, visibility, and a constituency"[35]— someone who is virtually guaranteed to break the 10,000-copy ceiling many books face.

Although Emeril had a regional constituency at this stage in his career, what really boosted the success of his cookbook was the media training he received prior to his book tour. "Authors who are media-genic are going to increase their chances ten-fold of being published and published successful," says publicist Lisa Ekus, who provided Emeril with his media training. Ekus finds that once her clients have gone through media training, they are much easier to book as guests on radio and TV shows, which can have a tremendous impact on a cookbook's sales.

In Emeril's case, he was media-savvy and his career and celebrity were on an upswing—a strong combination. His book tour went extremely well, leading to seven more books over the next 11 years, most of which were national best sellers.

Of course, his first cookbook had the greatest impact on his career. Once it was published, his credibility in the industry rose dramatically and the number of media outlets available to him jumped. It was also one of Emeril's first retail products.

Over the course of the next few years, Emeril the chef became Emeril the star, complete with TV show, restaurants, products, web site, and a track record of publishing success. And with each new level of success, his cookbook sales rose almost in concert. Emeril quickly built his platform—cooking is fun; he scored visibility in dozens of newspaper and magazine articles, TV and radio shows, as well as through public appearances in support of his cookbooks and charity events; and he developed a hard-core constituency sure to buy more of his cookbooks.

Interestingly, since Emeril's first cookbook, the market itself has become polarized between people who want to learn exactly how to replicate a recipe or technique and others who just like looking at the pictures. In fact, cookbook consultant Larry Chilnick reports that the segment of the population consisting of armchair chefs is huge. "There's a gigantic market of cookbook collectors," he says. "Half of the people buy cookbooks because they're collectors"[36]— rather than foodies. They appreciate the product but do not necessarily need to try the recipes.

One marketing tool that has become essential for publishers— and for chefs with cookbooks to hawk—is the Internet. Web sites are now an important tool for marketing and selling books, ranging from behemoth Amazon.com to sites created to sell one particular book. Individual chefs and authors, for example, can fairly easily create a web site to promote and sell their books. And with consumers frequently turning to the Internet to research products and services before making a purchase, as well as for recommendations, it is a necessary channel to be leveraged. It is also a powerful promotional tool that can quickly and efficiently link chefs with fans and potential cookbook buyers. Observes Ekus, "The Internet is a critical place for reaching your niche audience. And it hasn't been embraced nearly as seriously as it should be."[37]

Emeril, for one, is not in that category. His company's web site, Emerils.com, does everything from sell cookbooks to enable guests to make dinner reservations at any one of his restaurants. It also offers a database of recipes and provides personal background information on the chef.

Publishing a cookbook was an important means of leveraging Emeril's success to reach more potential customers and to position him for even greater long-term success.

4

EMERIL'S TIPPING POINT

Chefs that invent cuisine are far different and far more creative, and therefore potential television people, than chefs who are just good chefs.
—Judy Girard, president, Food Network[1]

A single phone call, from a television producer in Nashville, Tennessee, to Emeril in New Orleans one hot August day in 1993 would forever change the chef's future. Producer Alan Reid, of Reid/Land Productions Inc., had an idea for a cooking show and wondered whether Emeril would be interested in shooting a pilot. He was looking for an innovative and talented personality to lead the show and had heard Emeril might be a good fit.

Says Emeril in *Emeril's TV Dinners* (William Morrow, 1998), "When I got the call, I really didn't give it much thought. I was busy with the restaurants, and I had no idea of when I would have the time to go to Nashville where Mr. Reid was headquartered." But he went. Despite having no professional TV experience, the idea of being seen by millions of viewers was appealing to Emeril, who decided to pursue the opportunity.

That decision would vault Emeril into a new league of celebrity chefs. His evolution from chef to restaurateur to author had been methodical but relatively fast—adding television host to his resume would exponentially speed his transformation to celebrity.

The Food Network Comes Calling

Today, more than 10 years later, 80 million homes in the United States[2] and 11 countries have access to the Food Network, the equivalent of 90% of all U.S. cable and satellite households, according to Food Network parent, E.W. Scripps.[3] Its 621,000 average viewers pale by comparison with major networks like CBS, which has an audience of close to 11 million,[4] but it has gained impressive ground each year, with revenues climbing about 60% annually.[5] Ratings have also jumped, with the Food Network achieving a 20% increase from 2001 to 2002,[6] earning it a number one ranking among ad-supported cable networks based on year-to-year subscriber growth.[7]

Started on a shoestring by Reese Schoenfeld (the cocreator of CNN) in 1993, Scripps purchased a controlling interest in the Food Network four years later—which now stands at 70% ownership.[8] The Food Network is now part of the Cincinnati media company's fastest-growing business unit, helping the company post record revenues of $1.5 billion in 2002. Clearly, people are tuning in.

Perhaps more important than audience statistics, however, is the impact the Food Network has had on the American way of life. More than any other media outlet, this cable newcomer has shaped how we view cooking and food, redefining cuisine—haute or not. Transforming the drudgery of food preparation into entertainment, the Food Network has captured our attention in droves. And it has made a megastar out of its first employee, Emeril.

Observes brand expert Samantha Ettus, of Ettus Media Management, "Emeril's brand and the Food Network's brand have grown in parallel. His pilot was one of their first shows. When cable networks became popular and the Food Network launched, that's really when Emeril launched."[9]

How to Boil Water

Back in 1993, as Alan Reid worked to develop a new kind of cooking program, the Television Food Network, as it was then called, was a struggling start-up. Initially, it featured just six hours of shows a day—which it repeated four times to provide 24-hour coverage—for its six million cable subscribers. Some of the episodes were new, while some were reruns featuring such culinary stars as Julia Child and Dione Lucas, who specialized in classic recipes.

Reid's concept was a show named *How to Boil Water*, which was a program for people who knew nothing about cooking. The show was to be hosted by a relatively unknown professional chef teaching very basic dishes. Emeril was perfect.

At the time, Emeril was well known in New Orleans—very well known—but his fame faded the farther from New Orleans he traveled. What the Food Network executives were looking for was a fairly well known chef who could develop his own recipes and connect with the audience. Emeril's personality, energy, and magnetism made him a natural for the part, and he took it when it was offered to him.

Signing on with the Food Network would become a pivotal moment in his career and his business. But it was still a stepping-stone financially. Figures from the Screen Actors Guild, a labor union that protects the rights of performers, lists the going rate for weekly television performances as $2,206 per day back in 2001, the earliest figures it provides. As a beginning television performer with a start-up network, it is likely Emeril's pay was in this range.

Always looking to learn new skills, Emeril tackled his role as television host with intensity, pulling in members of his restaurant staff to assist. Admitting he knew little about television production, Emeril describes the busy time: "I figured what the heck. Here was something that I had never done before and I was willing to give it a try. I thought it would be fun trying to teach the rudiments of cooking. It was tough because we didn't really know what we were doing. Marti [Dalton, his director of marketing] and I were writing scripts and recipes on legal pads in our already-overcrowded restaurant office we shared with managers and chefs. Looking back, it was pretty crazy."[10]

Unfortunately, his TV debut would not be his shining moment. Emeril's lack of television skills and experience was evident in the first few episodes of *How to Boil Water*. In fact, the format showcased his lack of experience by placing him center stage, alone, reading lines from a teleprompter that someone else had written, cooking dishes that someone else had selected. He was stiff, constrained, and awkward—not at all like the Emeril of today. In fact, there was barely a hint of the charisma and charm he exuded in person.

It was obvious he was not enjoying his time on camera, and his discomfort was difficult to watch. Says Emeril, "I wasn't used to scripts and I told them [Food Network producers] to go get an actor to do these shows. I wasn't comfortable and I felt like Dracula with all that makeup."[11]

Not surprisingly, after one season, the show was canceled. But that was not the end of his TV career. Food critic Tom Fitzsimmons observes, "They seemed to recognize the star power they were wasting."[12] As Emeril tells it, "The president of the Food Network called and said, 'Emeril, I've got good news and bad news. The bad news is that we think you're a little overqualified for *How to Boil Water*. The good news is we think you've got some television ability and you're a heck of a cook. We want to try something else.'"[13]

The something else was a show called *Emeril and Friends*, which also failed. Like *How to Boil Water*, it had a predictable script that kept Emeril's true abilities under wraps. Even Emeril admits it was nothing to be proud of: "In the beginning days, when I stunk, there was a reason. Because I wasn't Emeril. Because it was all a script."[14] Finally, executives tried a third program, *The Essence of Emeril*, which gave Emeril the freedom to design the show around his talents.

Third Time Is the Charm

With *The Essence of Emeril*, the producers allowed Emeril to set the pace, choose the recipes, and use his own words—to be himself. Now able to control how his food was presented, Emeril as a television personality blossomed.

Control has been a key success factor for Emeril. In fact, he has experienced his biggest successes when he has controlled his environment. At Commander's Palace, despite the fact that he was in charge of the food served at the restaurant, it was not under his control. He needed to leave and fashion his own place, set his own standards, and create his own menu to really thrive—which he did. His cookbook, which reflected the type of cooking he enjoys most, was a success because it was a work of love. And his TV show, once it became a program he was proud to be associated with, developed a solid fan base quickly. The momentum grew once he hit on a format and presentation style he could call his own.

It was still low-budget, however. Emeril would steal away for a few hours each day to spend time with Anne Kearney, a chef from Emeril's who ran the test kitchen, to develop recipes for the show. Then he would return to the restaurant for the evening shift, while Kearney stayed to type up the material. Some weeks he would hop a late-night plane armed with an ice chest of local goodies—ingredients like crawfish, Creole seasoning, and Steen's Syrup—headed to New York to shoot some episodes.[15]

The production pace was crazy, with Emeril squeezing in taping between management of his two very successful restaurants. To keep time away from Emeril's and Nola to a minimum, Emeril initially scheduled tapings in Manhattan for Sunday, Monday, and Tuesday so that he could be back in town on Wednesday. The team would shoot five shows on Sunday, with Emeril arriving following a late night of cooking in New Orleans, seven shows on Monday, and seven shows on Tuesday.[16] "My schedule was insane," he admits.[17]

Trying to balance his roles as restaurateur and television host was tough, leading to many late nights and a frequently exhausted TV production crew. As the show became more popular, demand for more episodes increased, lengthening Emeril's day as well as his forays into New York City. It was during one of these late-night filming sessions, always without an audience, that Emeril's trademark phrases would emerge. He explains, "We were shooting eight shows a day, 32 shows in a pop. Sometimes 24 to 32 shows in three days so that I could go home. Unheard of! Four, five camera guys, stage manager, sound technician, boom, everybody else is in the control tower. Try doing like eight shows. So it was 'BAM!' to wake 'em up."[18]

The crew's reaction to hearing "BAM!"—jolting them awake and reenergizing them—was just what Emeril wanted. So he started using the term more frequently on the show whenever herbs or spices were called for. By boosting the amount of flavor in the dishes he was preparing, he was "kicking it up a notch," which became another famous catchphrase that he eventually trademarked.

In addition to keeping his crew from sleeping, Emeril's rallying cries also contributed to his gradual-then-sudden fame. As Malcolm Gladwell explains, "The tipping point is the moment of critical mass, the threshold, the boiling point."[19] It was the specific point in time when word of mouth about his cooking—whether through his restaurants, his cookbook, or his television show—gained so much momentum that suddenly audiences could not get enough of Emeril. They mobbed his book signings, jammed his restaurants, and bought his cookbooks hand over fist.

Since his arrival at Commander's in 1982, Emeril had been slowly gaining a reputation as a fine chef. That reputation translated into a solid group of local customers, supplemented with a growing list of out-of-town customers who came to enjoy his cooking. As time went on, Emeril's list of fans grew. But even a decade later, he was barely a national name. He had a popular cookbook that was selling nationally, but personally, he was still considered a regional chef. *The Essence of Emeril* changed that, transforming him from beloved Southern chef into national powerhouse in a matter of months. It took him years to reach that stage in his career and mere days to become a national celebrity.

Deciding to invest time in a pilot television show without any assurances that it would be picked up by the network was a classic Emeril move. He evaluated the situation as most successful entrepreneurs do, recognizing that there was risk involved, mainly involving his time, and saw that the upside potential was huge. Even with the original subscriber base of just 6 million viewers, that was probably 5.5 million more than were currently aware of his culinary talents. It was a step in the right direction when it came to promoting his restaurants, his cooking, and his cookbook.

At first, Emeril probably saw a stint on TV as good for his restaurants. The more people heard his name, the more likely they would be to eat at Emeril's and NOLA. Or for those viewers who could not make it to New Orleans, he now had a way to nationally market his cookbook. Emeril has always been a master of leveraging one marketing channel to benefit others, and this was most likely the case during the first few months of his new gig in New York.

But somewhere along the line, perhaps when *The Essence of Emeril* was created and he was given nearly carte blanche to develop it, Emeril started to see his television career as a stepping-stone to opportunities beyond the restaurants. It was a step toward developing a stand-alone brand with multiple channels. Yes, a successful television show would be good for his retail business, but it could also lead to new business deals separate and distinct from the restaurants. It was then that Emeril, celebrity chef, was born. It would take a couple of years before the rest of the world would catch up to Emeril's new vision for his career, but he saw the potential.

By 1996, everyone else did, too. *The Essence of Emeril* had become one of the network's highest-rated shows, and *Time* magazine named it one of the 10 best shows on television.[20] Emeril's notoriety as a professional chef, a talented chef, was suddenly eclipsed by his new image as a television star. At that point, he was known as the star of a cooking show first and foremost, not as the owner and chef of two of the country's best restaurants. However, instead of being frustrated by that shift, as many chefs would be, he focused on the enormous opportunity his new role presented. In front of millions of households on a daily basis, Emeril had the chance to teach viewers about cooking—his style of cooking.

The Essence of Emeril's success on the Food Network was the tipping point for the next phase of Emeril's career—the final impetus that propelled him from well-known to celebrity status. But it was still hard work.

Emeril's Personality Shines

After he had a couple of years of *The Essence of Emeril* under his belt, network executives decided Emeril was capable of even more. But rather than replace the very successful existing show, they wanted to supplement it with a second one. The format, however, was in question.

That question would be answered during a special taping of a show promoting his second cookbook, *Louisiana Real and Rustic* (Morrow Cookbooks, 1996). A new cooking game show was about to debut, and the network had rented a studio for production. Someone on the team suggested taping two one-hour shows to help promote Emeril's new book and make use of the space when it was not otherwise occupied.[21] Given only two weeks to pull it together, the production crew built a new set, planned menus, and decided to invite a live studio audience to participate.

Not sure what taping in front of a live audience would be like, Emeril was shocked at the enthusiastic reaction. "I'll never forget pulling up in the taxi and there's a line out the studio door and I'm like, 'What the heck's going on here? Jerry Springer?' "[22] he asked. No, fans were lined up to see him.

As taping began and Emeril ran out onto the stage, the crowd erupted in enthusiasm. Pumped by the audience's energy, Emeril performed like never before. And the Food Network had their new format, which would become *Emeril Live*.

Filming of *Emeril Live* started in January 1997—while *The Essence of Emeril* continued—and the show immediately differed greatly from its predecessor in several ways: It was an hour long, versus a half hour; it focused on more than one dish; it featured a jazz band and a live studio audience of 200 (sometimes screaming) fans.[23] Of course, the audience was the one element that made all the difference for Emeril. As he says, "That's when the magic came."[24]

The show was a hit, mainly because Emeril felt at home. He explains, "This is what cooking is all about, at least for me. You get to see people's reactions to the food—they can smell it, see it, taste it. Plus I didn't need a script. Here was something I could do off the top of my head."[25] Buoyed by the audience and the band, *Emeril Live* became much more than a TV show. Although he might read some initial remarks from the teleprompter, much of the show consisted of Emeril ad-libbing and joking with the audience. Unpredictable and unpretentious, viewers tuned in to see what Emeril would cook, and say, that day. Reporter Robert Sullivan aptly describes it in a *Travel & Leisure Golf* article: "It's an hour-long party with a band, a wild-and-crazy host and a lot of good food."[26]

It was also a watershed moment for the Food Network. Says Judy Girard, president of the Food Network, "From day one this show did better than the rest of the network did. It really carried the network for a couple of years. In the cable world, it only takes one show to make a network, initially. Then you build around it. And Food Network fortunately had Emeril to do that and so it began to raise the profile of the network."[27] Emeril's show was tremendously popular and unlike any other cooking show on the air.

Emeril's Cooking Philosophy: Keep It Simple

Although the entertainment is a draw, it is Emeril's encouraging message that keeps his audience tuned in. His life's work is to convince viewers that anyone can cook and that the act itself of preparing a meal is much less important than the gathering of the family around the table. "Make it the way you like it," he counsels during a show. "Share the love!"[28]

First and foremost, "Emeril makes cooking simple," says H.G. Parsa, professor of hospitality management at Ohio State University.[29] That is what makes him so popular. "He educates people on how to cook gourmet food at home," says Parsa. "Anyone watching the show feels they can do it." In other words, as Emeril says, "It's not rocket science."

He is also consistent and predictable, points out Parsa. You know exactly what to expect when you turn on his show. During each episode you are pretty much guaranteed to hear plenty of "BAM!" and "kick it up a notch," on top of "happy, happy, happy" when he drenches a dish in wine, or "oh yeah, babe" for emphasis.

Transforming the methodical, precise approach to cooking to an entertaining event is part of his mission. His message is that cooking does not have to be complicated and anyone can do it, which is what he tries to demonstrate with each show. Unlike old-school chefs, who use carefully measured ingredients in each dish, Emeril throws in a dash of this or a heaping of that. It is a more casual, light-hearted take on gourmet food than had previously been shown on TV, and audiences were happy to have it.

Of course, culinary purists complain about the dumbing down of the skill and science of cooking, with Emeril being the leader of that movement. Instead of appreciating the increased interest in fine dining and gourmet cooking that Emeril has certainly fostered, some of his colleagues have lost respect for him.

Critics, too, bristle at his showmanship. *Esquire*'s John Mariani says he finds Emeril annoying to watch. His trademarked phrases and quirks have started to grate on Mariani's nerves. He explains that Emeril's "deliberate mangling of the English language and constant repetition of sentences drives me nuts. It's embarrassing."[30]

Gone is the staid, snooty stereotype of gourmet chefs. Sure, they are still around, but their popularity has weakened. Today, the most popular of chefs is a gregarious, loud ham of a guy whose personality has a tendency to overshadow his culinary brilliance—at least to some industry observers.

At the Food Network, the shift away from a hard-line focus on the technical aspects of cooking jibed with an emerging consumer preference for lighter, more entertainment-oriented fare. *Emeril Live* was perfect for the evening hours, when viewers wanted to sit back and relax, while *The Essence of Emeril* continued during the daytime for viewers who might actually want to cook—rather than just watch him cook—some of his specialties.

Now, the Food Network has two tracks of programming, explains Eileen Opatut, senior vice president for programming and production. "We really are two channels. One for people who want to take ideas and do them themselves and one for those who just want to watch people cooking."[31] Although the channel started as more of a serious network for cooks, with Emeril's influence its programming has evolved to be more about the art of cooking.

Back in 1997, Emeril's innovative yet informative approach to *Emeril Live* earned a Cable ACE Award from the National Academy of Cable Programming for best original cable programming. To earn an ACE Award in the first year of programming is unusual and reflects the show's groundbreaking status.

Emeril's rising star was noticed by *Good Morning America* (GMA), which offered him a weekly slot as a food correspondent the following year, in 1998. Once again, he could not turn down a TV opportunity. As he says, "I was asked to do it and needed that job like a hole in the head. But what stoked me was the opportunity to reach even more people."[32] GMA's five-million-plus audience was too big a market to turn down.[33]

As a food correspondent rather than resident chef, Emeril did more than cook tasty meals. Instead of featuring preparation techniques or trendy recipes week after week, he also helped viewers understand how to identify the freshest produce and what kinds of ingredients work best for certain dishes.

A Stumble

Emeril may have been having so much fun on television that in 2001, when he was approached about starring in his own sitcom on NBC, he decided to have even more fun, and said yes. That was his first mistake. Perhaps the prospects of reaching an even broader audience—beyond the Food Network—and his sincere enjoyment of appearing in front of a TV audience clouded his judgment.

His biggest faulty assumption, however, was thinking that starring in a prime-time network TV show would be the same as working on a niche cooking show, or believing that acting would be as easy and effortless as he found cooking to be.

Before pursuing a brand extension, which a sitcom was for Emeril, most corporations typically assess whether the opportunity is a good fit, asking such questions as: Is it a natural outgrowth of an existing product or service? Does it match the company's long-term goals? Is it a good use of limited resources (i.e., Emeril's time), and does it leverage the business's core competency? Had Emeril asked such questions, he might have recognized that his core competency was cooking, not acting. He might have avoided the embarrassment that would come later.

NBC misjudged as well, says Robert Manasier, president of IFPFILMS.com, a fully integrated studio with branding expertise. Emeril had a following, and NBC thought they could piggyback on that asset. But they overlooked the fact that his strength is entertaining while cooking, says Manasier. Putting him outside his element—in a sitcom—was a disaster.

The half-hour comedy show, titled simply *Emeril* and loosely based on Emeril's life, was developed by veteran sitcom writers Linda Bloodworth-Thomason and her husband Harry Thomason, who was also the show's director. Although not much of a cook, Bloodworth happened to catch *Emeril Live* and was intrigued by the show and its host. After thinking about it for several months, the pair asked Emeril to work with them on developing and starring in the comedy.

Filmed in Los Angeles on Fridays and Saturdays, Emeril played a New York chef with a family and his own cable show. Surrounded by a cast of professional actors, the test pilot was panned by critics. Later, actor Robert Urich was added to liven up the dialogue, but the show never really took off as expected.

Going in, Emeril anticipated no problems making the jump from cable cooking program to prime-time comedy show. "It shouldn't be too difficult," he told NBC. "I play myself—passionate about food, cooking and making it all fun."[34]

Unfortunately, it *was* more difficult, and viewers noticed.

Apparently underestimating his appeal on prime-time TV, both *Emeril* the show and Emeril the actor struggled. Even with the help of a dialogue coach on set to assist him, the show was slammed by most critics. One of the most negative was Kevin Thompson of the *Palm Beach Post*, who wrote, "A talented trio of co-stars can't mask the fact that Emeril has the comic timing of a slug."[35]

Exhibiting the stiffness he showed on *How to Boil Water*, Emeril was hard to relate to. Viewers might have warmed up to him if his true personality had been written into the script. Even NBC was hoping that would happen, with then-president Jeff Zucker telling *Broadcasting and Cable*, "Quite frankly, what we want is Emeril to be himself and just play himself."[36] That proved harder than it sounds.

Unfortunately, Emeril's popularity as a chef did not carry over into prime time. His personality did not come through—probably because Emeril is, in fact, not an actor and is not used to following a script. The earlier failures of *How to Boil Water* and *Emeril and Friends* should have been an indication that a scripted sitcom would not make use of Emeril's strengths—his passion for food and his spontaneous nature.

The show was canceled.

Cynthia Sanz of *People* seemed to sum it up well, observing, "People like him. He has a very engaging personality, but a good personality doesn't make somebody an actor, and a good idea didn't make for good scripts."[37]

Part of the blame needs to rest on the shoulders of the NBC executives who had high hopes for the show—too high. Placed in the 8 P.M. Tuesday evening time slot, *Emeril* was positioned as the draw—the show that would pull viewers in and keep them on the channel for the evening. Had it been scheduled behind a lead-in show, such as *Friends*, it might have had a serious shot. But *Emeril* met the same fate as *The Michael Richards Show*, which had been placed in the same time slot the previous year: cancellation.

Fortunately, since Emeril appears to have been pursuing the acting job as a means of expanding familiarity with his name and his brand, the rollout of the show effectively accomplished that goal. Granted, his exposure would have increased as the number of episodes shown rose, but all the promotional activity in advance had a big impact. The print and broadcast promotion of the show before it even aired, as well as the advertising campaign leading up to and during its run, certainly heightened consumers' awareness of Emeril and his cooking. Nonfoodies who had never been to—much less heard of—Emeril's restaurants now knew who Emeril Lagasse was. That was an accomplishment, even if the television critics bashed the show.

Emeril the Celebrity

Suddenly, Emeril was everywhere, and fans could not get enough of him. Through his television exposure, he connected with millions of viewers, hooking them with his delicious recipes and building the relationship with his down-home, folksy personality, explains media consultant Michael Sands, of Sands Digital Media. "Being a celebrity is not about money, prestige, and power," Sands says. It's about being someone whom everyone wants to know. Emeril surely fits that description.

But when exactly did Emeril qualify as a celebrity? Shortly after *Emeril Live* debuted. That was when phone requests for tickets to the show blew out the switchboard in a small town in New England.[38] In its first season, more than 500,000 requests came in for tickets to the show—multiples of the number of tickets that were available. However, there were signs that a groundswell was building even during his 1993 book tour. In city after city, thousands of fans lined up for hours just to have the chance to meet him in person and get an autograph.

His celebrity status had been gained through a grassroots effort, explains Sands. Fans of his restaurants, his cookbook, and his television shows wanted more of him. His innate—and uncommon—ability to connect with people he has never met in person has greatly contributed to his success. Beginning with consistently good food at his restaurants, which was mirrored in the recipes in his cookbook and brought to life in front of millions of people on TV, Emeril leveraged his culinary talent to become a major celebrity.

And it is not just women, the traditional cooks in the family, who love him. Perhaps more than any other chef, Emeril reached a broad spectrum of consumers before celebrity chefs became common. Although most television shows have a fairly homogeneous audience—consisting mainly of men or women, young or old, straight or gay—Emeril's fans fall into all of those categories and more. From children to firefighters to teenagers and grandmas, Emeril is loved by just about everybody.

That fact is driven home on a daily basis in offices, at bars, or around the dinner table. When Emeril's name comes up in conversation, most people know who he is, points out Parsa. And the reaction is generally favorable. "People can relate to him. And they can talk about him with their friends."[39] Though they may never have eaten at Emeril's or seen his TV show, the large majority of Americans have some type of relationship with Emeril. That in itself is fairly remarkable.

Familiarity with Emeril transcends gender, age, or culture and is an accomplishment that speaks to Emeril's inclusive business and marketing strategy. That inclusiveness is reflected in a multitude of ways throughout his business—from his hiring practices at his headquarters and in the restaurants, to the members of his studio band, to the members of his studio audience. There is diversity that demonstrates his ability to relate to all cultures, says Parsa.

And beyond his diverse staff, Emeril also incorporates discussions regarding other cultures into his shows. When preparing an Italian dish, for example, he may relate information about a particular region or style of cooking that shows his admiration and respect for the culture. His very positive view of other ethnic groups endears him to a broad audience, as a result.

Emeril's Personal Brand Reaches the Tipping Point

While Emeril's rise to prominence was gradual, there was also a point in time when the pace at which he was becoming well known quickened. First he was simply known in New Orleans, then he was known among the hundreds of thousands of foodies who bought his cookbook, then he was known by the millions of cable customers who received the Food Network. And then, BAM!, he was everywhere.

As mentioned, that moment when he evolved from a simple restaurateur or TV host to a famed celebrity chef was his tipping point, the moment when his career suddenly took off, when his personal brand reached "critical mass, the threshold, the boiling point," as Malcolm Gladwell explains.[40] Products often experience a tipping point when, suddenly, they rise from obscurity to become so hot that retailers cannot keep them on their shelves. Think Palm Pilots, Cabbage Patch dolls, or fax machines.

The same is true of brands and personalities. Remember Julia Roberts in *Steel Magnolias?* Everyone wanted to know who she was, where she came from, how she landed such a major part, as well as when her next movie was. It was as if she had been plucked out of nowhere to land a leading role in this movie. *Steel Magnolias* was Roberts's tipping point—the moment when her career finally reached a boiling point.

Of course, she had been in other movies—*Mystic Pizza* and *Blood Red*, for example—as well as appearing in TV shows like *Miami Vice* and *Crime Story*. But suddenly everyone took notice once she was working next to established stars like Sally Field, Shirley MacLaine, and Olympia Dukakis. Julia tipped with *Steel Magnolias*. Her next film was *Pretty Woman*, and her career has not let up.

Emeril's tipping point was also a show—*Emeril Live*. It was so unlike any other cooking show, and Emeril was unlike any chef viewers had seen, that he stood out; he got people talking about him. And just like that, he was a hot property, after years of preparation.

Tipping points are characterized by dramatic moments when change happens suddenly, but they depend on three components: people, the brand or product itself, and/or the environment. Gladwell's terms for these players are *the Law of the Few*, the people; *the Stickiness Factor*, in this case, Emeril; and *the Power of Context*, or the environment. A tipping point is a function of one, two, or all of these factors.

The Law of the Few

In Emeril's case, the few people who had the largest impact on his celebrity were the people who led to his show—his cookbook publisher, the Food Network producers, and the restaurant and food critics who had been talking him up. This small group of people generally has the following characteristics: They are sociable, energetic, and knowledgeable and influential among their peers, says Gladwell. He names them *mavens, connectors,* and *salespersons.*

Gregg Lederman, managing partner of Brand Integrity, Inc., who uses the tipping point in his work with major corporations, explains that mavens are information specialists who act as brokers, sharing and trading the information they have accumulated with friends and associates. The connectors are people specialists who have an extraordinary knack for making friends and acquaintances and, consequently, have a larger network of contacts. And salespersons are persuasion specialists who influence others.

The Stickiness Factor

Sometimes the most powerful element is the person or product itself. In this situation, both Emeril's message (cooking is fun) and he himself are sticky. That is, they are memorable and make a huge impact on consumers. Emerilisms such as "BAM!" and "kick it up a notch," while annoying to some folks, are what make Emeril different. They reflect his energy and enthusiasm for cooking, as well as his unique approach to meal preparation.

In addition to what he says, the way he says it makes a difference— his New England accent is distinctive. His appearance is also a bit unusual, and it was even more so back in the late 1990s, before celebrity chefs became common. Seeing a solid, masculine man dressed in chef's whites talking about baking a soufflé was new. The images and sound bites stay with you.

The Power of Context

The power of context, explains Lederman, is everything that is going on in the environment that impacts Emeril's rise to celebrity-dom. That would include the dramatic rise in cable television networks and subscribers in the early to mid-1990s, as his TV career was taking off. Viewers were also in the mood for more entertaining programming, as their work life continued to grow more demanding, more frantic, and more draining. Americans' preference for nesting and cocooning at home, inviting friends over for entertainment rather than going out, also spawned a greater interest in cooking and all its accoutrements; it became trendy to cook. The rising popularity of New Orleans as a tourist destination heightened awareness of its culinary power and hometown chefs, including Emeril.

Surely there were other external influences at work during the years leading up to Emeril's wildly successful live cooking show, but these were some of the most significant in terms of television and cooking. Emeril's tipping point was made possible mainly by his own personal attributes, his stickiness, and the environment he was working in, the power of context.

Proper Preparation for Every New Venture

Like so many other aspects of his career, Emeril prepared for his success on television carefully, beginning with the media training he received before heading out on his first book tour. "Media training was important to landing a show on the Television Food Network," believes Lisa Ekus, who provided the training.[41] Recognizing the importance of his book tour, Emeril was committed to being the best possible representative for his publisher and sought training to ensure that.

In addition to his much-talked-about work ethic, Emeril is also known for planning and preparation before undertaking any new venture. The months of work he did planning and preparing for the opening of Emeril's Restaurant is one example, as is the media training for his book tour, and the dialogue coach he retained for his sitcom role. Although he has already achieved so much, Emeril never stops trying to improve every aspect of his business and his life, making regular investments toward that end.

As the concept of the tipping point suggests, some aspects of his career and success were squarely within his control, while others were out of his hands. What was happening sociologically, politically, and technologically in America in the 1990s, as his star began to rise, was essentially out of his control. Later, once his popularity tipped, he would start to make an impact, but before then, he was mainly at the mercy of his surroundings.

In contrast, he had more control over the stickiness of his message and persona, which he essentially created for television audiences. And the law of the few who would influence his career was the result of connections he had made professionally and personally during his training and early career.

Emeril and the Food Network: Reciprocal Success

Just as Emeril worked to ensure his TV success, the Food Network had a similar struggle—first determining what kind of programming would work, finding chefs who fit their needs, and producing low-budget shows that audiences would actually watch. Ultimately, "the Food Network owes a lot of its success to Emeril," says Samantha Ettus. Emeril set the standard for the network, bringing new viewers to the channel regularly and increasing general interest in cooking as an activity.

Could the network have succeeded without Emeril? Maybe, but it would likely have taken the company much longer to reach profitability.

And would Emeril have become such a star? "If the Food Network had bombed and not been successful, we don't know if Emeril would still be a household name," says Ettus. Since both brands began working together in their respective infancy, at the start of an important technological trend—climbing cable usage—and hit upon an untapped interest in cooking as entertainment, it is hard to say whether either could have succeeded without the other.

Now together, there are no plans to part. In May 2003, Emeril signed a five-year contract with the Food Network to produce 90 new episodes of *Emeril Live* a year, as well as 26 episodes of *The Essence of Emeril.*

Interestingly, as Emeril's popularity and paycheck have grown—thanks in good measure to the Food Network—the network's own corporate budgets have remained capped, or at least limited. "The shows are very low budget," says Manasier.[42] While Emeril has been perfecting his performances, the Food Network has been polishing its own ability to manage resources. "It's a very efficient company," observes Manasier, who praises the way it maximizes economies of scale.

All five shows for the week are shot in one day, reducing labor costs significantly, and with four kitchens built on one set, little real estate is needed in which to operate. The company's return on its investment in property and performers has been huge, largely due to its top-notch resource management. "They don't spend money unless they have to," confirms Manasier.

The bar may actually have been set by Emeril back in 1993, when, due to his own time constraints, he required that his shows be filmed back-to-back. By packing the taping of several shows into one day, he could more quickly return to oversee his restaurants. That schedule, although exhausting for everyone involved, may have become the Food Network standard, making it possible to crank out several shows for far less money than any other television network. Its low-budget but highly popular shows surely contributed to the company's decade of rising profitability.

And just as Emeril has leveraged his TV shows to market his other products—restaurants, cookbooks, spices, cookware, cutlery, clothing, personal appearances, you name it—the Food Network has branched out, too. Over the years it has pursued a number of new chefs to feature on its shows and to build shows around. That variety has served it well, offering viewers a range of methods, styles, and personalities to choose from. It has also reduced the network's chance of failure by building its stable of celebrity chefs, rather than continuing to rely on only one or two stars (recall what happened to Martha Stewart Living Omnimedia's stock price when her scandal hit?).

Julia Child's Impact

Emeril's career as a cooking show host was made possible in part by legendary chef Julia Child.

"There is only one Julia," says Emeril. "That lady is just amazing."[43] Although he worked with her only briefly as a cook in the 1970s,[44] in many ways Julia paved the way for Emeril's later success.

Unlike Emeril, Child's introduction to cooking came later in life. Born in 1912, raised in Pasadena, California, Child attended boarding school in San Francisco and college at Smith, and enjoyed an early career working for the Office of Strategic Services in Washington, D.C., during World War II. Having met future husband, Paul Cushing Child, on a work assignment in Sri Lanka, the two were married following the end of the war. When he was sent to Paris, she accompanied him.

Having grown up in a well-to-do household with cooks mainly responsible for meal preparation, Child's exposure to cooking was limited. Her interest in cooking only surfaced as she attempted to fit into the role of housewife. She threw herself into the challenge, devouring information on French cooking and signing up for classes at the famed Cordon Bleu cooking school. She was the only woman in her class.

She later started L'Ecole des Trois Gourmands with Simone Beck and Louisette Bertholle, which taught Americans visiting Paris how to cook French dishes.

After returning to the United States and settling in Cambridge, Massachusetts, Child continued to teach cooking classes and in 1961 finally published a cookbook she had been working on for 10 years—*Mastering the Art of French Cooking*. The lengthy book was both

detailed and encouraging to readers, making even the most complicated French dishes seem doable. Its goal was to teach Americans,
with access to American ingredients and tools, how to prepare traditional French cuisine. It was a success.

The cookbook earned rave reviews in the *New York Times* and an
appearance on the *Today* show. Her popularity soaring as a result of
the book, Child was asked to do a TV interview for WGBH in
Boston. The response to the interview was so overwhelming that the
station asked her to tape a pilot cooking show, *The French Chef*, which
spawned several other cooking series, such as her *Master Chef* programs.[45] She won awards for her cookbook and her shows, which
truly shaped American culture and cuisine. During her career, she
wrote nine cookbooks.

In addition to introducing classic French dishes and cooking
techniques to an audience that had never experienced them, Child
made cooking accessible to the common man, much like Emeril
does today. Her engaging personality and friendly demeanor proved
a winning combination for TV.

Interestingly, during the rise of the women's liberation movement
of the 1970s, Child began to see the inequities of her field and spoke
out about it. "It wasn't until I began thinking about it that I realized
my field is closed to women! It is very unfair. You can't teach in the
Culinary Institute of America! The big hotels, the fancy New York
restaurants don't want women chefs!"[46] Ten years later, those same
hotels and restaurants had decided they did not want American-born
cooks either, shutting Emeril out until he had some French training
under his belt.

5

HITCHING HIS CAREER
TO NEW ORLEANS'S GROWTH

The Pied Piper of the pan has become to cooking what baseball legend Babe Ruth is to the home run.

—Hollywood Reporter[1]

U nbeknownst to most New Orleanians in the late 1990s, there was a major celebrity in their midst.

Ironically, despite Emeril's growing popularity, one city that *did not* carry the Food Network was his own town—a town steeped in culinary tradition. So while he was certainly quite popular locally, area residents may have had little sense of the absolute pandemonium he was creating outside their city. Thousands of fans were lining up to see him at public appearances, and even more were jamming phone lines trying to get the few tickets there were to his show. He was fast becoming a major star, right in their own backyard.

Emeril was certainly not the first Louisiana chef to become famous. Paul Prudhomme, Emeril's predecessor at Commander's

Palace, had opened his own restaurant (K-Paul's), published cook-books, and developed branded products such as spices and cookware, just as Emeril would do. The one thing Emeril had that Prudhomme did not was his own television show, but since most New Orleanians had never seen it, few would place him at Prudhomme's level.

"In Louisiana and New Orleans, the chefs are stars," explains Stephen Perry, president of the New Orleans Metropolitan Convention and Visitors Bureau, Inc.[2] Everyday conversation typically revolves more around culinary happenings—a shocking menu change at a popular eatery, drama in the kitchen at another restaurant, or a frank assessment of a new chef—than around sports, current events, or Hollywood celebrity news. In New Orleans, the biggest celebrities are the men and women running local fine dining establishments.

Despite the fact that local residents may have been oblivious to Emeril's rising star, the town itself was benefiting from his fame. "Every time he appears on TV, he's an ad for New Orleans," confirms Perry. Given the significant increase in local tourism in the last decade, it is obvious that Emeril has been good for New Orleans. "Emeril and New Orleans were the ultimate love affair," he says.

Coming to See Emeril in New Orleans

"Emeril came into his own when New Orleans was becoming a tourist economy," observes Brett Anderson, food critic at the *Times-Picayune* newspaper.[3] The 1984 World's Fair was held at New Orleans's Rivergate Exposition Hall; afterward, the hall was expanded and renamed the Ernest N. Morial Convention Center. The fair had drawn attention to New Orleans, which was a catalyst for tourism growth. The convention center reopened in 1985 to brisk business from conventioneers and trade shows. When demand for the site exceeded expectations after a few short years, work began to again expand the center, which was completed in 1991.

As work was beginning on the second phase of the convention center expansion, Emeril decided it was the right time for him to go out on his own and add "restaurateur" to his resume. While New Orleans's popularity as a convention and trade show destination was already rising, Emeril's own reputation and fan club were beginning to heighten interest in the Louisiana city. Although on parallel paths, the two entities—Emeril's organization and New Orleans's tourism agencies—were working toward the same goal: attracting more guests to visit and spend money in town.

New Orleans has a long history as one of the top destinations for Mardi Gras celebrations, fine food, and jazz music. Vacationers have flocked to the city for years, partaking of the fine cuisine and entertainment. But the city's appeal began to grow beyond that of individual and small group excursions to include large corporate events, such as industry trade shows.

Part of the reason behind New Orleans's draw was the capacity of its convention center. The size of national trade shows mushroomed during the 1980s and 1990s to the point that only a handful of centers could accommodate larger shows. New Orleans was one of the largest venues, mainly because it had expanded in anticipation of growing demand, rather than waiting until shows outgrew the existing convention center. In fact, in 2002, the Ernest N. Morial Convention Center was named a top 10 site for the largest 200 trade shows that year.[4]

The number of visitors to New Orleans rose from 8,401,000 in 1990—the year Emeril opened his first restaurant—to a high of 10,620,850 in 2000, reflecting a 26% increase. Following the events of September 11, 2001, the total number of visitors dropped to 9,842,479 in 2002, but the figure still represents a cumulative 17% jump from 1990.[5]

Convention attendance also rose consistently during that period, with no drop due to terrorism. Total convention attendance in 1990 was 1,128,434, climbing 25% to 1,408,265 in 2002.[6]

During the period from 1990 to 2001, visitor spending also grew substantially. Tourists spent $2.8 billion in New Orleans in 1990, but by 2001 that figure had risen a remarkable 81%, to $5.1 billion. Average spending per visitor also rose annually, from $334 in 1990 to $530 in 2001, the last year the figures were reported, representing a healthy 59% increase, perhaps due in part to the city's growing ranks of fine dining establishments.[7]

As New Orleans's reliance on tourism grew, hoteliers attempted to meet the associated demand for rooms. Between 1996 and 2002, a total of 47 hotels and 8,206 rooms were added in the city. And instead of falling because of the larger supply of rooms, hotel occupancy rates remained stable, hovering near 70% throughout this period of growth.[8]

The Convention Center, as well, expanded in 1999 to 1.1 million square feet of contiguous exhibit space, 140 meeting rooms, two ballrooms, and a state-of-the-art 4,000-seat auditorium. It is currently the seventh-largest convention facility in the nation and is about to undergo yet another expansion, Phase IV, which is expected to attract 280,000 more out-of-town visitors through increased conventions and meetings.[9]

New Orleans was not the only city experiencing tourism growth during this period, however. New York City, by comparison, saw its tourist visits jump by 55% from 1991 to 2002, in part because of the number of day-trippers into the city. In total, those visitors spent $14.1 billion, up 47% from $9.6 billion 11 years prior.[10] Las Vegas, too, the longtime site for such major trade shows as the Consumer Electronics Show, with more than 129,000 attendees, saw tourism climb 22% from 1996 to 2003, the number of visitors rising from 29.7 million in 1996 to an estimated 36.2 million in 2003.[11]

Explains Michael Hughes, associate publisher of *Tradeshow Week,* "The convention and tradeshow industry grew considerably in the 1980s and 1990s in terms of the number of events and total attendance. The number of convention centers in the U.S. and Canada expanded from 269 in 1986 to nearly 400 by the late 1990s. Total convention center exhibit space expanded from 42 million square feet in 1986 to 66 million square feet by 2000."[12] At the same time, corporations were beginning to recognize the value of face-to-face interactions with prospects, and business partners and employees sought out shows where professional development opportunities and industry networking were readily available.

The economy was growing, the stock market was rising, and companies were sending their employees to trade shows, business meetings, and conferences as a regular part of doing business. Most major cities, if not all, saw the number of travelers rise.

One of the biggest draws in New Orleans was its cooking. Virtually anyone who came to town wanted to enjoy the nightlife and the much-vaunted cuisine there. Increasing consumer interest in cooking and in Emeril drew people to New Orleans to sample his food and enjoy the many activities the city has to offer. Emeril was good for New Orleans.

But the reverse is also true. New Orleans was good for Emeril. He might never have made it as big if he had hailed from anywhere else.

A Catalyst for New Orleans's Growth

The question of who was a catalyst for whom is almost a chicken-and-egg story. Did Emeril's locating his flagship restaurant in the struggling Warehouse District bring more attention to the area, resulting in economic revitalization? Or did Emeril happen to choose a site in an area that would have flourished anyway? That is hard to say.

According to Stephen Perry, "[Emeril's] opened when tourism boomed, and as the tourism industry grew, he grew with it." Because of where he chose to locate the restaurant, one important event where Emeril was concerned was the addition of hotel space at the convention center in 1991, the year after Emeril's Restaurant opened.

From there, hotels sprang up to satisfy visitor demand for rooms, bringing hungry travelers within easy reach of his popular establishment. One thing is sure, according to Perry, "[Emeril's] impact on the economy is worth tens of millions of dollars."[13]

There is no doubt that Emeril influenced tourist decisions to visit and dine in New Orleans, but his influence on the local restaurant scene was no less important. "New Orleans is still very much a provincial place," says Brett Anderson, "where restaurant-goers are skeptical of new things"—meaning new restaurants, new chefs, and new entrées. "The joke used to be that New Orleans was a city of 1,000 chefs who could all cook the same ten dishes," laughs Anderson. Emeril played a major role in changing that.

Commander's Palace, where Emeril received the most substantive training as chef and restaurateur, is a very risk-taking restaurant, says Anderson. From the bright blue exterior paint job to the innovative menu, 200-year-old Commander's set the pace for the city in many ways. "The same could be said about Emeril," says Anderson. Under his leadership at Commander's and later at his own restaurants, Emeril challenged local chefs to stay at the top of their game. He also trained and mentored others who would later open their own eateries in the city.

But, again, part of that competitive shift can be attributed to the increasing importance of out-of-town visitors, some of whom expect to be wowed during dinner; local restaurateurs were challenged to meet those lofty expectations. Out-of-town guests want and expect a memorable dining experience—unlike what they get back home—which is hard to provide if the chef is preparing the same dishes that have been on the menu since the place opened. Emeril set the bar high by constantly challenging himself and his chefs to use only the best ingredients and to develop inventive, seasonally tied menu items.

Keeping pace with Emeril has meant expanding wine lists, adding tasting menus, developing specials based on seasonal ingredients, and providing wait service training to ensure a pleasurable meal that guests will write home about.

The difference in cooking primarily for a local crowd as opposed to cooking for a transient audience is that the pressure to satisfy every customer frequently varies according to the chance of a return visit. Or, as Anderson puts it, "The incentive for a restaurant to continually 'wow' people diminishes with tourists versus a hometown clientele."[14]

Neighborhood Revitalization

The World's Fair being held in New Orleans in 1984 was a catalyst, too. Once the fair left the city's Warehouse District at its conclusion, local community members were worried about what would happen next. "There was a great deal of concern that the area would begin another downward spiral after the fair evacuated," said Patty Gay, director of the Preservation Resource Center,[15] which supports and encourages refurbishing of existing buildings in the area.

To encourage greater community involvement and interest, a federal tax incentive of 25% of rehabilitation costs on area buildings was offered during the mid-1980s. The incentive became a magnet for developers, one of which was RCB Builders, Inc., which bought its first warehouse in 1984 and converted it into new apartments. Emeril was one of their first tenants.

Soon after, Henry Lambert of RCB had dinner at Commander's Palace, where Emeril was executive chef, and mentioned that he had the perfect building for a restaurant, should Emeril ever want to go out on his own. Although he did not really expect Emeril to be interested, they discussed the possibility until 1990, when Emeril left Commander's to strike out on his own.

The top floors of the building, now called the Rotunda, had already been renovated and converted into apartments. But the first floor of the pharmaceutical storage building was left for commercial use—for Emeril's use. In preparation for his restaurant's opening, Emeril renovated the entire floor, retaining the exposed brick and glass exterior walls from the old warehouse, but tearing out every-thing else and creating a spectacular space.

Although he could have opened a restaurant anywhere in New Orleans and it probably would have been successful, Emeril's deci-sion to locate in the Warehouse District was a smart move. As men-tioned, Emeril had been envisioning for years what his own restaurant would be like—what it would look like, feel like, sound like—and the only way he could hope to achieve that degree of control over its design was to start from scratch. The space in need of renovating was perfect, plus he was in a strong negotiating posi-tion with RCB, which would receive the tax credit (which was reduced from 25 to 20% in 1986[16]) as building owner. But if he waited too long, the opportunity might be lost as other tenants moved in.

As Emeril describes the neighborhood back then, "it was hip and kind of Soho-ish"[17] but lacking in any real basic services. His men-tor, Ella Brennan, questioned his sanity for wanting to set up shop in such a barren area, believing that a more established and well-trafficked area like the French Quarter or the Garden District would be a better choice. But he persisted, somehow knowing that the Warehouse District would turn around.

It was still risky. "I had established a huge clientele—more of an elderly clientele—at Commander's. I had established this very pro-gressive food because of my philosophies of from-scratch growing and we were on the cutting edge of doing whatever cuisine-wise. But I was moving to this neighborhood that [his clientele at Comman-der's] didn't really identify with. It was a very, very scary transi-tion."[18] But Emeril saw a need, was confident of his cooking, and took the leap.

Of course, Emeril's was a hit. And it bolstered the area. "When Emeril's came, the whole neighborhood really took off. It was quite dramatic,"[19] says Arthur Roger, who owns an art gallery by the same name that opened years before Emeril's did. As the excitement sur-rounding the area took off, Emeril eventually bought an already renovated building and converted it into one of the first single-family homes in the district.

In the years since, several new galleries and museums have set up shop in the neighborhood; the National D-Day Museum is down the block, as is the Contemporary Arts Center. The 30,000-square-foot Louisiana Children's Museum, located next door to Emeril's, had already opened in 1986, but has since incorporated new exhibits in response to suggestions from their well-known neighbor. A music club, the Howlin' Wolf, opened and other casual and moderately priced restaurants have moved in, including Restaurant August, Mulate's, Vic's Kangaroo Café, and Warehouse District Pizza. High-end dining, however, is Emeril's domain.

While bringing in commercial tenants has provided an important backbone to the neighborhood, it is the residential work that has taken the lead in terms of renovation. Although work to spruce up the neighborhood continues, "Without Emeril, it would not be the exciting place that it is today," maintains Gay.[20]

Paul Prudhomme Lays the Groundwork

Although Emeril arrived at Commander's a couple of years after Chef Paul Prudhomme had left, his predecessor would still play a role in his success.

Like Emeril, Paul Prudhomme knew from a very young age that he wanted to be a chef. Raised in Louisiana's Acadiana country, Prudhomme was taught to cook by his mother, beginning around age seven. Without electricity in the home, the family ate what was available nearby—fresh vegetables, meats, and fish, seasoned with herbs and spices from the garden.

After graduating from school, Prudhomme began traveling for several years, learning as much as he could about cooking in the various parts of the country, in a wide range of restaurants. It was during these experiences that he honed his knack for seasoning dishes.

He remembers, "Sometimes when I thought the food was too bland, I'd sneak in a few dried herbs and spices. When customers complimented the dishes from my station, I'd try to remember exactly what I'd used, but that was hard, so I began keeping little notes on good mixes in my pockets."[21] Prudhomme and Emeril are kindred spirits when it comes to kicking dishes up a notch.

Eventually Prudhomme returned to New Orleans as executive chef at Commander's Palace, where he continued to develop as a chef. He also made his mark on the restaurant, which became well known for Cajun food during his tenure; blackened meats and fish were standard fare. But after a few years, he decided to open his own restaurant. So in 1979, he and his late wife, K Hinrichs Prudhomme, established K-Paul's Louisiana Kitchen, a small, casual eatery in the French Quarter.

Although originally developed to appeal mainly to local clientele, K-Paul's quickly gained a following among tourists as well as area residents. Two of his most famous dishes—Blackened Redfish and Blackened Steak—have been widely adopted.

His first cookbook, *Chef Paul Prudhomme's Louisiana Kitchen* (Morrow Cookbooks, 1984), which was released in 1986, sat on the *New York Times* best-seller list for weeks and was followed by six other cookbooks. Two of his cooking videos were also at the top of *Billboard's* chart for 53 consecutive weeks.

In addition to running the restaurant, which has since been expanded, Prudhomme branched out into catering, with K-Paul's catering division, and created a separate company to manage the development, production, and marketing of his renowned blends of herbs and spices. Named Magic Seasoning Blends, the all-natural herbs and spices are sold worldwide to consumers and institutional customers through his business.

Prudhomme's most significant contributions to Emeril's career were his ample use of spices, heightening local and national interest in Cajun cooking prior to Emeril's arrival in New Orleans, and his success as a restaurateur following his tenure at Commander's.

Knowing that Prudhomme's career had been enhanced, not damaged, when he opened his own restaurant encouraged and inspired Emeril to do the same.

Opening a Third Restaurant in New Orleans

Having already opened Emeril's and NOLA in New Orleans (as well as several other restaurants in other cities), Emeril rounded out his collection of New Orleans restaurants in 1998 when he purchased the Delmonico restaurant, which had closed in 1997 after a hundred-year run. The Delmonico was a more traditional restaurant that had become a bit dated, but Emeril's plan was to bring back many of the features that he felt had been lost, including "club service, some tableside cooking, great sommelier, great wine program, and a lot of those classic New Orleans dishes: en Papillote, caramel cup custard, ice cream bombes."[22] The two former owners couldn't have been more thrilled.[23]

After spending $4 million to renovate the "spectacular" building, eand the concept, stimates local food critic Tom Fitzmorris, he reopened the restaurant as Emeril's Delmonico in 1998.

Fitzmorris counts Emeril's purchase of the Delmonico as one of the turning points in his career. "When Emeril opened his first restaurant, he had to hustle for dollars to do it, since it was his first independent restaurant. His second restaurant, NOLA, was opened in partnership with the man who owned the building and wanted something in it, so it was, again, not a risky undertaking for Emeril,"[24] explains Fitzmorris. But taking over the Delmonico was an ambitious—and very visible—project with no other backers. Emeril would make it or fail totally on his own.

Says Fitzmorris, "At the time, I thought that he was trying to build another Commander's Palace: a restaurant with both a lot of history and tradition, but also a cutting-edge aspect. While [Delmonico] is very different from Commander's, I do think he succeeded in that."[25]

The interior design, exceptional wine list, and classic menu combine to offer a traditional meal on a grand scale, just as the Delmonico had been known for.

Serving appetizers as varied as House Made Chorizo Sausage, Oysters Brochette, and Morris Kahn's Filet Mignon Tartar, Emeril's Delmonico attracted guests looking for a taste of traditional New Orleans, both in cuisine and in style. Entrées included Wild Mushroom-Ricotta Cannelloni, Braised Colorado Lamb Shank, Rosemary-Garlic Grilled Chicken Breast, and Sautéed Rainbow Trout, among several others. And the desserts, totaling more than a dozen, included Bourbon Vanilla Crème Brûlée, Cinnamon Crusted Roasted Apple Bread Pudding, Hot Double Chocolate Praline Pie, and New Orleans Bananas Foster. The menu, along with the ambiance, service, and wine, was a true winner.

"Delmonico moved [Emeril] from the realm of hot chef with a personal restaurant to that of the restaurant entrepreneur in the highest levels of the local business,"[26] summarizes Fitzmorris. The Delmonico was a true test of whether Emeril had the vision and the staying power to be more than a small restaurateur, and he passed with flying colors.

It also solidified his ties to New Orleans and further served to link his business success to that of the city.

Emeril's Homebase: In New Orleans

Although his thick New England accent gives away his roots in Massachusetts, for more than 20 years New Orleans has been Emeril's home. Today he says he feels he has always been in New Orleans—it is that much a part of his life and his soul. But his love of and commitment to New Orleans goes well beyond simply enjoying the place and its people—Emeril has put down personal and professional roots. His local investments, which total more than $15 million, include his three restaurants, his corporate headquarters, and his home and that of his parents, whom he convinced to join him in his adopted hometown.

While his restaurants surely generate hundreds of thousands of dollars in tax revenue for the city of New Orleans, it is Emeril's Homebase, his corporation's offices, that signifies his long-term plans to remain based in Louisiana. Originally a one-room office, Emeril's corporate space has evolved into a 46,000-square-foot, $3.5 million building that was converted from an old bowling alley into a sleek, state-of-the-art facility for Emeril's use.[27]

Like virtually every other facet of his business, here, too, Emeril retained strict control over the design of the space to ensure it would match his vision. "Emeril knew exactly what he wanted when we began working on the building," confirms Jim Farr, a partner with the architectural firm of Farr + Huson, who managed the project. "Everything from the state-of-the-art test kitchen and shipping department to a large room for a food reference library received his scrutiny."[28] And although the offices are made of mahogany and glass, Emeril's are no larger or fancier than anyone else's. According to Farr, Emeril said, "Make it just like the rest."[29]

This one building on St. Charles Avenue holds everything from the company's administrative offices to recipe development space, product shipping, and a retail storefront. His entire administrative staff, test kitchen workers, writers, marketing and PR pros, dot-com operations, and warehouse are all housed there; those workers plus everyone who works in his restaurants total 1,400 employees companywide.[30]

Like the growth of tourism in New Orleans, Emeril's operations have expanded as well. Beginning with 37 employees,[31] the company now boasts multiples of that, with more than 200 based locally. That is more than 440% growth in less than 15 years just in New Orleans, and 36,800% growth overall. Not bad for an industry where failure is more common than success.

Along the way, it would be a surprise if Emeril had not been offered tax incentives to put down roots in New Orleans. Generally,

such programs involve offering tax abatements or credits for companies willing to commit to locating their headquarters in a particular
locale. Sometimes those incentives include a provision for the creation of a certain number of new jobs, or there may be additional
incentives for such new jobs. Having seen the exponential growth of
his employment rolls, Emeril would likely have applied for such
credits if they had become available. And given New Orleans's love
affair with the celebrity chef, it is probable that they granted them.

New Orleans Style

"[Emeril] has made serious food accessible to everyone," says Brett
Anderson, food critic at the *Times-Picayune*, "which is also very New
Orleans." "In New Orleans, people's appreciation of food transcends
class,"[32] he continues. Residents of all education levels, employment
stature, races, and genders participate in the local debates about all
things cuisine-related. New Orleanians love their food, and they
love sharing it with others. Anderson contrasts food's unifying element in New Orleans with the elitism of East Coast cooking, where
culinary knowledge and appreciation are assumed to increase with
income.

In keeping with that appreciation of good cooking, food afi-
cionados in New Orleans treat themselves frequently to quality
meals at some of the more expensive restaurants the city has to
offer, says Anderson. Enjoying a fine meal prepared by a talented
chef is a pleasure New Orleanians do not like to deny themselves.
This is another reason Emeril has done so well in this city—they
appreciate him.

According to Anderson, "His food tends to be very much an
extension of his personality, which is to say, it's in your face. The flavors are very bold and strong. It's very accomplished cooking, but it's
not something that you need to have an educated palate to appreciate." That universal appeal is what makes him good for New Orleans.

"I would defend him, at the very least, as someone who is very good for restaurants in this city," says Anderson.[33]

Emeril can also be credited with bringing the pendulum back to Creole-based dishes, after Prudhomme swung it toward Cajun. He developed his own niche and reputation by blending Asian and Portuguese techniques with traditional Creole fare. This evolution of the locals' beloved dishes was enough to catch their interest but not so much as to turn them off.

New Orleanians' willingness to eat out regularly at high-end restaurants surely contributed to Emeril's financial success. It is likely that local residents spend more on meals out than typical residents in other cities, making New Orleans a great spot for a chef to operate in. It is also a city in which generating word-of-mouth advertising is easy—New Orleanians nearly obsess about food, making fast work of getting the word out about a hot new eatery or a bistro to be avoided. Chefs can become stars almost overnight in New Orleans if the food is consistently good, as it is with Emeril.

Setting the Bar: Emeril's Influence on Other Chefs

When Emeril joined the staff at Commander's Palace in 1982, at the unheard-of age of 23, he followed in the footsteps of very talented, well-known, older chefs. He was an untried, unknown chef—an anomaly—at a restaurant with a long tradition of excellence and experience. But Commander's was also known as something of a risk-taking restaurant, and hiring a twenty-something chef was not out of the realm of possibilities.

After having worked with Emeril for more than seven years, Ella Brennan may have begun to recognize the advantage of bringing in a more malleable chef who could build a following at the restaurant as his or her culinary talents grew. "Every chef that's come after Emeril at Commander's has been young and unproven," observes

Anderson, as if to suggest that Brennan had recognized the wisdom of that approach and adopted it as the new tradition.

Emeril trained young Jamie Shannon before turning over the executive chef mantle to his 29-year-old protégé back in 1990. Shannon had begun his career as a busboy and moved up to cook when he decided to make his career choice official by enrolling at the Culinary Institute of America. From there he went to work at Trump Plaza Hotel in Atlantic City and then to Commander's Palace,[34] where he started as a saucier and moved up to executive chef upon Emeril's departure.

Shannon's biggest impact on Commander's was insisting on purchasing ingredients from local purveyors, claiming later that 70% of the ingredients used at the restaurant were drawn from within a 100-mile radius of New Orleans. It was that kind of commitment to quality and freshness that earned Shannon the James Beard Foundation's Best Chef in the Southeast honors in 1999.

The executive chef for a total of 11 years, Shannon later trained Tory McPhail, Commander's executive chef since 2001. McPhail trained under Shannon at the New Orleans restaurant but then headed east to the Breakers in Florida, and later to London, where he worked at the Picasso Room and L'Escargot. After returning to the fold to run Commander's Palace Las Vegas, he was recruited at age 28 to return to the New Orleans flagship to assume Shannon's duties following his sudden death in late 2001.

Although placing the responsibility for running the kitchen of such a large restaurant on the shoulders of a twenty-something chef might have made Ella Brennan nervous in 1990, the advantages must have been apparent as well—namely, that the Brennan clan could continue the young chef's training in-house, helping him rid himself of bad habits, such as Emeril's volatile temper, while adopting the Brennan approach. Not to mention the fact that younger chefs are less likely to leave after a short time to run their own restaurants—it may happen later, as it did with Emeril, but not as quickly.

Certainly, Emeril was good for Commander's. As the new chef, he was probably something of a curiosity for loyal patrons, who made reservations to see what all the fuss was about. Then, after having tasted his specials, they made plans to return to see what he would come up with next.

In addition to his cooking, the guests at Commander's also began to fall in love with Emeril's personality, which was more gregarious and personable than those of the previous two chefs, Paul Prud-homme and Gerhard Brill, who had filled in before Emeril was hired. The warm, friendly way he greeted diners by name, thanking them for their patronage and making every effort to meet their needs, won a solid customer base. In seven years, Emeril's cooking made Commander's *the* place to eat; it was well known before he arrived, certainly, but it is even more so today. More than a decade since he left, the restaurant is better known because of Emeril's tenure.

6

EXPANDING THE BUSINESS AND BUILDING A BRAND

Clever cooks train replacements, get out of the kitchen and watch their empires grow.

—*Forbes* magazine

I t's a great crowd. It always is here,"[1] said Emeril as he signed copies of *From Emeril's Kitchens: Favorite Recipes from Emeril's Restaurants* (Morrow Cookbooks, 2003) in Vero Beach in December 2003. More than 3,000 people had begun lining up at the Vero Beach Book Center as early as 8:00 A.M. for his 4:00 P.M. book signing. The crowd was probably the largest the store has ever had for a visiting author, estimated the owner, with the second-largest turnout being Emeril's previous visit, back in 1997.

Despite having the flu that day, Emeril signed books and did media interviews until 8:15 that night, attempting to grant each customer's wish for an autograph. Taking a conservative guess, the Book Center's owner estimated the day's sales at more than 2,000 copies, a sure sign of Emeril's popularity.

Although Emeril may draw thousands to buy an autographed copy of his book, most book signings draw far fewer attendees. Many authors even question the value of such events when audiences can be as small as 5 or 10 people. But Emeril is unusual, appealing to such a broad spectrum of consumers that thousands of fans in virtually any part of the country will show up just to see him.

It is not surprising that Emeril got his start in New Orleans. After all, it is the one town most notable for its cuisine. The more than 3,000 restaurants in the city earn rave reviews from food and restaurant critics nationwide year after year. It is a kind of culinary mecca that enhances a chef's resume like no other.

Expectations are also higher. In a city with more gourmands than usual and a culture centered on food and music, too many missteps can slow a career. Conversely, a talented chef with an ebullient personality can quickly gain national attention if he or she is from New Orleans. That was the case with Emeril.

His popularity grew quickly with locals and tourists, building his reputation as a skilled chef. And when the awards started pouring in, his stature in the culinary community was sealed.

Winning Restaurant Awards and Honors

Emeril always knew he would be a successful chef, but when he earned one of the top honors given a restaurant just a few months after opening Emeril's in New Orleans, Emeril himself may have been a little surprised. Being named Best Restaurant of the Year by John Mariani of *Esquire* may have actually set him up for some disappointment. Where do you go from there once you have already won the top prize right out of the gate?

The next year, in 1991, *Food and Wine* magazine named Emeril one of America's top 25 new chefs and the prestigious James Beard Foundation nominated Emeril for its highest honors, Outstanding Chef and the Outstanding Service Award.

Although Emeril's Restaurant and his subsequent venues were widely praised over the next few years, it was not until *Emeril Live* made him a mainstream television star in 1997 that the awards started flowing. Suddenly he was hot again.

That same year—the year he tipped—the James Beard Foundation again nominated him for Outstanding Chef honors and its Outstanding Service Award. In 1998, *GQ* chose Emeril as Chef of the Year and *People* magazine crowned him one of the Most Intriguing People of the Year. The National Restaurant Association, the major association for his industry, awarded him the Salute to Excellence Award as well.

In Las Vegas, Emeril's New Orleans Fish House was named Best New Restaurant by Zagat's and was awarded Best Seafood Restaurant by *Las Vegas Review Journal*. Emeril's Delmonico Steakhouse, his other Las Vegas establishment, won Best Steakhouse in *Las Vegas Life* magazine three times in the early 2000s.

Back at home, Emeril's Delmonico received four stars from AAA and the *Mobil Travel Guide* in 2003. Emeril's Orlando garnered Best Restaurant honors from *Orlando* magazine, and DiRoNA awarded an Excellence in Dining Award.

A New Territory: Las Vegas

On a winning streak in New Orleans, in 1995 Emeril decided to open his third restaurant, in Las Vegas, another city known for its convention traffic, but not necessarily for its haute cuisine. In the mid-1990s, business travelers, foreign tourists, wealthy locals, and the millions of convention goers were the primary target audience for fine dining restaurants, of which there were few. All-you-can-eat buffets represented the lion's share of local dining establishments.

Las Vegas's convention attendance and residential development were growing at an astounding pace during the early to mid-1990s, with the Las Vegas metropolitan area being named the fastest-growing region in the country in 1996. The area's population had grown 41% in six years and welcomed 32 million visitors annually.[2] "The size of the market is amazing," says Todd English, who owned five Boston-area restaurants at the time and now runs Olives Las Vegas in the Bellagio. "There's got to be gold in them thar hills. You need just a tiny fraction of the people who live there or come to visit to make Las Vegas a dining destination as well as a gambling destination,"[3] he observed back in 1998. Demand for services was growing, and smart restaurateurs like Todd English and Emeril had taken notice.

Simultaneously, the construction boom of the 1990s put pressure on existing hotels to spruce up their image in order to hold onto their customers. With the $1.5 billion Bellagio hotel and casino on its way, some hotel owners were looking for a way to distinguish themselves. One of their solutions was to partner with superstar chefs.

Wolfgang Puck was the first celebrity chef to open up shop, in 1992, with a carbon copy of his Los Angeles hot spot, Spago. It did so well, grossing nearly $12 million a year, that hotels began trying to align themselves with the nation's hottest chefs in order to grab a portion of that upscale money.

Charlie Trotter was actually the second major chef to move into Las Vegas, in 1994, where he set up shop at the MGM Grand. Unfortunately, after a strong start, with a very high-end concept, MGM management apparently pushed Trotter to change the whole approach—enlarging the space, changing the menu, and cutting prices. After just a few months, Trotter asked for a buyout and returned to Chicago. When Steve Wynn offered a new opportunity at the Bellagio, Trotter rejected that, too, saying, "I got the impression that he's too much hands-on. I got the impression that he might come in and say, 'Serve this,' which is not something I could cope with,"[4] sounding as if he was describing the reason for his falling out at the MGM Grand.

Shortly thereafter, Emeril moved into the space Trotter had left.[5] Emeril's New Orleans Fish House takes up 5,500 square feet and seats 160 in the dining room, plus an additional 18 at the seafood bar. Designed by Emeril's second wife, Tari, the restaurant cost $800,000 to build, not including the kitchen improvements, which the MGM Grand paid for.[6] Featuring bare floors with black-and-white photos of Cajun country,[7] Emeril's shied away from the glitz that is usually found in Las Vegas. This, his third restaurant, was his second experience partnering with another organization. He first partnered with the owner of the building in which NOLA is located.

The menu at Emeril's Las Vegas venue includes a variety of seafood, from fish to shellfish, as well as nonfish fare. The seafood bar is a popular choice, offering New Orleans Style Po Boys and Baked Seasonal Oysters, just to name a couple of dishes. For dinner, guests can select from Sweet Barbeque Atlantic Salmon, Pan Fried Sole, Pecan Roasted Texas Redfish, Creole Spicy Boiled Maine Lobster, or Grilled Jumbo Gulf Shrimp, on the seafood side. Meat lovers may prefer the Grilled and Roasted Double Cut Pork Chop, the Roasted Half Chicken, or the Louisiana Cedar Plank Campfire Steak. For dessert, Triple Layered Coconut Cake, Emeril's Banana Cream Pie, and Sweet Potato Pecan Bread Pudding are the standouts among several delicious options.

Echoing the menu at the original Emeril's without mirroring it, Emeril's New Orleans Fish House won fans for its fresh, original creations.

With the larger tourist base and captive audience at the MGM Grand, Emeril's third restaurant was almost sure to be a hit. As usual, it was. "The response has been unbelievable,"[8] reported Emeril just days after the restaurant opened.

Publishing Success

Following the success of his first three restaurants, adding to his chain did little to raise Emeril's professional stature. Perhaps more important for his industry credibility at this point were his cookbooks, which reflected his individual take on cuisine and American culture.

Emeril's New New Orleans Cooking, his first cookbook, presented consumers with Emeril's approach to cooking at his namesake restaurant. His second, released in 1996, contained recipes more likely to be found at NOLA, his second restaurant, which is known more for experimentation and innovation. Food critic Tom Fitzmorris considers *Louisiana Real and Rustic* a turning point for Emeril. "It's one of the best Louisiana cookbooks ever published," he says. Written with a local chef, Marcelle Bienvenu, who introduced Emeril to country Cajun traditional cooking, *Real and Rustic* was a step up from *New New Orleans Cooking*, which Fitzmorris notes had some recipes that did not work.

Although the books were widely praised for increasing the awareness and appeal of Creole and Cajun cuisine, it was Emeril's third cookbook, released the following year, in 1997, that proved his breakout work. Following his two more general cookbooks, *Emeril's Creole Christmas* (Morrow Cookbooks) was a more specialized title geared to holiday cooking. It was also his first national best seller.

Continuing his pace of one cookbook a year, in 1998 he published *Emeril's TV Dinners* (William Morrow, 1998), leveraging his success on *Emeril Live*, which had by then won a Cable ACE Award and was seen in millions of homes nationwide. It, too, became a best seller.

In 1999, he published *Every Day's a Party* (Morrow Cookbooks), also a best seller, followed by *Prime Time Emeril* (Morrow Cookbooks) in 2001, which did not reach best-seller status, most likely because of the significant downturn in the publishing industry following September 11. No one was buying books at that point.

In 2002, his seventh cookbook suggested a change in Emeril's perspective, with a book of recipes developed just for children. *Emeril's There's a Chef in My Soup!* (HarperCollins) became a *New York*

Times best seller within two weeks of its release. He had hit a chord with his fans. It was about that time that his third wife, Alden, announced she was expecting their first child.

His eighth cookbook, *From Emeril's Kitchens,* contains 150 recipes for the most-requested dishes in his nine restaurants. Published in 2003, it also quickly became a best seller.

Due to the overwhelming response to his first children's cookbook, *Emeril's There's a Chef in My Family! Recipes to Get Everybody Cooking* (HarperCollins, 2004) will be his ninth book.

Beyond his success as a chef and writer, Emeril's cookbooks provide a timeline for important events in his life. Beginning with books that explain his personal style and palate, publishing is another medium to spread the gospel of cooking according to Emeril. Once his Cajun-Creole roots were established with his first couple of books, he moves on to recipes that build on the success and popularity of his television shows. Having married again in 2000 and looking forward to the birth of their new baby, his third child, he releases a cookbook especially for his youngest fans. Finally, wanting to demonstrate the scope and breadth of recipes in his many restaurants, he publishes instructions for how to make the most popular dishes.

While certainly an important means of strengthening Emeril's brand and industry reputation, publishing also serves as a lucrative profit center for his company. Assuming industry-standard royalties of 10% of the cover price, Emeril earns between $2.60 and $3.00 for each book sold. And with more than 3.5 million in the hands of consumers, cookbooks have netted him several million at the very least.

Additionally, on top of any advance, each cookbook sold at his company web site, Emerils.com, or at the retail outlets in his restaurants or headquarters, nets an even higher profit margin. Retail booksellers can typically purchase books at a wholesale cost of 50 to 56% off retail. Assuming Emeril was able to negotiate the same terms, he garners approximately $13 per book sold through his web site.

With such a strong fan base, TV shows through which to market products like his cookbooks, and retail outlets in which to sell them,

Emeril's only challenge when it comes to publishing is just finding the time to work out the concept and assign workers to get it done.

More New Restaurants

Following a slew of awards and industry recognition for his ground-breaking culinary skills, Emeril's attention returned to New Orleans, where (as mentioned in Chapter 5) the chance to open a third local restaurant had just arrived. Never one to reject a great opportunity there for the taking, in 1998 Emeril bought the Delmonico and invested heavily to renovate and reopen it as Emeril's Delmonico.

Tackling the challenge without outside partners and facing expectations that had been set by the 100-year-old establishment, Emeril once again proved his business savvy and culinary expertise. In no time Emeril's Delmonico was named one of the best places to eat in New Orleans.

After partnering with the MGM Grand in Las Vegas, Emeril recognized the value of having a popular hotel or resort as a landlord and agreed to be one of the first restaurants to set up shop at City-Walk, the entertainment district at Universal Orlando in Florida. In addition to expanding his fan base beyond New Orleans and Las Vegas, getting in on the ground floor at the theme park's dining and shopping complex presumably meant a better financial deal; City-Walk's vice president and general manager alluded to such partnerships in a 1998 *Orlando Sentinel* article.

Alongside Jimmy Buffett's Margaritaville and the NASCAR Café, you get the sense that the sophistication of Emeril's Restaurant may be lost on visitors. But the food and ambiance follow along the same lines as the existing Emeril's Restaurants, with Creole fare serving as the backbone. And the advance reservation required, as long as six to eight weeks during peak dining hours, rival those at his other locations.

Just a few months later, Emeril opened his second Las Vegas

eatery, the Delmonico Steakhouse, which is located in the upscale Venetian Hotel/Resort/Casino. Described as an oasis away from the glitz and glitter of typical Vegas eateries with "simplicity, under-statement and rustic Spartanism," Delmonico has been highly rated as a steakhouse on the strip, with *Las Vegas Life* repeatedly naming it the best steakhouse in town in the early 2000s.

As you would expect, the restaurant's dinner menu is heavy on steaks, from rib eye to bone in steak to strip steak, filet mignon, chateaubriand, and sirloin. But lobster, shrimp, chicken, pork chops, salmon, and lamb are also available for those not in the mood for beef. With foie gras as an appetizer, it is clear this restaurant is for those who are serious about good food. However, more standard alternatives, such as shrimp cocktail, bruschetta, and steak tartare are also listed.

Similar but different—an amalgamation from several of his other restaurants—the Delmonico Steakhouse keeps Emeril in a class by himself.

Emeril the Pioneer

In many ways, Emeril is a talented chef much like other talented chefs—Wolfgang Puck, Jacques Pepin, Alice Waters, to name a few—displaying mastery of culinary skills combined with a flair for the unusual. And in other ways, he is a pioneer—the first to achieve the status of celebrity chef, the first to bring the fine dining experi-ence to the masses, and the first to effectively reach both male and female audiences on the topic of cooking.

Although he may never have planned to be a pioneer, Emeril gained a sizeable competitive advantage by being one. Researchers at Northwestern University report that, in many ways, market pio-neers like Emeril have the opportunity to shape the perception of their brand and of the entire market category in which they operate.

By achieving celebrity chef status before anyone else, Emeril effectively defined what it means to be one. He is the standard by which other celebrity chefs are judged.

Gregory Carpenter, Rashi Glazer, and Kent Nakamoto of the Kellogg School of Management at Northwestern University found: "As brands enter the market sequentially, buyers learn about them. The pioneer plays a special role in the buyers' learning process. Being the first entrant, the pioneer has the unique opportunity to become perceptually distinctive, defining buyer notions of value for the entire category and influencing the choice process."[9] In layman's terms, by being first, Emeril assumes the responsibility for educating the market about what it means to be a celebrity chef, without interference from other sources. He is in control.

Essentially, with nothing else to compare the pioneer (Emeril) to, consumers define the whole market category (celebrity chefs) by him and his brand. Say the researchers, "[Consumers'] experience is limited to the pioneer, so the pioneer becomes more memorable, more vivid, and often the pioneer and the product category become closely related in buyers' minds, sometimes synonymous." Since consumers remember and recall the pioneer more clearly and frequently than any competitors, the pioneer's brand is then more frequently chosen.

This "pioneering advantage" creates a significant and enduring barrier to entry. In fact, subsequent competitors—would-be celebrity chefs—will be able to achieve only a fraction of the market share that the pioneer obtains as a result of being first to market.

Following Emeril, there have been many chefs to develop and star in cooking shows on the Food Network, but none that have garnered the fan base that Emeril has. Others, such as Wolfgang Puck, may have a similar combination of restaurants, TV shows, and products but have not managed to win the hearts of American consumers to the degree Emeril has. In many ways, he is the Michael Jordan of the culinary world and, like Michael, so far there is no one who has been able to step into his shoes—not that Emeril is thinking of retiring.

By securing the market leader position, Emeril is in the driver's seat when it comes to determining his next move. His competitive advantage is almost impenetrable. Everyone from hoteliers to product manufacturers to publishers, consumer product marketers, fundraisers—you name it—wants to affiliate with this powerhouse brand. Success breeds success.

Interestingly, his failures have had a lot to do with his current champion position.

How Emeril's Failures Paved the Way for Success

By 1998, Emeril was an A-list celebrity who could do no wrong. His success was staggering, his popularity soaring. And yet it was his failures, not his accomplishments, that had positioned him for the rewards he was receiving. In fact, *because* of his failures, he was now successful, says celebrity expert Michael Sands, of Sands Digital Media.

Looking back to his early days in the profession, one of Emeril's first failures was his inability to land a job in New York City. Even armed with awards and one of the best culinary arts degrees around, he still had difficulty. But rather than accepting failure and moving on to something else, either by relocating to a different city or falling back on his musical talents, Emeril challenged himself to further improve his skills through an internship in Europe.

That one decision, to continue investing in himself, to better his professional skills, encapsulates Emeril's whole approach to life— look past failure to the opportunity that is just around the corner if you can kick your skills up a notch. He refuses to view failures as such, but, rather, as opportunities to learn and grow. His inability to land a job was just a sign that he needed more skills, he thought. So he went out and got them.

Soon after moving to New Orleans to assume the head chef position at Commander's Palace, his first marriage fell apart and his wife and two daughters moved back to Massachusetts. He experienced a different kind of failure, personal rather than professional, and Emeril again focused on bettering himself because of it. He poured his heart and soul into making Commander's even better than it had been, which was hard to do, given the restaurant's solid track record. But he succeeded, moving Commander's into a new level of fine dining and winning an even larger following. By purposely turning his attention away from his personal hurt, Emeril made possible an even greater success for Commander's.

When he decided to open his own restaurant but failed to convince Ella Brennan to partner with him on a Warehouse District location, he did not give up on the idea altogether. He stuck to his vision and vowed to find another way to make a go of it. That meant pursuing financing on his own. Unfortunately, attempting to secure financing for a start-up restaurant—not the safest of investments from a lender's perspective—led to a series of failures. Time and again, lenders turned Emeril down. But he did not give up, each time contacting one more bank regarding a loan. And when he was almost out of options, one of the most conservative banks around, Whitney National Bank, agreed to lend him the money he needed.

Those bank rejections tested Emeril's resolve and made his approval that much sweeter. It also impressed upon him the need to stay in close contact with his banker to ensure that future applications for financing would be less onerous.

Several years later, after having remarried, Emeril again experienced heartbreak—a second divorce, in 1998, which was worse this time because he and Tari had also been business partners. She had been the driving force behind the award-winning ambiance created within Emeril's and NOLA, as well as handling many of the administrative tasks. But months apart due to restaurant openings, television commitments, and book tours had taken their toll on the relationship.[10] In order to hold onto his company, he had to arrange a financial settlement that was a temporary setback to his business.

Says Emeril about the experience, "I wouldn't wish divorce on my worst enemy. . . . There's no good time. It stinks, it's a lousy thing. It's probably a wake-up call in a sense. It's probably the closest thing to death that you'll experience."[11] Even his daughter Jessica noticed a change in her dad, commenting, "I think that after his second divorce, he took a step back and sort of had to re-evaluate and reposition himself and figure out what he needed."[12]

The price of divorce was high, but he managed to survive and move on, perhaps changing some of his contractual relationships in order to avoid such a situation again.

A second divorce might have soured most men on love, especially with the business impact factored in, but Emeril found it again, with Alden. They married in 2000. She, too, is a partner, but in every sense of the word; she and their son are at Emeril's side constantly, providing both the family connection and the career support that he needs.

It was around the same time as his wedding that Emeril was approached about appearing in his own sitcom on network television. As mentioned in Chapter 4, this show was inspired by events in his life: The comedy revolved around a cooking show host and his friends and business associates. But because it was a different genre and required a different skill set, the show failed. Emeril had assumed that his experience of hosting his own cooking show would apply to comedy, but despite coaches, script changes, and a major effort on his part, the show was canceled. The critics had been unkind, questioning his acting ability, and Emeril moved on, but with a bruised ego.

On the plus side, millions of consumers who had never before seen his cooking shows now knew who Emeril was, compliments of NBC. Consumers without cable TV had a sense of what Emeril was all about. His popularity broadened, despite the show's cancellation. Few of his fans thought less of him because of the show's failure—his cooking shows were still in production, still extremely popular.

These failures, some major, some minor, could have caused Emeril to leave the field, shut his business down, or take other drastic action in response. But he did not. Like other wise business owners, he saw his failures for what they were—learning experiences.

As bCentral.com business columnist Jeff Wuorio states, "Failure offers insight. It's an opportunity to identify what went wrong and highlight greater issues that we all need to be reminded of from time to time."[13] Describing failure as a teacher, Wuorio points out several ways failure can improve a business:

- A willingness to fail can encourage innovation. Says Richard Farson, author of *Whoever Makes the Most Mistakes Wins* (Free Press, 2002), "Improvements only happen when you try things differently."[14]
- Although failure can be caused by risk taking, both are necessary for innovation and creativity to thrive.
- Failure and mistakes can prompt introspection that lead to improvement.
- Studying your own failure, as well as those of other business owners can show you how common it is. Says Al Vicere, executive education professor of strategic leadership at Penn State University in Wurio's bCentral article, "It's important to study how others failed. That can help you build patterns that can prove exceedingly useful."
- A failure may reflect an idea that is ahead of its time. "Failure can also derive from strength," points out Wuorio. Revamping the strategy may be all that is needed to reach success.
- A failure can lead to an overall evaluation of the business, forcing the owner to look beyond the immediate situation. "Thinking about what went wrong really pulls you up to a more strategic view," says Vicere.

In Emeril's case, his failures consistently led to a reassessment of the situation, development of a new strategy, and an appreciation for what he had learned along the way.

Although Emeril projects an image of success, positioning himself as a leading chef and culinary mind, it is his failures that truly distinguish him from the stereotypical image of a chef as being arrogant, curt, and inaccessible. Perhaps in part because of his struggle for everything he has, Emeril is nothing like that. By all accounts, he is warm, personable, and slightly shy.

While his successes highlight what makes Emeril different from his fans, his failures underscore what makes him similar. Failures forge a bond with his customers, viewers, guests, and neighbors that endear him to them and strengthen his image as an ordinary person with extraordinary skills, according to Sands, who says that it is the failures throughout his life that have made his current success possible.

How Emeril Stacks Up against Industry Standards

In positioning his company for greatness, Emeril determined what the best practices were in the industry and established standards that exceeded them. Throughout his company, from the design of the kitchens in his restaurants to the speed with which guests' drinks are delivered to the table to the interactive capabilities of the corporate web site, Emeril set performance expectations. Even operationally, Emeril's Homebase is well above average.

Using figures provided by the National Restaurant Association's 2003 *Restaurant Industry Operations Report*, it becomes clear how and where Emeril surpasses the competition. Restaurants at the high end of the dining spectrum, in this case categorized as "Full Service Restaurants with an Average Check Per Person $25 and Over," still represent a wide range of levels of service even within the category of white-tablecloth dining. With 53.5% of the restaurants in this category having average check values of less than $32.99, there obviously are eateries in a different league than Emeril's restaurants, where it would be rare for one person to dine for less than $32.99, much less a whole party.

That said, the majority of respondents to the association's survey have been in business more than five years (64%; represent a single, independent unit (85.5%) versus multiple units (14.5%); and are profitable (60.5%)). Also like Emeril's operations, nearly 70% of the restaurants queried are located in less than 7,500 square feet of space and have fewer than 200 seats. The bulk are privately held corporations (61.1%) like Emeril's, although 40% of those responding reported revenues of less than $2 million.

Within the category of high-end fine dining, median food and beverage sales per seat total more than $10,000 per year. However, if that were the case at Emeril's restaurants, where the number of seats hovers around 160, the restaurants would be generating less than $2 million a year—far less than what industry insiders believe the sites are earning.

Or, calculated another way, the association learned that median total sales per square foot are $300 in this category, which would mean the 5,500-square-foot Emeril's New Orleans Fish House generates approximately $1.6 million per year. The true figure is probably multiples of that.

Emeril's is clearly a standout in many ways, but either the industry has begun to copy the chef's formula for success or he is relying on tried-and-true methods to gain an edge. Not that it is a competition, however. In fact, Emeril frequently refers guests to other area restaurants he respects.

Grassroots Marketing to Loyal Customers

Emeril has worked hard for his success, but his customers have helped tremendously. Probably without expecting it, Emeril has created his own corps of customer evangelists—volunteer salespeople and customers who buy from him regularly and rave about it, encouraging others to as well.

"Customer evangelism is a philosophy about customers," say Ben McConnell and Jackie Huba in their book *Creating Customer Evangelists*

(Dearborn, 2002). "Inside a business thriving with customer evangelists, everything is designed to keep customers coming back. These
companies deliver memorable experiences that compel customers to
share their knowledge with others." Which is exactly how Emeril
positions his company when he attempts to deliver the perfect dining experience.

Behind this commitment to building long-term customer relationships that generate buzz about his company is the understanding that it costs five times more to acquire a new customer than to
keep an existing one.[15] Aiming to delight his current clientele makes
fiscal sense as well. Most important, loyal customers spend more
money than infrequent customers and help to drive new business to
their favorite places. They do that by raving excitedly about Emeril
to their families, their friends, their business associates, as well as the
lady in line behind them at the grocery store or the man next to
them on the plane. They may gush about the dinner they had at one
of his restaurants last week or the out-of-this-world appetizer they
prepared based on a recipe at his web site. They may urge a friend to
try one of his spices or purchase a cookbook to give as a gift. They
spread the gospel of Emeril to everyone they know, and to some
they do not know, because they feel a connection to and an appreciation for his talents. "Customer evangelism spreads by word of
mouth," say McConnell and Huba, reinforcing the power of the personal referral.

But this emphasis on the customer experience does not start with
customers, it starts with the company's leader. Emeril sets the standard for his company by setting customer delight as the expectation,
and he demands that his employees go above and beyond to achieve
that. That is the kind of boss who earns customer evangelists.

Peer Review from Other Chefs

Of course, earning customer raves does not necessarily mean that
Emeril wins kudos from his colleagues. But he does.

Renowned chefs from Julia Child to Charlie Trotter to Wolfgang Puck express their own admiration for his skills and business acumen. Child observes, "He's made cooking fun, which I think is very important because that brings people into the kitchen. Anyone that can bring people into the kitchen in their own home I'm for."[16]

Friend Charlie Trotter, of Charlie Trotter's in Chicago, says, "I think he's one of the finest, if not the finest, chef-operators in America today. The type of creativity he exhibits is exciting," adding that in the 10 years they have known each other, he has never seen Emeril make the same dish twice.[17]

Norman Van Aken, of Norman's, comments, "He's so good at every angle, whether it's cooking or the business end of running a restaurant."[18]

Emeril does have his critics, however.

Lewis Beale, of the New York *Daily News* says, "I think that the main criticism of Emeril is that the shtick tends to overwhelm the presentation. It is as if you are locked in a room with him forever and ever and there were an endless loop of 'BAM!' and 'Kick it Up a Notch' running through your head. It would drive you crazy. And I think it drives a lot of food writers crazy and a lot of people who take food seriously crazy because they think the show biz aspect overwhelms the food aspect."[19]

Even Anthony Bourdain, the outspoken Food Network host and author of *Kitchen Confidential* (Bloomsbury, 2000), admits Emeril is good at what he does. "I hate Emeril's show and his cuddly persona, and his audience like the Moonies," says Bourdain. "That said, Emeril Lagasse can really cook."[20] Coming from someone like Bourdain, whose role is to be critical, that is high praise indeed.

Despite some dissatisfaction, or jealousy, in the ranks regarding the impact of his television shows on the perception of the culinary industry, most industry leaders recognize that Emeril has become their unofficial spokesperson. Through his visibility and frequent public appearances, Emeril has drawn attention to cooking as an art and a science, boosting interest in the activity both as a vocation and as an avocation. Applications to cooking schools are up, as are requests for admittance to specialty training sessions, such as knowledge of wine.

Because of, or in spite of, this, several leading culinary organizations have invited Emeril to become involved. He now serves on the National Advisory Board of the James Beard Foundation and is frequently involved in activities and fund-raising events in support of organizations that have helped him, such as Johnson & Wales University, in addition to other culinary programs, such as the hotel school at Cornell University. Although his business focus is on his clientele, he remains visible to his peers through professional involvement and volunteering.

The Emeril Brand: Reaching Maturity?

Despite his work to position himself as a brand rather than as an individual, there are signs that both are on their decline. A bad review here, falling media coverage there—nothing major—but an inkling that Emeril's rise to prominence may have plateaued.

This was to be expected, of course, since all brands and products eventually experience a slowdown in demand. All brands follow a life cycle that leads from development to introduction and growth, on to maturity, and eventual decline. "The Emeril brand is reaching maturity," says Dennis Reynolds, the J. Thomas Clark Professor of Entrepreneurship and Personal Enterprise at the School of Hotel Administration at Cornell University. "This doesn't mean it will die soon, but it will diminish as the brand becomes more omnipresent in the marketplace."

The development stage of Emeril's brand began during his tenure with Dunfey Hotels, when he earned a reputation as a chef and turnaround restaurateur. Those skills led to his position at Commander's, where his status rose. But it was not until he disassociated himself from the Commander's Palace brand name, with the opening of his own restaurant, that the Emeril brand was born.

During this introductory phase, Emeril's goal was to generate interest in and awareness of his restaurant and cooking skills. His brand name was just emerging as an entity unto itself, and demand for his services was rising exponentially. Although most new products and services do not gain momentum as quickly as Emeril's Restaurant did, the growth curve during this phase is typically steep.

Once his name and reputation went national with the launch of *Emeril Live*, Emeril was officially in the growth phase of his brand's life cycle, typically a period of rapidly rising revenue. It is during this phase that brands are extended and distribution channels expanded just to keep up with customer demand. Emeril took the opportunity during this time to roll out branded products, add to his line of cookbooks, and open several new restaurants.

Through synergistic marketing using one profit center to promote others (and vice versa), Emeril's empire grew more vast. But once the pace of sales began to slow a bit, due in part to the sizeable customer base, the brand had become mature. Although sales typically slow during this phase, profits still increase due to lower marketing costs; with a larger customer base characteristic of a mature brand, fewer marketing dollars need to be allocated to generate sales.

Brands necessarily become mature after exponential growth and exposure, a phase that can last anywhere from a few months to many years. Following maturity, a brand either reverts to the growth phase by virtue of a new product, marketing approach, or trend or progresses into decline, during which sales fall off due to market saturation or a shift in customer preferences.

Think about the personal computer, for example. It took years to reach maturity, but the market pushes itself back into growth mode with revolutionary product additions that entice consumers to replace the models they have. On the other hand, Tab, once a leading diet cola, is all but extinct now, save for a small band of loyal fans. It is hard to find retailers that carry the brand, thanks in part to Diet Coke, the 300-pound gorilla. The introduction of Diet Coke grabbed market share away from Tab, causing sales to fall and shifting consumer preference toward the Nutrasweetened diet cola.

Shifting customer preference, in a nutshell, is Emeril's biggest threat. Consumers everywhere love him, but at some point, will he become passé? If that time comes, his brand will be in decline and he'll need to invest in rejuvenating it.

By virtue of his current leadership position in the industry, Emeril routinely receives opportunities to hobnob with fellow restaurateurs, chefs, restaurant critics, and foodies. And it is that culinary network that gives Emeril industry credibility.

7

MANAGING THE EMERIL EMPIRE

Emeril has a unique ability to bring out the best in people. He can see talent in someone and just make it flourish.

— Tony Cruz, director of finance, Emeril's Homebase[1]

Almost three years went by and I began realizing that we were getting the sort of core people that were extremely professional—because we didn't hire actors or actresses or students. We wanted people to be waiters or waitresses. You know: professional people," says Emeril. "And we were getting this core of people that were very serious. We'd built this rock core and I didn't want to become the revolving door for the industry, so I realized we had to create some opportunities," he explains.[2]

That realization led Emeril to open a second restaurant, NOLA, in order to provide advancement opportunities for members of his staff, whom he didn't want to lose (as mentioned in Chapter 3). Valuing his staff—at every level—and offering opportunities to learn new skills and rise within his company are what have given Emeril's Homebase a significant competitive advantage, as well as made Emeril himself a success. One measure of that success is his company's low employee turnover rate, which is reportedly far below national averages. In fact, some of his employees have worked with him for more than 20 years—an anomaly in an industry where the average tenure is far lower.

In 2003, the average turnover rate for employees at fine dining restaurants was 45%, according to the National Restaurant Association; the average rate for salaried employees was slightly less, 38%, and for hourly employees slightly more, 53%.[3] But perhaps because there is so much competition for a position in one of Emeril's restaurants, most employees choose to stay put. When Emeril's Atlanta opened in August 2003, for example, there were nearly 1,000 applicants for just 160 spots.[4] A few months later, in Miami Beach, there were 800 applicants for 110 jobs.[5]

Making the effort to keep employee turnover down has several benefits, including improved operational efficiency, because the business does not have to constantly hire and train employees, and costs can be reduced. Les McKeown, author of *Retaining Top Employees* (McGraw-Hill, 2002) and president of Deliver The Promise, reports that it costs between 1.2 and 2.0 times a worker's annual salary to replace him or her.[6] In the typical fine dining restaurant, where the average worker is earning $18,767, according to the National Restaurant Association, that equates to a replacement cost of more than $28,000.

That $28,000 covers the hard costs a restaurant incurs each time someone leaves and needs to be replaced, including the administrative costs of processing the exit; increased unemployment tax; cost of additional overtime for others to cover hours the employee was scheduled for; criminal, credit, and reference checks on replacement applicants; the cost of an interviewer's time; the cost of any orientation and training; and lost productivity within the organization while the individual is being replaced, explains McKeown.[7] No wonder Emeril tries to avoid having to go through this too often!

Building an Effective Staff Organization: Seven Key Factors

Emeril has proven himself a businessman with a vision for his organization and well-developed standards of performance he expects everyone to live up to. This vision and set of standards has led to years of superior customer satisfaction and profits. But part of what makes Emeril so successful is not just his business strategy, it is how he implements it. Says Jeffrey Pfeffer in his book *The Human Equation: Building Profits by Putting People First*, "Successful organizations understand the importance of implementation, not just strategy, and moreover, recognize the crucial role of their people in this process."[8]

Employees, though critical for success in just about any industry, are even more so in food service, where the quality of the meal service is more important to guests than the food itself, according to a 1999 Zagat Survey, which showed 62% of customer complaints are about the service and only 11% are about the food.[9] If food were the most important part of the meal, that percentage would be reversed. That observation bears itself out at Emeril's places as well, about which Hugh Rushing, executive vice president of the Cookware Manufacturers Association, says, "You can find finer cuisine, but you can't find a finer experience"[10]—a refrain heard almost universally.

Pfeffer, a professor of organizational behavior at Stanford Business School, has identified seven dimensions that characterize successful companies. By "successful," he means businesses that produce profit through the careful selection, retention, compensation, and management of their employees. The seven dimensions are as follows:

1. Employment security
2. Selective hiring of new personnel
3. Self-managed teams and decentralization of decision making
4. Comparatively high compensation contingent on organizational performance

5. Extensive training
6. Reduced status distinctions and barriers
7. Extensive sharing of financial and performance information throughout the organization

1. Emeril's Homebase Offers Employment Security

In the past 10 years, corporate policy regarding human resources shifted at many of the nation's largest employers, which has had a trickle-down effect on companies of all sizes. Where lifelong, guaranteed employment was the norm in the early- to mid-1900s, by the 1980s, that commitment to workers had begun to erode and layoffs and downsizing became almost de rigueur.

Today, in the early 2000s, announcements of cutbacks and layoffs appear in the media weekly, to the tune of tens of thousands of workers. Granted, many of those firings ebb and flow with the economy, with a down market causing more downsizing in order to trim a company's largest expense line items—salaries and benefits. But even in the 1970s, organizations provided a level of job security that is virtually unheard of today.

Unfortunately, by viewing employees as expendable assets, companies frequently run into trouble. Focusing on managing expenses—rather than generating sales—as the key to survival, many businesses are doomed. Lack of any kind of employment security creates a pool of workers who are short-term-oriented and who put job preservation before their employer's needs. Understanding this, it is easy to see why some companies routinely go through round after round of layoffs. Eastman Kodak Company, for example, has cut its workforce at its main facilities in Rochester, New York, from a high of 60,400 in 1982 to 20,600 in 2003 through widespread layoffs every three years; the company also announced further reductions of 12,000 to 15,000 within the next three years.[11]

On the other hand, there are a handful of companies that commit to providing employment for their workers, assuming top performance, and have avoided recent layoffs. In his book, Pfeffer describes the tactics used by the Lincoln Electric Company, a successful arc welding and electric motor manufacturer, to provide employment security. Years ago, it began offering guaranteed employment to its workers after three years on the job. It has also not had a layoff since 1948. Despite business downturns, the company refused to divest itself of its most valuable asset—its experienced employees. Instead, the company redeployed them, transferring some production workers into the field as sales reps (and increasing its market share in the process). Pfeffer summarizes, "Over the years, Lincoln has enjoyed gains in productivity that are far above those for manufacturing as a whole, and its managers believe that the assurance workers have that innovations in methods will not cost them or their colleagues their jobs has significantly contributed to these excellent results."[12]

Although Emeril's Homebase lacks Lincoln Electric's long-term track record, having been started in 1990 versus 1895 for Lincoln, the companies' perspectives on human resources are quite similar. Emeril recognizes the importance of well-trained, experienced employees who are in it for the long haul and goes so far as opening other restaurants in order to provide ongoing opportunities for growth within his ranks. He'd rather grow, and deal with the associated challenges, than lose workers who have been with him for years to the competition. He looks for and rewards employees who want a long-term position with the company.

Once an employee has been with Emeril's Homebase for a few years and has been promoted into management, some even get the opportunity to become part owners in one of the restaurants, providing added employment security as well as an incentive to stay.

But employment security is the foundation of all other organizational policies in successful companies, which rely on the assumption that staff members have the company's best interests at heart. Pfeffer explains, "Employment security is fundamental to the implementation of most other high performance management practices, such as selective hiring, extensive training, information sharing and delegation . . . delegation of operating authority and the sharing of sensitive performance and strategy information requires trust, and that trust is much more likely to emerge in a system of mutual, long-term commitments."[13]

Fortunately, Emeril seems to get this. Rarely do you hear of someone being fired or leaving his employ, probably because he takes such pains to find the right people from the outset—another characteristic of the most successful companies.

2. Emeril's Homebase Practices Selective Hiring

Another secret of Emeril's success has been his careful selection of employees. Not content to hire the typical food service workers—students, part-timers, struggling artists, people between other jobs—Emeril limits his waitstaff to individuals who truly want to work in the industry. Many stay for the money—waitstaff in fine dining establishments can do quite well financially—while others see a waitstaff position as a stepping-stone to an eventual manage-ment position at the company.

Although it may be assumed that food service is an easier indus-try in which to land a job, that is not the case at any of Emeril's restaurants. Using the Emeril's Atlanta applicant figures, where nearly 1,000 applicants vied for 160 slots, only 6% of those who apply land a job. By comparison, Harvard University's undergradu-ate class of 2007 admitted 2,094 of its 20,987 applicants, or 10% of the applicant pool.[14] Yes, getting a job at one of Emeril's restaurants can be even harder than getting into Harvard, believe it or not.

However, at Emeril's restaurants, experience in fine dining and an interest in working there are just the first-round qualifiers. Those seriously being considered for coveted waitstaff positions must prove their ability to get along with others; chemistry is a major part of the hiring decision, reports a former employee, who applauds Emeril's hiring criteria. Because of the emphasis on teamwork, any-one unable to work cooperatively is out of the running.

Most companies look for experience and technical skills first and interpersonal attributes later, whereas smart companies, like Emeril's, search for those qualities that cannot be taught—such as a willingness to work hard, an ability to work cooperatively, friendliness, and a voracious appetite for learning. How to take a drink order or manage 10 tables at once can be learned; attention to detail cannot.

Pfeffer offers several recommendations for the selective hiring process:

- Get a larger number of applicants per opening available (which Emeril does by attending job fairs and advertising openings).
- Screen for fit and attitude rather than learnable skills (chemistry is more important than anything else at Emeril's restaurants).
- Identify and specify the most critical skills or attitudes needed for success and narrow the list to a small number for use in screening (a short list is used).
- Set up several rounds of screening to build commitment and communicate the importance of making the right hiring decision (more than one interview is often required).
- Involve senior managers in the hiring process to signal the company's view of the importance of strong hiring decisions (Emeril is personally involved in various aspects of hiring and training employees, while general managers frequently make local hiring decisions).
- Regularly assess the process and results used in recruiting and adjust accordingly.[15]

Since most of Emeril's staffers are under age 45,[16] bringing in workers who are comfortable with a younger workforce is important.

3. Emeril's Homebase Relies on Decentralized Decision Making

"One of the things we do is we trust each general manager," says Emeril. When hiring employees for the new restaurant out of town, he explains, "Eric Linquest, my vice president, and I didn't go to the job fair in Atlanta, for example. They had 450 or more the first day and interviewed over 500 people the second day. We trusted the management team to hire the right people."[17] That is typical of Emeril's reliance on his restaurant staff, 98% of whom have been promoted from within.[18] Although he is called a very hands-on manager, in that he takes a personal interest in every aspect of how the profit centers of his organization are being run, he is also confident enough of his employees' abilities to be able to let go of tasks. Each of the nine restaurants is run by a self-managed team, with oversight from Emeril.

Few decisions, however, are made individually. At Emeril's, employees work as teams, both on the restaurant floor and behind the scenes. And together, teams decide on changes that need to be made or work that needs to be done.

Study after study has shown that teams outperform individuals. In addition to improving the quality of performance and results, team members also enjoy higher job satisfaction and the potential for higher compensation, due to performance-based pay. At Emeril's restaurants, workers are trusted to make decisions that are in the best interest of the company. Not only does such responsibility and authority make employees truly feel important to the organization, but shifting more responsibility for decisions to employees has allowed Emeril to continue expanding his operations.

Emeril explains, "I know what motivates people. The foundation of a relationship with someone is built on how you treat them. I never ask people in my organization to do things I haven't done or wouldn't do. When you do that, folks want to contribute. And when you have people who contribute, it's like a family."[19] This would also explain why no one wants to leave.

4. Emeril's Homebase Offers High Compensation

To a large degree, a company's compensation plan reflects the value it places on its people—either they represent the organization's most prized asset or they do not, says Pfeffer. Smart companies make sure they pay above-average salaries to retain their carefully selected, well-trained, high-performing employees.

Industry observers believe that some members of Emeril's waitstaff routinely make six figures annually through a combination of salary and tips. This level of pay is well above the National Restaurant Association average of $18,767 per full-time equivalent employee in restaurants generating more than $2 million in sales.[20]

Assuming one of Emeril's restaurants generates total revenues of $12 million, at a conservative tip rate of 15%, the restaurant's waitstaff is dividing a pool of $1.8 million a year in tips—on top of a salary. But perhaps even more telling is the fact that 98% of restaurant positions are filled from within at Emeril's Homebase—employees obviously want to stay with the company, presumably in part due to higher-than-average compensation.

But benefits are more than just the amount in a paycheck, and employees at Emeril's company are no exception in what they receive. Workers are offered health insurance, a 401(k) plan, and a 25% dining discount[21]—essentially the industry-standard offerings.

However, an important aspect of the company's compensation plan is the performance-based profit sharing available to senior employees who have partnered with Emeril on a restaurant. Although such arrangements can take many forms, it is likely that participating employees are required to make an up-front payment—a buy-in amount—in exchange for owning phantom stock in the restaurant. Although Emeril's organization does not release such information, for comparison's sake, Outback Steakhouse's buy-in amount is $200,000. Phantom stock works by giving an employee a percentage ownership in a business, based on how many total shares have been issued for the company. However, if the employee leaves the company, he or she likely forfeits the buy-in investment and stock ownership, and the stock reverts back to the company, where it can be redistributed or resold.

By combining employment security with above-average wages and a group-based form of compensation, such as profit sharing or partial ownership, companies like Emeril's Homebase leverage their human assets, rewarding employees for their individual contributions as well as their participation in the organization's success.

5. Emeril's Homebase Provides Extensive Training

Being "Emerilized" is how the company describes its intensive training program. The three- to four-week session, which Emeril leads off, teaches waiters and waitresses how to think, work, talk, and walk.[22] It is also a major investment for Emeril, who spends approximately $200,000 just to "indoctrinate waiters, reservationists, bus boys and dishwashers into the ways of Emeril."[23]

From the larger issues of what constitutes customer service to how to present a menu to a guest, Emeril's performance standards are drilled into the waitstaff until the Emeril Way becomes second nature.

In contrast, most U.S. companies view training as a frill that can be cut during economic downturns, reports Pfeffer. Only the best-performing organizations understand that it is a source of competitive advantage to be leveraged.

6. Emeril's Homebase Reduces Status Distinctions

"Make [my office] just like the rest," Emeril told his architects as the company headquarters was being built. Wanting to be perceived as another team member rather than the CEO, Emeril chose to have his office designed no larger than anyone else's. Granted, he doesn't spend much time there, with his hectic schedule, but the message was important—"We're all working together to create something special," the implication being that he is no more important than anyone working to serve the company's customers.

Although people frequently use dress as a means of distinguishing between different levels of employees, Emeril does all that he can to blend in rather than stand out. He'll don his chef's uniform when working in one of his restaurant's kitchens—but this is mainly for the customers. Otherwise, he is in casual dress, feeling no need to distance himself from his workers.

It may seem like a minor point, but encouraging the sense that everyone is working together for a common goal, from which everyone will benefit, is actually very important for peak performance, says Pfeffer. Emeril seems to instinctively know this.

7. Emeril's Homebase Shares Corporate Information

Most privately held companies, like Emeril's Homebase, cautiously guard information about the internal workings of the company, fearful that details of its financial performance may leak out and somehow damage the business. Fortunately, Emeril recognizes how incongruent that practice is with trusting your employees—either you trust them or you do not. It makes no difference whether we are talking about corporate financial ratios, money in the cash register, or names in the reservations book. Sharing sensitive information demonstrates to employees that they are trusted, that they are part of a team working cooperatively to succeed.

From a practical side, sharing information also enables team members to understand what their goals, strategies, and tactics are. Without details regarding profit margins on products the restaurant serves, waitstaff are less effective at selling high-margin items. Providing internal information is like providing tools that allow employees to do their best work.

At Emeril's, restaurant managers know how their location stacks up—they have their own budgets to work with and are challenged to do their best to achieve superior performance. In turn, that information is communicated throughout each restaurant to assist workers in contributing to the company's success.

Setting a Steady Pace for Growth

To some observers, Emeril's branching out into other markets—Las Vegas, Orlando, Miami, and Atlanta—signaled an aggressive growth push. But others disagree. "Nine restaurants in twelve years is not fast growth," says Isidore Kharasch, president of Hospitality Works, an international food service consulting firm. "He's growing at a pace that's comfortable for him and his team, which seems to be working well," adds Kharasch.[24]

Slow, steady growth is Emeril's strategy, in part due to his employees. He keeps his hiring and training costs low by hiring from within and carefully mentoring new talent. That, of course, takes time.

"We don't hire general managers or chefs de cuisine to run our restaurants, we build them," says Emeril. "That includes everyone from the front-of-the-house to the back-of-the-house. We just started it last year for sommeliers."[25] He has also instituted a new management development program for employees with leadership aspirations.

Emeril has avoided the temptation of expanding too quickly, Kharasch contends. To be successful at opening another restaurant, it takes a management team in place, a smoothly running operation, and positive cash flow. "Many restaurateurs jump too soon," explains Kharasch, by opening a second restaurant once the first hits the break-even point, rather than waiting for a growing positive cash flow. "But the first restaurant becomes your bread-and-butter," says Kharasch. It provides the cash flow needed to sustain the first *and* second restaurants during the first year, when the new restaurant is generally a cash drain on operations.

In contrast to too-eager restaurateurs, Emeril has moved slowly and methodically to open new restaurants, carefully choosing locations and concepts to fit the local market. "We could be international. We could be in Japan. We could be in London. But that's not what we are," explains Emeril.[26] Although, if he wanted to, he could open a restaurant just about anywhere, Emeril sticks a select few in warmer climates. He chooses carefully and moves slowly.

The most restaurants Emeril has ever opened in one year is three—hardly a blistering expansion pace by comparison to other chefs' chains, such as Wolfgang Puck's Express eateries, which set up 30 outlets in 10 years with plans for a total of 300 more in 4 years.[27]

Emeril's original plan had been to open one new restaurant in 2002, Tchoup Chop, and two in 2003 in Atlanta and Miami Beach. Instead, he opened none in 2002, following the events of September 11, 2001, and three the following year. In fact, Tchoup Chop's opening at Universal Orlando was delayed following the Bali terrorist attack, where many of his furnishings originated. But Emeril had plenty of product licensing work to keep him busy while he waited for everything to be completed.

Waiting can be a useful business tool, actually. By waiting until his existing restaurants are running smoothly—operationally and financially—Emeril lowers his risk of failure. He also provides time for his employees to settle into their new positions.

Fortunately, consumers are on his side. Each year since 1974 the percentage of meals eaten in U.S. restaurants has increased, from a low of 34% to a high of 46% in 2002, according to Piper Jaffray analysts.[28] The average annual expenditure on food away from home also grew, from approximately $1,750 in 1973 to more than $2,500 in 2002.[29] Those figures do not count business-related meals, however, which are more likely to be eaten in high-end restaurants.

As consumers have become accustomed to dining out more frequently, in part due to the quickening work pace that leaves little time for leisurely dining and entertaining, the expectations have also risen. With far more restaurant dining experience than previous generations, the bar is set increasingly higher for restaurateurs hoping to make their mark on foodies. Which is why Emeril's record of success with every restaurant he has opened so far is quite remarkable. Satisfying the varying tastes and preferences of residents in multiple markets with the common ground of excellent service is an accomplishment few chefs and business owners can claim.

Selecting Sites for New Restaurants— in Tourist Destinations

With a 59% failure rate among restaurants in the first three years, according to new research by Professor H.G. Parsa at Ohio State University,[30] Emeril's portfolio of eateries is doing very, very well. With nine restaurants in five cities and no closings, he is definitely above average, says Isidore Kharasch.

After successfully opening a second restaurant in New Orleans, Emeril moved beyond his hometown and into Las Vegas, 1,750 miles away, then on to Orlando, Atlanta, and Miami. There are many techniques used to select a strong restaurant location, says Kharasch, but some of the standard rules do not apply to places with a celebrity chef's name over the door. Customers will drive farther and spend more to eat at a restaurant run by a well-known chef, he says, making some of the general location guidelines more forgiving when it comes to restaurants such as Emeril's.

But Emeril's site selection process and philosophy are quite simple: "We want to be where we want to do business," he says. "Not because it's cool. It's not a quantity thing; it's a quality thing."[31] And because he is a hot commodity, Emeril can do that.

Most restaurateurs evaluate the demographics of an area or city first to determine whether there are enough potential customers to keep the place busy. Of course, fast-food restaurants are more interested in teens and twenty-something consumers, and fine dining establishments are more concerned with older residents and potential business clientele, but there needs to be enough of a market segment to make a concept work. For upscale restaurants, the local business climate also plays a major role in weeding out potential sites; recent layoffs and budget cuts will mean less money to be spent on client dinners, catered events, or holiday parties.

In addition to customer demographics, other factors include the number of businesses in a particular area, the amount of build-out still needed, and the amount of traffic, explains Kharasch. While a celebrity chef may worry less about build-out or development in an area, traffic is always a concern. The location still needs to be easily accessible to a large percentage of people in the region.

Just looking at the cities in which Emeril's restaurants are situated, you get a sense of Emeril's primary location strategy—tourist destinations. The benefit of locating in cities with high tourist traffic is that more money is often spent on meals; business travelers need a white-tablecloth restaurant in which to entertain guests, and vacationers do not scrutinize the bill as closely while away from home. Marty Kotis, president and CEO of Kotis Properties and president of the Council of International Restaurant Real Estate Brokers says, "We've found that if you hit a strong tourist destination or make it extremely convenient for business travelers, you get more of those types. To do really big numbers, you need to capture those two markets."[32]

So far, Emeril has chosen wisely in this regard. "In Atlanta, you would pick Buckhead—which is where Emeril went," observes Kotis. "In Vegas, you would pick a very strong hotel/casino"[33]— again, where Emeril went, with restaurants at the Venetian Resort/Hotel/Casino and the MGM Grand Hotel and Casino. However, choosing a location off the beaten path will not necessarily reduce business, as Emeril's Restaurant in New Orleans proves. "It's a cab ride versus a walk," explains Kotis, which does not seem to deter guests in the least. And of the 40 million visitors to Orlando each year, many spend time at Universal Studios Orlando, where Emeril's two restaurants are situated.

Focusing on attracting tourists and business travelers does not mean that local customers are unimportant, however. Far from it, says Kharasch. In fact, wowing local customers may be even more important in a tourist mecca.

Since local residents will frequent a restaurant much more than tourists, it is essential that an upscale restaurant cater to *their* needs first and foremost. "If a restaurant doesn't satisfy the local clientele, it will be branded a tourist trap," says Kharasch. When that happens, restaurants lose out on local word-of-mouth advertising. Typically, when area residents cannot recommend a restaurant to their friends, they will not recommend it to tourists, and the restaurant ends up failing.

One of the biggest issues for out-of-town restaurateurs is maintaining the same level of quality and service that guests have come to expect. As Emeril has added to his list of eateries, he has had to reduce the amount of time he can spend in any one place, putting at risk his restaurants' reputations.

Given the amount of time Emeril spends in New York City taping his shows, opening a restaurant there would seem to make perfect sense. But so far he has no plans to do so, despite the fact that he is presented with hundreds of opportunities each year, many of which are based in Manhattan. Sticking with restaurants in warmer climates is his preference, perhaps because they are more likely to be year-round tourist destinations.

Marketing via Emerils.com

Yes, he has two television shows, a guest spot on *Good Morning America* each Friday, and a Crest commercial, but even Emeril, as well known as he is, still needs to invest in marketing to keep sales growing. According to the 2003 *Restaurant Industry Operations Report* from the National Restaurant Association, fine dining establishments market primarily using newspaper advertising, Yellow Pages advertising, the Internet, newsletters, and community involvement. About 75% of the full-service restaurant operators reported an intention to advertise in a newspaper in 2003, and 70% planned to advertise in the Yellow Pages. However, restaurants with higher per-check averages relied more heavily on Internet advertising, customer-produced newsletters, and sponsoring community events than restaurants with lower check values.[34] In most respects, Emeril's marketing tactics mirror his high-end counterparts nationally.

One of Emeril's strongest marketing tools is Emerils.com, the corporate web site. Given the large number of out-of-town clientele, the business's web site provides a means of maintaining a connection with fans.

Launched in 1997, the initial purpose of the web site was to enhance customer service by giving fans access to more than 3,400 recipes, offering useful cooking tips, and providing personal information about Emeril. A secondary goal was to promote the restaurants. By developing the site in-house and keeping it simple, it cost less than $15,000 to get it up and running.[35]

Within a couple of years, however, fans were demanding more from the site. The Internet had continued to evolve, and computer users were becoming more dependent on web sites for information. So Emeril decided to get serious and totally overhauled the site, spending $5 million on servers, software, phone banks, and staff to design it, set it up, and support it properly[36]—providing the same level of service online that his clientele had come to expect of him offline. The investment was a smart move, both from a revenue-generating and from a brand-building perspective.

In 2001, Emerils.com went higher tech, incorporating Macromedia's Flash product into the display for improved ease of use. Within two weeks of the site relaunch, sales jumped 8% and the number of registered users climbed 6%, while maintenance costs dropped 85%. Following the upgrade, sales were expected to rise 21%.

As Emeril's empire has grown, so has the company's web site, expanding to incorporate online product sales and restaurant reservations on top of regular cooking-related columns and content. Now fans can do more than just read cooking information; they can take steps to start cooking. Virtually all of Emeril's branded merchandise is available for purchase, including cookbooks, chef apparel, pots and pans, knives, and seasonings.

Managing Hands-On

"Emeril's still very hands-on," claims former executive sous-chef Brian Deloney. If you make a mistake, "he will tear you up," he says.[37]

But apparently not too horribly, because Deloney has worked in Emeril's restaurants for six years, starting at Emeril's flagship, where he stayed only briefly, and then moving to NOLA for five years, where he rose from line cook to executive sous-chef, before transferring to Emeril's Delmonico Steakhouse in the Venetian Resort/Hotel/Casino in Las Vegas.

Although Emeril travels constantly from restaurant to restaurant, to New York and back weekly, as well as to special events and charity functions, he keeps careful track of issues in each restaurant using a folded piece of paper and a telephone. Not one to micromanage his team, he still likes to be kept abreast of any problems that crop up or areas that need improvement.

After all, it is his name over the door at most of his restaurants, and his reputation is at stake every time a meal is served. His continued involvement in the details of his restaurants may be why his standards are holding steady, with restaurant guests, for the most part, continuing to receive the quality service and food they associate with Emeril, even though he may not have been in the building for weeks.

Rallying the Troops

When he is in town, however, his presence is surely felt. Arthur Brief, professor of organizational psychology at Tulane University, remembers watching Emeril in action a few years ago, leading a waitstaff meeting before the dinner rush at Emeril's. "Emeril was in back giving what appeared to be the nightly meeting with the waitstaff. And he was cracking jokes, being silly, and trying to infuse the waitstaff and pump them up,"[38] remembers Brief. Anyone else watching might have questioned Emeril's antics, but Brief marveled at his managerial style.

Research has shown that laughing, joking, and putting employees in a good mood can impact the service they provide customers, says Brief. In essence, energizing employees increases the odds that they will share that positive energy with customers, leading to a more enjoyable buying experience. "It's a wise thing to do," says Brief.

"One of his best qualities is that he knows how to get people to perform," says a former employee.

Attending such premeal meetings is also a way for Emeril to demonstrate the importance of each and every worker and to express appreciation for their efforts in making the company successful. Organizations where senior executives, such as Emeril, are visible frequently achieve higher financial performance. And he understands the effect his appearance can have on the staff, which is why he makes the rounds at each restaurant, showing up to invigorate the workers and thrill the clientele.

Ensuring the Perfect Dining Experience

The carefully selected and trained employees working in the front of the house, the behind-the-scenes helpers, and the highly visible culinary crew all work together to provide each guest with a dining experience well beyond their expectations. Rather than approaching that task by emphasizing just one element of the day's or evening's happenings, Emeril chooses to break down each aspect of a guest's activities in the restaurant to try and make a positive impression on them at every step.

Says Emeril, "When the customer calls to make a reservation, or pulls up to the valet—that's when the whole process starts."[39] Name recognition is the first commandment that employees strive to adhere to—workers attempt to greet guests by name to make them feel welcome and important.

Using the in-house computer system, waiters and waitresses try to anticipate a customer's drink preference and have it waiting at the table even before the customer arrives. If you had a vodka tonic at your last visit, for instance, you will likely be asked if that is what you would like this time.

During the evening's premeal meeting, all the employees working the dinner shift meet in the dining room to review information about who will be arriving, what they prefer to eat and drink, as well as what they dislike. Each member of the team is assigned a task to help make every guest's night special, whether that means having a certain type of wine waiting at the table when they arrive or serving a specially prepared dessert to cap the night off.

Other tactics, carefully planned and well-rehearsed, include having umbrellas ready at the front door to escort guests to and from their car, which is valet parked; placing a special doormat at the front door for customers to wipe their feet clean before entering the restaurant; greeting the guests by name—a member of the waitstaff arrives at the table to greet them within 30 seconds of everyone being seated; using signals to alert other staff members if a drink order has already been taken; and wishing the customer good night by name.[40]

During the day, waiters and managers mail notes of appreciation to customers to further the connection with the restaurant and to encourage a return visit. It is personal touches like these, beyond the meal, that stand out in the minds of guests, many of whom return regularly to enjoy the attentive yet respectful service.

Emeril says he spent 10 years developing his dining concept in his head, picturing how customers would be treated, what would be served, what the space would look like. Borrowing from best practices at many U.S. and French restaurants, Emeril created his own set of standards and guidelines to impress guests at every meal, succeeding in besting even the best in the business.

But to be sure that his exacting standards are maintained when he is not in the building, Emeril has a thorough evaluation process in place. Consultants secretly visit and review the quality of service at his restaurants each month, reporting on everything from how reservations are handled to their good-bye from the valet. This report gives Emeril a sense of what might need to be improved. Those issues and others are discussed during quarterly meetings and at an annual summit.[41]

Monitoring—and Maximizing—Profitability

While Emeril's first priority may be to provide each and every guest with an exceptional dining experience, making sure his restaurants are profitable is a close second, as it should be. More restaurants go out of business because they fail to understand the fundamentals of making money.

Fortunately, even during a sluggish economy, Emeril's restaurants continue to grow, producing a 1.5% increase in business in 2003 from 2002.[42] Considering the rising unemployment rate, slew of corporate layoffs, slowdown in travel, and poor overall economy, that is quite an accomplishment.

With beverage sales generating 15% of Emeril's restaurants' revenues,[43] the remaining 85% is composed of food and retail sales—probably in the neighborhood of 80% food and 5% retail, which includes Emeril-branded products sold on-site, such as hats, shirts, and aprons. That's an 80/15/5 split.

Kharasch's goal with his consulting clients is an 80/20 split, with 80% of sales coming from food and 20% from beverages. However, when the percentage of food sales rises higher than that of beverage sales, explains Kharasch, profits are generally lower, because the cost of food is higher than that of beverages. Although the margins vary by the type of food served—with steaks, for example, providing less profit than chicken or pasta dishes—beverages generally provide 75 to 80% profit.

The National Restaurant Association reports that the median total cost percentage for fine dining restaurants is 32%, meaning that food and beverage costs average out to 32% of the total cost of the meal.[44]

Although Emeril's Homebase is privately held and does not release restaurant revenues, insiders estimate the revenues per restaurant at well over $5 million. Emeril's Orlando is said to generate in the neighborhood of $12 million, and it is not even the company's most popular—Delmonico in Las Vegas is, says an employee. By comparison, the Cheesecake Factory consistently earns $10 to $12 million per restaurant, giving credence to the reported figure for Emeril's.

One reason Emeril's operations grow every year is that Emeril focuses on the long-term picture where his business is concerned. By fretting over every meal that comes out of his kitchen, Emeril demonstrates his recognition that each customer sitting in one of his restaurants is worth far more than the $115 or so he or she will spend that evening on dinner for two; the lifetime value of a loyal Emeril's customer is in the thousands, if not tens of thousands, of dollars. Making sure they are satisfied—no, thrilled—with their experience chez Emeril increases the likelihood that they will return. It also increases profits.

Researchers at Northwestern University report that studies indicate increasing customer retention by 5% can result in a 100% increase in profits.[45] Focusing on bringing customers back again and again drives up the lifetime value of that customer, as well as the net profit to the company. Not to mention the lower marketing cost required to entice them back.

With an operation that clearly appears to be humming along, garnering awards and profits, Emeril could decide to take it easy. But that is not him, not him at all. Emeril is the man who wakes up each morning, thankful for the opportunity to try to do a better job today than he did yesterday. Always interested in learning, Emeril soaks up knowledge and finds ways to apply it to his company.

He also is rarely satisfied for long. What was popular three years ago is likely in need of a makeover by now, and Emeril is the first to recognize it. Whether it is his web site or a restaurant location, Emeril routinely invests millions of dollars to keep every aspect of his business fresh and state of the art.

"Kick it up a notch" is not just a fun phrase he uses, it is the way he approaches life and work.

8

THE ART OF PARTNERING

Great food and great people equal profit.

—Emeril Lagasse[1]

A couple of years ago [around 2001], Tom Williams [chairman and CEO of Universal Studios Recreation Group] calls me and says, 'We're doing this partnership with the Loews hotel group and we've been racking our brain how you can do a signature restaurant for us,' " says Emeril. With an Emeril's Restaurant already at Universal Studios, as well as an existing steak house, thereby nixing the possibility of a Delmonico Steakhouse, Williams was not sure how he could get another Emeril eatery in his resort.

"Look, you don't have to go any further," Emeril tells him. "I've got this concept."[2] That concept was Tchoup Chop, a Polynesian-inspired property furnished with handmade items from Bali—everything from ceiling treatments to tables, woodcarvings, and tikis at the bar. The food would be Cajun-Asian fusion, outfitted with a Benihana-style teppanyaki grill that fit perfectly with the Royal Pacific Resort location Williams was looking to fill.

With a menu unlike that of any of his other restaurants, Tchoup Chop aimed to attract foodies with a taste for something a little different. Instead of grilled or nut-encrusted fish, dinner guests at Tchoup Chop can order Banana Leaf Steamed Fish of the Day. Kiawe Grilled Rib Eye Steak sports a homemade teriyaki sauce alongside the entrée and vegetable side dishes. Tchoup Chop's Clay Pot of the Day, served with steamed rice and seasonable vegetables, can only be found here, as is the case with the Hawaiian Style Dinner Plate, including Kiawe Smoked Ribs, Kalua Pork, Teriyaki Grilled Chicken, Chorizo Potato Hash, and Baked Macaroni—all for one person. Tchoup Chop is a step in another direction for Emeril, but it seems like he is still on course.

Beyond the new restaurant concept that later debuted at Universal in 2003, this process of proposing a concept to a current landlord reflects Emeril's commitment to partnerships, such as that with Williams. Says Emeril about the relationship, "I feel good about him, his vision, his team, his quality. That's what it's all about. It's not about quantity for us. I'm about quality. That's why we get along so well."[3] However, Emeril seems to get along famously with most, if not all, of his landlords, suppliers, service providers, and employees.

Many companies brag about partnering with this corporation or that celebrity, but in many cases, the relationship is vague and undefined. When Emeril talks about his partners, whether he is referring to members of his management team, his manufacturing suppliers, his hotel landlords, or his wife, he takes that association very seriously. Although the level of specificity about the alliance varies, Emeril is the master of partnering. His partnerships are more than just deal making, they are personal relationships that engender loyalty and trust. In many ways, they epitomize the Emeril brand. They are also quite rare, especially in today's business climate.

Current Partners: Complementing Emeril's Strengths and Weaknesses

The word *partner* is used to describe a wide range of business relationships, from an official joint venture in which two or more organizations pool their resources in pursuit of a common goal, to a close, more casual relationship with a major customer, and just about anything in between. Essentially, anytime two or more people or companies are supporting each other's goals, they are working in partnership.

"All businesses need resources," explains attorney Curt Sahakian, founder of partneringagreements.com, which includes capital, people, products, and distribution. But some lack the proper balance, he says. Start-ups, for example, may lack capital, but have plenty of new product concepts. Other companies may have an incredible distribution system set up, but lack new products to enter the pipeline. In the food service industry, qualified people are typically the weakest link and the area where partnering can make the biggest difference.

In Emeril's case, he identifies his area of weakness and then pursues partners to fill the gap. He leverages something he has a lot of—credibility—in order to acquire the resources he lacks, explains Sahakian. And while Emeril's partnerships all seem to be friendly, mutually respectful relationships, they do not have to be to work.

Partnering with Financiers

One of Emeril's first partners was his banker, whom he had to woo. When he lacked capital he needed to open his first restaurant, he approached lenders in the hope of gaining their financial support. Other partnering opportunities existed with outside investors and venture capitalists, but Emeril shunned those in favor of retaining complete control of his business. And it worked, when Whitney National Bank came through to provide the money he needed. Over time, as Emeril shared information about the growth and profitability of Emeril's Homebase with his partner, Whitney National was willing to lend more. That partnership has endured, with Emeril presumably negotiating better lending rates as his company has grown and his power as a partner has increased.

Partnering with Customers

The other side of the financial coin is Emeril's customers, who provide the cash flow necessary to sustain his operations. Emeril routinely gives credit to his team for his success, admitting that he could not have done it all alone, but, in fact, his customers deserve a lot of the thanks. Without their loyalty and support—such as when they rave to friends and colleagues about the quality of his food—Emeril's empire would never have existed.

Over the years, Emeril's customer base has exploded as he has provided the food and dining experience his clientele has asked for and they, in turn, have paid whatever price he was charging for the opportunity. The partnership has worked because of Emeril's visibility and brand strength, creating a steady stream of new customers eager to have the chance to sample his cooking. And while he could certainly have raised his prices in order to cull the ranks of his customers, making it unaffordable to some, he has insisted on keeping prices comparatively reasonable. By effectively keeping switching costs low for his customers, they have little reason to go elsewhere.

Partnering with Employees

Although talented people are some of the most difficult resources to identify and retain in the food service industry, Emeril does so by turning to his culinary network for candidates and by offering incentives to stay once an employee is hired. Explaining that "there's no substitute for an ownership interest," Sahakian says that Emeril's partnering with his employees makes sense. It builds in a switching cost—the employees lose all or part of their equity investment—if they leave Emeril's employ, subsequently reducing the number of senior staffers who decide to go elsewhere. In addition, the higher income that is possible as a partner is another means of tying employees to the company.

Another component of retaining employees, says Emeril, is

loyalty. "Loyalty is the secret of building a great team to support what-ever you do. It means a lot to me when people talk about my loyal management staff, who have been with me since the early years. I am loyal to them; they are loyal to me."[4] They get what they want and he gets what he wants—by all accounts, it is an effective partnership.

Partnering with Suppliers

Although partnerships are nothing new, the extent of the loyalty that Emeril displays to the people and companies he aligns himself with is unusual in modern times. This applies to his suppliers as well as his employees. For example, when William Morrow and Com-pany agreed to publish his first cookbook, *Emeril's New New Orleans Cooking*, a bond was formed. Despite offers from other publishers, Emeril has stuck with Morrow, now part of HarperCollins, for his subsequent eight books.

Products as they relate to Emeril's business fall into two cate-gories: ingredients used at his restaurants and commercially branded consumer products sold through retail outlets. In both cases, Emeril has established strong partnerships that provide him with the items he needs when he needs them at a price that yields a tidy profit.

One-half of Emeril's formula for success, great food, is achieved through a network of ranchers, farmers, fishermen, and growers who supply Emeril's restaurants with the freshest ingredients available. It is those ingredients that determine what specials will go on the menu, in fact. It is these suppliers who provide Emeril with access to items necessary to run his business. He also works closely with them to ensure they grow exactly what he needs so that they can maximize their bottom line, too.

But control is another reason for partnerships. Instead of being beholden to one company or individual, Emeril reduces his depen-dence on any one supplier. Spreading out his purchasing needs gives Emeril the control he craves over his business. Rather than being at the whim of the market, Emeril's partners ensure that the deliveries they make have the fruits, vegetables, herbs, meats, and fish used to prepare his award-winning dishes.

And if the products are not fresh enough, he has been known to reject them. As mentioned in Chapter 1, one poor fisherman had his catch kicked into the street by Emeril early in the chef's career.

When he decided to develop a line of branded consumer products to sell, Emeril turned to potential manufacturing partners for assistance. In exchange for permission to use his name and likeness on products they produce, Emeril receives royalty payments tied to sales. He also meticulously oversees and approves the development of the merchandise along the way, vetoing any that fail to meet his quality standards.

Partnering with Landlords

Some of his most important partners on the restaurant side of his business are his landlords—the hotels, casinos, resorts, and building owners who rent him space in which he operates his eateries. Those relationships have shaped the type of clientele he attracts and the reputation he has built.

When Emeril ventured out of New Orleans and into Las Vegas in 1995, opening Emeril's New Orleans Fish House inside the MGM Grand, he was breaking new ground again. He was one of the first celebrity chefs to partner with a hotel on one of his branded restaurants. Says Emeril, "I think the MGM was really smart, in the beginning days, when they were the first ones who wanted to find restaurant people to do restaurants."[5]

Today, it is so common as to be almost overdone. Fine dining restaurateurs aiming to capture tourists and business travelers are partnering with established resorts and hotels left and right. Having a built-in audience is one of the biggest advantages of locating the restaurant within a hotel, says Mauricio Andrade, director of operations for Emeril's Homebase. And to leverage those captive hotel guests, 10% of the seats at Emeril's Tchoup Chop in Orlando are held for hotel guests until 10 A.M. But employees give priority to guests staying at any of the Loews Universal hotels,[6] a bonus for the hotel chain, which will surely benefit from repeat guests looking for an in at Emeril's.

From the hotels' perspective, a celebrity chef restaurant provides instant name recognition that can be a draw to drive up food sales and room reservations. "In a lot of cases," says Dan Bendall, of Cini-Little International, Inc., "a very low percentage of guests eat in hotel restaurants. This is a way to bring them back."[7] Beth Grant, food and beverage director at Loews, reports that the advantage to the hotel is that having Emeril's name on the restaurant guarantees people will hear about the hotel.

On average, food and beverage sales account for approximately 29% of a full-service hotel's revenues[8]—a substantial amount that can significantly impact a hotel's bottom line. With a name-brand celebrity chef partner, however, that number can go higher.

Since it opened in 1999, Emeril's Orlando has become one of the company's most successful, reports Andrade, who says Emeril's turns away "300 people a day"[9] who are hoping to dine there. But instead of building from scratch, Emeril's opened a smaller place inside Loews in Orlando.

Preferring to partner on projects than go it alone, almost as a rule, five of Emeril's nine restaurants—the majority, that is—operate within existing hotels and resorts. First was Emeril's New Orleans Fish House in Las Vegas in 1995, at the MGM Grand Hotel and Casino, and later, in 1999, Delmonico Steakhouse at the Venetian in Las Vegas and Emeril's Restaurant Orlando at Universal Studios in Florida. In 2003 he opened another restaurant at Universal Orlando, Emeril's Tchoup Chop in the Royal Pacific Resort, and Emeril's Miami Beach at the Loews Miami Beach Hotel.

For celebrity chefs like Emeril, the financial arrangements are often lucrative, and the built-in clientele appealing. Instead of having to invest millions to renovate or build a high-class eatery, hotels and resorts offer major incentives to attract the quality and name recognition of a chef like Emeril. Industry experts say that celebrity-quality terms may end up costing the restaurateur very little to set up shop.

In some cases, the property owner puts up all the funds for the building, improves it, and pays a tenant allowance—essentially, cash paid to the restaurant—for the privilege of having the celebrity chef operate within its walls. In return, the tenant then pays a percentage of the restaurant's sales as rent, or a fixed rent plus a percentage of sales over a certain breakpoint, or a base rent plus an amortized payment.

The advantage of such arrangements is that each party is bearing partial responsibility for the success of the restaurant, and both will benefit if it does well. That is at the crux of successful partnerships—shared blame and benefit.

For smaller hotels, the benefits are even larger. "It's very difficult for an unknown, stand-alone hotel restaurant to break through the competitive clutter and bring in anything but the captive, stay-in audience,"[10] says Michael Sansbury, regional vice president for Loews Hotels, which operates three hotels at Universal Orlando, where Emeril's Orlando is located.

The same could be said about unknown, stand-alone restaurants. That is the power of partnerships.

Partnering with His TV Producers

Another partner critical to Emeril's current visibility and fame is the television network that gave him his own show. When producers from the Food Network and Emeril, the rising star chef, met, each party had something the other wanted. The Food Network had a vehicle for distributing Emeril's brand and image nationwide to millions of households, while Emeril had a unique talent for making cooking come alive as no one else could; his show would become their new jointly developed product.

Interestingly, in the beginning of their partnership the Food Network seemed to need Emeril more than he needed them. As described in detail in Chapter 4, the fledgling company needed a show and a host that would attract viewers in droves; without talented chefs on board, the network would have failed. Emeril was not the only chef to get his start on the Food Network. However, with six hours of new programming daily, one of which was Emeril's show, he accounted for a larger percentage of that block. Conversely, Emeril would likely have succeeded without the Food Network; it just would have taken longer. His enhanced visibility made possible by TV hastened his celebrity, but his reputation was already growing in the early 1990s, around the time of the Food Network's launch, as a result of the positive restaurant reviews he had received and the professional awards he was winning.

More than a decade later, as both parties are in their heyday, the tables may have turned in the Food Network's favor. While the network has diversified, reducing its reliance on Emeril's popularity, Emeril's main television gig is still on that network. Without that level of continued exposure, his star would certainly fade. Perhaps that is why he inked a five-year contract in late 2003, guaranteeing him his own time slot through 2008.

The Pros of Partnering

Few businesses have the financial resources to expand quickly into new markets without the assistance of partners such as suppliers, distributors, investors, and customers. Emeril is not alone in this respect. With each new restaurant, Emeril has had to turn to his partners for support in making each location a success. With each new cookbook, his partners have stepped in to increase sales and availability. With his foundation, Emeril has leaned on his partners to help provide support in the form of their participation or financial underwriting. Although the names of the partners change depending on which aspect of his business is being discussed, Emeril clearly works in tandem with others.

But there are other reasons to partner, as well, according to the

Corporate Partnering Institute. Effective partnerships allow one or both participants to do the following:

- Seize limited-time opportunities
- Access a new market
- Increase market share
- Adapt to changing market conditions
- Acquire a new skill or area of competence
- Overcome existing organizational weaknesses
- Obtain financial, or other, resources necessary for success[11]

During his career as a chef and restaurateur, Emeril has leveraged partnerships to achieve all of these benefits.

Seize Limited-Time Opportunities

Following the success of Emeril's Restaurant in the early 1990s and the push from employees for him to provide a career progression, Emeril began to consider opening a second location. He had not quite determined where that should be when space opened up on Rue St. Louis in New Orleans.

The building owner was eager to quickly get a new restaurant into the space and made Emeril quite a deal, say observers— low-cost rent in exchange for a partner role. Essentially, the building owner traded the space for little or no rent for future earnings, and NOLA was born.

The time was right for Emeril to expand—his first restaurant, which he opened two years earlier, had settled into a routine that comes with solid management—and he was looking for the right opportunity, the right space, for his second location. He might not have been able to afford to debut a second restaurant so quickly had it not been for the availability of the space and the offer from the building's owner. But Emeril recognized this as an opportunity to be seized, and he did.

Likewise, when he was approached about hosting a television cooking show for a yet-to-be-formed network, Emeril recognized the upside potential of such an opportunity and agreed to participate. However, since the network had a small viewing audience and was starting from scratch, Emeril was effectively a partner. If his show, as well as others, succeeded, the Food Network would prosper. If not, it would shut down. By the same token, if the Food Network succeeded, Emeril's visibility would skyrocket. The relationship was codependent, just as a partnership is.

But the partners he was leveraging at that stage in his career were really his staff, including behind-the-scenes cooks and chefs who collaborated with him in order to develop scripts and recipes for the show. Without them, Emeril would have been unable to pursue the opportunity while still running his restaurants.

Access New Markets

Once Emeril had temporarily saturated the local fine dining community in New Orleans, it was time to venture into new markets. Without partners, it would have been too costly to consider. In New Orleans, Emeril had a strong and loyal customer base, a well-trained staff, and up-to-date kitchens and dining rooms. Elsewhere, he had nothing more than a potential customer base.

However, in the early 1990s, Las Vegas's MGM Grand Hotel and Casino approached Emeril about opening a restaurant within the hotel. Wolfgang Puck's Spago, which opened at Caesar's Palace in 1992, was doing a brisk business and other hotels wanted to get in on the action.[12] In 1994, the MGM Grand had spent $4 million developing a top-of-the-line restaurant for Emeril's friend and colleague Charlie Trotter, but after a management decision to totally overhaul the restaurant's approach, Trotter demanded a buyout and went back to Chicago.[13] Soon thereafter, in 1995, Emeril's New Orleans Fish House opened. At that point it was just the second celebrity chef–run establishment in Las Vegas, though today it has plenty of competition. Despite the myriad other dining options, guests still flock to the MGM and the Venetian, where Emeril opened the Delmonico Steakhouse in 1999.

Working in partnership with hotels has been Emeril's entry strategy in Las Vegas, in Orlando with Universal Studios, and in Miami Beach, where he operates out of a Loews property. The only city he has gone into alone is Atlanta.

Using partners, who generally agree to finance some aspect of his market entry, Emeril can establish a presence more quickly, with a much better chance of success, than if he entered new geographic markets on his own. Partnering with recognized hotel and resort names improves his own reputation as well.

Increase Market Share

In cities where Emeril already has a restaurant presence—including New Orleans, where he has three restaurants, and Las Vegas and Orlando, where he has two each—partners have enabled him to increase his market share, grabbing a larger percentage of the fine dining revenues with additional locations.

However, partners have made an even bigger impact on the retail side, with Emeril's licensed products. Suppliers, who partner with Emeril by providing the manufacturing and distribution end of the product equation, are a means to more quickly gain access to consumers through established distribution channels. In fact, his supplier partners are his sole means of increasing sales through such retail outlets as supermarkets, warehouse clubs, specialty stores, department stores, and discount retailers. Again, the relationship is codependent, with Emeril totally reliant on his partners for production and distribution and the suppliers beholden to Emeril for the continued brand recognition and demand.

Adapt to Changing Market Conditions

Working in partnership with major hotels and resorts buffers Emeril's restaurants from changing market conditions, providing him with a built-in clientele on a regular basis, as long as the resort or hotel continues to draw travelers, that is. In the wake of September 11, as American travelers scaled back their long-distance jaunts, all travel-related companies have had to adjust to a smaller customer base. Working collaboratively, however, gives Emeril and his partners a distinct advantage over stand-alone hotels and restaurateurs.

One of Emeril's fine dining establishments located inside or on the periphery of a hotel is a reason for a traveler to choose to stay at the MGM Grand in Las Vegas or the Loews hotel in Miami Beach rather than a similar-quality complex with a no-name eatery. And since hotel guests frequently have priority when it comes to nabbing a seat at the hotel restaurant, that is one more plus in the hotel's favor.

Emeril's colocated restaurants benefit from the in-house, almost captive audience at a casino or hotel, which provides a steady stream of guests. So when the economy takes a turn for the worse and consumers choose to dine out less frequently, his restaurants will experience less of an impact than those occupying space in the business district, for example.

Partnering on licensed products enables Emeril to move more quickly to grab a share of the growing cookware and kitchen accessory market. With consumers eating in and entertaining at home more, sales of cookware, appliances, and kitchenware are growing. By aligning the Emeril brand with some of the top names in the industry, he not only enhances his image, but he gets a running start when it comes to rolling out products. He is able to be more responsive to changing market conditions than celebrities who choose to set up their own manufacturing and distribution operations, such as Paul Prudhomme chose to do with Magic Seasoning Blends. Working through established channels, Emeril can get his products to market faster and more easily with the help of his licensing partners.

Acquire a New Skill or Area of Competence

One product chefs typically develop to promote their particular culinary approach is the cookbook, something with which Emeril had had no experience when he met an acquisitions editor at a conference years ago. That meeting led to a contract for his first cookbook, *Emeril's New New Orleans Cooking*, which laid out Emeril's take on New Orleans cuisine. Since then, Emeril has published seven more cookbooks with the same publisher, William Morrow and Company, now part of HarperCollins.

Sticking with the same publisher gives Emeril more power as a chef and author, explains Susan Barry, literary agent with the Barry-Swayne Literary Agency. "Bookstore buyers know what to expect from him and his publisher, which makes a huge difference," she says. Through a long-standing relationship, Emeril establishes a rapport with his publisher's sales reps—they become more comfortable with him and are better able to sell his cookbooks to their network of booksellers. Additionally, they can build effective sales incentive programs with booksellers that are typically unavailable to one-off authors.

For Emeril, his long-term relationship with his publisher partner gives him access to a revenue stream and distribution network he would have been unable to establish on his own. Lacking expertise in publishing, Emeril turned to one of the biggest names in the business for guidance. With nearly four million books sold, the partnership appears to be going well.

Overcome Existing Organizational Weaknesses

The biggest obstacle or challenge restaurateurs face industrywide is employee turnover: having to recruit and train new staff members on a regular basis in order to stay in business. Although Emeril's reputation and success have significantly reduced the turnover his particular company has faced, he has also taken steps to partner with culinary schools that can provide trained employees. Granted, the affiliation is a loose one, but it is a connection other restaurateurs have not necessarily mined.

In Las Vegas, culinary students from the University of Nevada at

Las Vegas (UNLV) are solid candidates for positions at his two eateries in the city, for example, and the culinary schools in each of the other cities in which he operates have functioning culinary academies or programs as well, including the culinary arts program at the University of New Orleans—not to mention his alma mater, Johnson & Wales, and its campus in North Miami.

Obtain Financial, or Other, Resources Necessary for Success

Emeril has built his company slowly, without outside investment, in order to retain control of its operations. But in order to keep top employees, he does offer partner status to senior managers within his restaurants. Most restaurateurs require a down payment for the opportunity, which provides the organization with additional cash, in exchange for a percentage of future profits. While the money is not significant compared to the restaurant's total sales, it solidifies the relationship between the key employee and the company,[14] which is a bigger challenge for Emeril today than securing funding.

Partnering with hotels and resorts is a financially savvy move, in part because Emeril's landlords generally offer financial incentives to locate there. From reduced rent to renovations or a kitchen upgrade at no charge, such partnerships reduce Emeril's financial burden and risk.

Partnering Pitfalls

Of course, there are always downsides to partnerships, the biggest of which is "not paying attention to the exits," says Curt Sahakian, meaning that partners need to avoid being forced to remain in a partnership beyond its useful life. "You don't go into a partnership unless you have to," explains Sahakian, citing having to share revenue as the main reason not to. And entering a business relationship when in need of something, whether it is capital, people, products, or distribution, puts a company at a disadvantage. Recognizing their power position, some senior partners may try to use that to their advantage, locking their junior partner in.

At the core of the issue of exiting a partnership is switching costs, or what it costs to replace the customer or supplier. From a vendor's perspective, "you never want the relationship to end," explains Sahakian. Having to replace a customer is time consuming and costly (high switching costs) and suppliers dread it. Conversely, customers want to be able to easily transfer their business elsewhere (low switching costs) to retain control over the relationship and ensure that the vendor or supplier remains responsive and cost effective.

Emeril's partnerships with his customers and bank, sources of money and employees—the people aspect, and with his landlords and his product suppliers, which provide both products and the means to distribute them, comprise his core partner relationships. In all cases, he has worked to establish long-term alliances in order to reduce his switching costs, while retaining the option to exit when necessary.

That is the recipe for a successful partnership, says Sahakian. "Know what you want [out of a partnership], pay attention to what your partner wants, and when you get what you want, leave." In these cases, Emeril continues to get what he wants and has no reason to leave.

One of the few times a partnership turned out badly for him was his second divorce, from Tari Hohn. Hohn had become a formal partner in Emeril's Homebase, helping Emeril land the financing he needed to open Emeril's and then NOLA, Emeril's New Orleans Fish House, and Emeril's Delmonico. But when the marriage ended, to dissolve the business partnership Emeril had to pay his former wife for her involvement. Not anticipating a divorce at the start, Emeril presumably did not build in a means to retain any investment she made in his business should she leave, as he now does with his employee partners. So he compensated her for her substantial contributions.

Emeril's history of few partnership terminations means that he either negotiated the relationship in his favor and has no reason to go elsewhere or he is locked into an arrangement he cannot get out of. Given Emeril's business savvy and history of success, it is likely the former.

Building Goodwill through Community Outreach and Charity Work

Beyond the logistical aspects of lining up resources to run his business, Emeril partners to enhance his image. As a partner to charitable events and organizations, he frequently volunteers his time and talents. In some cases, he is the featured guest; in others, he uses his fame to encourage other people to participate.

Stephen Perry, of the New Orleans Convention and Visitors Bureau, tells of a time that Emeril and several other local celebrities pitched in to phone meeting and convention planners nationwide to encourage them to hold their event in New Orleans. Recognizing the benefit that his business receives from strong tourism and convention attendance, Emeril stepped up to the plate to support the organization. Although a loose partnership, both organizations benefit from the association they enjoy.

In addition to his long workdays, Emeril donates time and money to organizations in New Orleans as a way of giving back to the community that supports him month in and month out. Through his own charitable organization, the Emeril Lagasse Foundation, Emeril supports the work of local groups that match its mission—"Inspire, mentor and enable our future."

Emeril's community involvement extends beyond New Orleans, into the cities in which he owns restaurants, as well as in towns where he has a personal connection, which is just about everywhere at this point. His name can generally be found on the roster of many celebrity charity events, such as those sponsored by Andre Agassi, or in conjunction with one of his suppliers such as Fetzer Vineyards or his employer, the Food Network.

By establishing a foundation, Emeril has positioned himself as a serious philanthropist—someone committed to improving the lives of residents in the communities in which he operates. In New Orleans, foundation funds benefit St. Michael's Special School for Exceptional Children, which serves mentally challenged children between the ages of 5 and 21 who have major learning difficulties; the Louisiana Philharmonic Orchestra; and the Lynn Meadows Discovery Center in Gulfport, Mississippi.

When Emeril was selected to participate in the celebrity version of *Who Wants to Be a Millionaire,"* he named St. Michael's as the beneficiary of the $125,000 he won that evening. The check he hand-delivered to the school the following week was in addition to the $22,000 he had donated the month before from a fund-raiser.[15]

Emeril's support of the Louisiana Philharmonic Orchestra (LPO) arises out of his own love of music and his interest in introducing young people to it. The 70-member orchestra has teamed with the Emeril Lagasse Foundation to present the Young People's Concert Series, which reaches more than 12,000 schoolchildren in Greater New Orleans and in outlying rural areas. But his support goes beyond just lip service; Emeril actively participates in fund-raising in order to encourage others to provide support as well. In 2004, Emeril helped spearhead the Cookin' With Music concert for the LPO, which included a cooking demonstration along with a concert. He also appears on the orchestra's web site.

The connection to the Lynn Meadows Discovery Center came through Emeril's wife, Alden, who was a close friend of Lynn Meadows; they played tennis together in high school and during summer camps. Sadly, Meadows was killed in a car accident during her freshman year of college. The Lynn Meadows Discovery Center is the first children's museum in Mississippi and provides children in the community with opportunities for interactive play and learning, as well as hosting exhibitions and performances. Emeril and Alden are chairing the organization's current $2 million capital campaign.

Affiliations with nonprofit organizations, especially those supporting children, are likely matches for Emeril's corporation and
foundation, whereby he benefits from exposure as a generous human
being and the local area organizations share in any fund-raising
done on their behalf.

Being an involved corporate citizen builds goodwill that can
temper negative publicity, should it arise. Like a bank account into
which one deposits good deeds, community service can yield a big
payback if a damaging situation were to occur.

But Emeril also furthers his benevolent image by speaking highly
of fellow chefs and by referring his clientele to their restaurants. Not
only does he put himself in their league when he suggests that his
customers will find their menu of equal caliber, but he fosters a sense
of community and collaboration. By helping each other out, chefs
and restaurateurs improve the fine dining market as a whole.

The Ultimate Partnership: Mentoring

Once again, however, perhaps the epitome of partnering is Emeril's
relationship with one of his mentees, Bernard Carmouche.

Carmouche was in the eleventh grade when he took a job as a
pot washer at Commander's Palace not long after Emeril had taken
over as executive chef. He was there to make money to be able to
buy a car, a $200 Dodge Dart, from one of the restaurant's bar-
tenders. But when his work was finished, Carmouche would help out
in the kitchen, paying close attention to how things were done.

One day, after summoning the courage, Carmouche told Emeril
that someday he would like to be a chef, too. So Emeril made him a
deal. Carmouche remembers, "He told me he'd teach me how to
cook, but I had to finish school. The agreement was I had to bring
my report card to him."[16] For each A on his report card, Emeril
rewarded Carmouche with $20, and $10 for each B.

"Commander's and Lagasse turned my life around," says
Carmouche in an interview with the *Times-Picayune*. "I grew up in a

neighborhood where it was very hard to do the right thing. . . . I was at a dangerous kind of stage, because I couldn't afford all the things I wanted and I couldn't do what I wanted to do. I needed something."[17] Emeril showed him the way.

After graduating from Walter L. Cohen High School, Carmouche became a prep cook, learning culinary basics, such as knife techniques. He moved from salads up to the hot line, the back line, first cook, and sous-chef under Emeril at Commander's. Even after Emeril left Commander's, Carmouche stayed, working for three years at the Brennan family restaurant in Houston before returning to become sous-chef at the Brennans' Palace Café back in New Orleans.

Despite no longer working together at the same restaurant, the mentor-mentee relationship continued between Carmouche and Emeril. They talked regularly, and Carmouche stopped by frequently for a meal at Emeril's. So it was no surprise that Carmouche said yes when Emeril offered him a position with his operation.

One of his first assignments was an internship with renowned chef Roger Vergé at his Moulin de Mougins restaurant in the south of France. During his time there, Carmouche was as studious as Emeril had been during his internship years before, noting how food stations were set up, the procedures waitstaff used for servicing the clientele, and how Vergé communicated with his staff and guests.

Fast-forward four years, as Emeril made plans to open Emeril's Orlando and chose Carmouche, his protégé, to lead the restaurant as chef de cuisine. It took some convincing to get Carmouche to relocate, but he has settled in nicely.

Now driving a snazzy Acura, Carmouche reports, "I really like Orlando and my focus is Emeril's right now. I get opportunities I want here, but someday I'd like to open a small place." Once he does hang out his own shingle, he will likely have some mentees of his own. Sounding even more like his mentor, he says, "Whatever is taught to you, you teach the next person."[18]

Partnerships Plus

In addition to the one-on-one relationship that Emeril maintains with his suppliers, agents, and customers, Emeril also aims to leverage those partnerships for greater gain by cross-pollinating the relationships and resources. Instead of the typical win-win goal between partners, Emeril looks for the opportunity to weave several of his partnerships together for greater gain all around.

For example, Emeril's partner Fetzer Vineyards, which has developed a line of wines for him, also holds an annual fund-raiser, Fun in the Harvest Sun. Emeril participates in that as a way of heightening his visibility and demonstrating his allegiance to Fetzer. But in addition to supporting Fetzer, he also sells the wine on his web site and presumably serves it in his restaurant, simultaneously promoting both Fetzer Vineyards and his own brand.

9

MANAGING HIS IMAGE

Emeril is the McDonald's of the culinary arts.
—Professor H.G. Parsa, editor, *Journal of Foodservice Business Research*[1]

B ack around 1990, Joe Kahn, who operated the New Orleans School of Cooking, invited Hugh Rushing, now the executive vice president of the Cookware Manufacturers Association, to go check out "this new guy," who had just opened a restaurant on Tchoupitoulas Street. During the exquisite meal, Emeril brought out dish after dish to demonstrate his culinary skills, asking Joe's and Hugh's opinions of each one, colleague to colleague. Rushing remembers the meal with true pleasure.

Fast forward 13 years, to 2003: Rushing had the chance to dine at Emeril's in New Orleans a second time. And Emeril himself happened to be in the restaurant. Rushing took the chance to say hello and asked, "I'll bet you don't remember me, but . . ." Emeril looked at him and said, "Yes, I do. You were here about a week after we opened, with Joe Kahn."

It is that kind of memory that strengthens and sustains Emeril's likability. It is what helped make him a star, and what keeps him there. "It's the secret of his success," says Rushing.[2]

Brand Building 101

What does it take to create an image of a celebrity that is so positive that he becomes the gold standard for others in his industry—an image that stretches beyond who he is as an individual to the brand he has become? That's Emeril's story. And although few people achieve the level of success that Emeril has, his story of hard work, setbacks, and ambition is one that many Americans can relate to.

"Research has shown that brands somehow connect emotionally and maintain that connection over the long haul," explains H.G. Parsa, professor of hospitality management at Ohio State University.[3] "Emeril has become a brand in himself," says Parsa, by virtue of the connection he has made with millions of consumers who have dined in his restaurants, watched his television show, read his cookbooks, or bought his spices, cookware, cutlery, or wine.

Although his rise to prominence may seem recent and easy, it was actually long in coming and required dedication. But that effort worked in Emeril's favor. Instead of begrudging him success, fans, friends, and colleagues celebrated with him when it came. Emeril has become like a family member, explains media expert Michael Sands, of Sands Media. And that family member has become so popular that he has morphed into a powerful brand.

Two elements of a successful, sustainable personal brand are talent and charisma, says Samantha Ettus, brand expert and president of Ettus Media Management. Both are needed in order for a brand to transcend the individual's identity. Fortunately, Emeril has plenty of both.

His ability to pair seemingly disparate flavors and textures to create culinary masterpieces is what earned him the laundry list of awards as a chef. And the fact that his protégés have also won similar awards suggests that it is not a fluke—Emeril really does know how to cook.

He also does it with style and panache. As he is demonstrating a particular technique or instructing TV viewers on the finer points of red velvet cake, his demeanor and personality draw people in. He is charming, warm, funny, and engaging to watch—all of which make him the perfect brand representative.

In addition to his well-developed culinary skills and personal charm, Emeril excels at business because he manages his time well. He gets more done than most because of his energy level and ability to complete dozens of tasks in mere minutes.

Emeril has worked hard for what he has accomplished, beginning at a very young age. His parents were hardworking role models, as were the Portuguese bakers and the many chefs he worked under, here and in France. Now he serves as a role model for his staff, some of whom may aspire to run their own restaurants someday. Says Mauricio Andrade, who started as a waiter at Emeril's and is now director of operations, "Emeril is a person who inspires his staff. He's up earlier and works later than anybody, and he creates an atmosphere of leadership that has been a key ingredient of his success."[4]

Says Emeril about his go-getter attitude, "You have to get up early if you want to fit everything in. I do cram a lot into each hour and each day, but then I have always had a strong work ethic. I started working hard as a kid, and I still have the same enthusiasm. Of course, now I need a scheduler to keep everything going. We all have the same number of hours in the day; it's how we use them that makes a difference."[5]

On a typical day back in December 2001, Emeril tells a *New Orleans* magazine writer that he got up at 4 A.M., prepared for his appearance on *Good Morning America*, and filmed his spot. Then it was on to an appearance on *Live with Regis and Kelly*, and 16 radio interviews by telephone.[6] Once those were wrapped up, he probably still had time to check in with each of his restaurants before grabbing lunch. Yes, he is a multitasker extraordinaire, says his wife.

He is a multitasker because his company is multifaceted, requiring him to jump from one role to the next quickly. One minute he may be in one of his restaurants, the next he is on his way to his headquarters to sign cookbooks to be shipped to customers, and the next he is making phone calls to talk about shipments of his branded products.

But he does not try to do everything himself, and he is happy to give credit frequently to his hardworking staff. "It's not just Emeril Lagasse," he says. "Super Bowls aren't won by just one person. Super Bowls are won by having a great team."[7]

The Secret to Brand Longevity

At this stage, his brand has so many potential touch points—ways in which customers can come into contact with Emeril or any of his products and services—that it is somewhat surprising he has not faltered. There are a number of reasons his brand continues as strong as ever, say the experts, including the following.

He Delivers What He Promises

Customers are generally dissatisfied or disappointed with a product or service when it does not live up to set expectations, when it promises a certain level of performance and fails to come through. Emeril has such a vast number of fans and supporters primarily because he never disappoints, and that is because he never promises more than he can give.

"Emeril doesn't oversell," explains Professor Parsa. "He delivers what he promises."[8] He promises an extraordinary dining experience, and that is what guests enjoy. He promises an entertaining hour of cooking, and that is what viewers see. He promises a bottle of seasoning that will enliven a dish, and that is what consumers get when they add it to their meals. He does not say that his restaurants are the best in the world; he leaves that to his guests to decide on their own. He does not claim that his shows are the best cooking shows on TV or that his seasonings are the most unusual on the market. He describes his offerings realistically and then asks folks to try them, which they do, knowing they probably will not be disappointed.

He Is Consistent

There is comfort in consistency, in giving customers exactly what they expect. McDonald's is the epitome of consistency, with restaurants all around the world—the hamburgers served in London or Moscow taste the same as those prepared in Paris, Texas. That is why customers choose McDonald's over an unfamiliar restaurant—because they know what they can expect at McDonald's. It may not be as good as what they could have had somewhere else, but sometimes the known is better than the unknown. That is the value of consistency.

Viewers who turn on *The Essence of Emeril* or *Emeril Live* know exactly what to expect with each episode. There are few surprises, which is comforting to Emeril's fans. Even the use of his famous phrases— from "BAM!" to "hey, now"—is consistent; he uses the same message, even the same words, time after time.

That repetition is smart, says Professor Parsa, who maintains that people remember brands through lingo, through the words and phrases used in conjunction with them.

But consistency applies to all aspects of Emeril's operations, by design. By establishing performance standards across his company, Emeril has built in a level of consistency that is unusual in food service businesses. He uses existing employees to train new ones at his restaurants, he relies on the same suppliers for his ingredients, and he turns to the same publisher for each new cookbook he develops. It is unusual for Emeril to make a change when it comes to suppliers or employees because consistency is so highly valued within his organization.

He Makes Cooking Easy

Although the dishes he cooks may be high end, the ease with which Emeril explains the cooking process and the low-key, friendly manner in which he demonstrates it on his cooking shows makes it appear easy to even the most novice of cooks. That encouraging demeanor and helpful tone are appealing to viewers.

During a time when families feel stretched too thin, unable to accomplish all that is on their agendas, a message of simplicity is attractive. Consumers want to know more about how to deliver quality meals without spending all day in the kitchen. They want to wow their dinner guests without having to have the event catered by professionals.

"Food has really become theater," says Jack Hayes, southeastern editor of *Nation's Restaurant News.*[9] And nowhere else is that more the case than on *Emeril Live,* where the whole point seems to be entertainment, with a little cooking on the side.

Emeril is a showman extraordinaire, making food and cooking fun. "Even his entrance is like a WWF [World Wrestling Federation] entrance," says Professor Parsa, laughing. Part chef, part entertainer, Emeril lets his viewers choose to learn or just be entertained by his programs. And in either case, the experience is enjoyable.

He Is Friendly

People relate to Emeril in part because he does not look like a stereotypical chef. Explains Professor Parsa, "Old English chefs have a moustache and beard but Emeril takes his hat off, is clean shaven, and people can relate to him better." He makes an effort to look just like everyone else, rather than trying to distinguish himself—or distance himself—through his dress and facial grooming.

"For him the show is secondary; relating to people is most important," observes Professor Parsa. He connects to the millions of average Joes who are watching.

He also surrounds himself with friendly people, especially on his television shows. Emeril brings on special guests to help him cook, such as Patti LaBelle or fellow chef Charlie Trotter, livening up the show from time to time. And on *Emeril Live,* his band is part of his success, says Professor Parsa. The bandleader, Doc Gibbs, talks to him like a friend, furthering the image of the show as more of a gathering of friends than anything else. The addition of special musical guests, such as Al Jarreau, adds to the entertainment value of the program.

He Is Mainstream

Another reason Emeril continues to remain atop the culinary ladder is that he has transformed the formerly esoteric form of gourmet cooking into an activity that even children can participate in and enjoy. Haute cuisine has gone mainstream under Emeril's leadership, making it appealing and open to just about anyone.

The Emeril Lexicon

One of the challenges celebrities face once they reach that point of universal recognizability is to sustain it. Without a multifaceted program to remain in the public eye and consciousness, A-list celebrities gradually fall to being B- and C-list stars. Many of these folks continue to turn to the same medium for attention, whether it be television, print, or radio, to boost their popularity and notoriety, rather than branching out to reach new markets. Fortunately, Emeril knows better.

Rather than being satisfied with the exposure he receives through his two television shows and weekly guest spot on ABC, where he is essentially guaranteed to be seen by millions of fans each week, Emeril also pursues opportunities in other media. He is regularly seen in magazine and newspaper articles profiling or quoting him, routinely nets Internet coverage, does radio interviews, and enjoys one-on-one interactions with his fans at book signings, at charity events, or in his restaurants. He remains foremost in our minds because he is everywhere, almost literally. Everywhere you turn, Emeril is there—heck, even if you do not watch his shows, he is now regularly on network TV in the Crest ads.

However, although he remains very visible to consumers, what ensured the longevity of his celebrity status are the additions he has made to our everyday vocabulary—the aural component. Emerilisms like "BAM!," "kick it up a notch," "it isn't rocket science," "happy, happy, happy," "hey, now," and "pork fat rules" have helped make Emeril a potentially permanent influence on our normal speech patterns. Each time a common Emeril catchphrase is used, we are reminded of Emeril and, as long as the association is a positive one, it strengthens his brand image.

He has even gone so far as to trademark "BAM!" and "kick it up a notch," so that whenever the phrases are used, credit must be given to Emeril. "It's built-in advertising," says Donna Jo Napoli, professor of linguistics at Swarthmore College.[10] The small trademark symbol that appears next to the words also helps to draw additional attention to them.

Phrases like these stick in part because of the frequency with which they are used or heard, says Napoli. Whether they stick is partly determined by, as Napoli says, "how clever or appealing these phrases are" and partly by something "purely capricious"; that is, no one can really explain why they catch on. When they do, they start to be used routinely and strengthen the connection with the originator, in this case Emeril. Remember Wendy's ubiquitous slogan "Where's the beef?" The popular commercial featuring the little old lady asking this question became so well known that years after the commercial was shelved, consumers still make the connection with

Wendy's. On the other hand, younger generations who never saw the commercial have no idea why the question is so funny.

And that is the downside of such popular phrases—they lose their oomph. Napoli explains, "Generally when a phrase comes into the language in a particular context, if it sticks around long enough, it will start to be used in more contexts. Eventually, it will become so diluted and hackneyed that people will start avoiding it—it won't be cool anymore."[11] And maybe that is why Emeril has trademarked these catchphrases—to try to limit their usage in order to delay the inevitable downward spiral.

Corporations with product names that have come to represent whole product categories routinely issue warnings and requests to note an associated trademark, in order to retain their protected trademark status. Brands like Xerox, Rollerblade, and Kleenex are now used generically, rather than with an associated term such as photocopier, in-line skates, or facial tissue. Overuse has devalued the trademark in some cases, which may be what Emeril is trying to prevent.

Most important for his image is ensuring that Emeril is the chef associated with the terms. Second, trying to limit usage may help keep the phrases in use longer than a few months or years, before they are deemed out of fashion. Remember "Whassup?" or "Don't go there"? Use of such quips in their heyday proved you were cool, but once their expiration date had passed, using them branded you as behind the times or, worse, an embarrassment.

Of course, some industry observers suggest that scaling back on their usage might be in Emeril's best interest. "I find him difficult to watch," says John Mariani, *Esquire*'s food and restaurant correspondent. He cites the main reason as Emeril's blatant pandering to his TV audience, throwing out "BAM!" and "Hey, now" in every other sentence.

Developing and using catchphrases are part of Emeril's strategy to remain visible, which is smart. But going so far as to trademark them appears to be an attempt to hang onto his popularity even as it begins to wane. The tactic may ultimately have the opposite of the desired effect, reducing rather than lengthening their life span.

The Showman

Much of Emeril's notoriety is due to his television success. And like his many other efforts, Emeril carefully studied and planned his on-air persona. He prepared for his role as TV host through the media training he received, taking to heart Lisa Ekus's counsel regarding his energy level and presentation. "It's really just an evolvement of myself," he says.[12]

But as John Mariani sees it, "He's playing Emeril at this point. He's an actor"[13]—which may or may not be a good thing. In fact, culinary insiders snipe that Emeril has so little to do with the cooking that his company is based on that it is laughable. Claiming that his test kitchen staff develops all of the dishes prepared on his show and his chefs de cuisine create the restaurant menus, Emeril focuses on playing his role as TV show host and corporate CEO.

Called a "visionary" who defines what the company should be and do, Emeril's involvement in the day-to-day activities of his business has declined as his star has risen. Surrounding himself with top performers allows him to devote himself to the larger issues of brand building and extension, to spreading his message that food can be fun and anyone—even young children—can participate.

But Emeril the chef and restaurateur is apparently playing the role he has created just for himself. On TV, he is the loud, boisterous show host with boundless energy who encourages the audience's participation in his shtick. In fact, he feeds on it, says Mariani. "He plays to the audience too much. They're dying to hear him say 'BAM!' 'it's not rocket science,' 'oh yeah, babe.' " The whole show is a constant stream of Emerilisms, applauded and encouraged by his fans in the studio seats.

From his colleagues' perspective, Emeril the actor makes Emeril the celebrated chef look like an idiot. His over-the-top performances lessen his credibility as a talented chef, it has been suggested. Although Emeril does not seem to care, some observers question his current level of skill.

Of course, Emeril's true personality is apparently unlike that of the television star. Friends and colleagues use words like "subdued," "shy," and "quiet" to describe him.[14] However, on camera he is energetic, welcoming, extroverted, and loud. The difference in the two personalities reflects the creation of an on-camera persona that represents the Emeril brand; it is not the real Emeril, but it is the chef his fans have come to expect. Not wanting to appear inconsistent or disappoint, Emeril puts on his game face each time he goes in front of the camera.

Off-camera, he is much more restrained. That is the Emeril who toils late into the night wrapping up projects and the Emeril who loves nothing more than to stay home and cook for his wife and kids.

Emeril the Family Man

Family has always been a big part of Emeril's life. This includes his parents, who now live down the block from him in New Orleans; his two grown daughters, with whom he has maintained close touch; and his third wife and one-year-old son. Although he started his career as chef and restaurateur without his parents' blessing, his father now works with him and his older sister works in the business office at Emeril's in Orlando.[15] Throughout his career, he has presented cooking as a means of spending time with and enjoying the company of one's family.

Perhaps because his first two marriages failed and he missed out on family time with his daughters, now in their 20s, he has come to value setting aside time to spend as a family unit. Although his parents made a point of cooking and eating together, Emeril was not able to strike that balance until he married Alden in 2000. Now she and their young son, E.J., travel with Emeril constantly so that the family is not separated when he heads to New York to tape his shows or when he needs to spend time in one of the restaurants outside New Orleans.

With increasing frequency, Emeril talks about bringing back the family table—the tradition of families regularly dining together at home. He grew up around a family table, where food brought everyone together at least once a day. And now with Alden's commitment and involvement, his family is able to enjoy that again.

Reflecting his new focus on family, Emeril has initiated a number of products and projects in support of children and families. As described in Chapter 8, he established the Emeril Lagasse Foundation, which supports the work of organizations creating developmental and educational programs for children. In 2003, the opening of Emeril's Tchoup Chop, a more family-oriented restaurant at Universal Orlando, signaled an even greater appreciation for time spent with family. And the development of chefwear for kids, as well as his cookbooks *Emeril's There's a Chef in My Soup!* and the soon-to-be-released *Emeril's There's a Chef in My Family!* strengthened that child- and family-friendly aspect of his brand and his company.

But Emeril's commitment to family goes beyond his immediate kin to include his family of employees, who have worked together so long that many truly are like family members. And just as he supports his own blood relations, he also tries to support his extended family at Emeril's Homebase.

The Emeril Alumni Network

Where less confident restaurateurs might try to prevent competition from former employees looking to follow in their footsteps, Emeril is happy to help. Few employees leave Emeril's Homebase, but those who do almost always receive his blessing and assistance. In many ways like a proud papa, Emeril brags about their culinary aptitude and success, referring his own guests to the new restaurants his former employees have established. Such is the case with Tom Wolfe of Wolfe's of New Orleans and Anne Kearney of Peristyle.

Tom Wolfe grew up in a household filled with a passion for food and for sharing it with others, much like Emeril did. Wolfe's weekly family gatherings gave him a regular opportunity to assist his mother in preparing traditional New Orleans dishes for the two dozen or so attendees. In addition to his mother, family friend Henry Schmitt also fostered Wolfe's fascination with food and cooking by introducing him to fresh sausage and seafood.

His professional career began with the establishment of his own catering company, which taught Wolfe firsthand about owning a small business and led to his enrolling in Delgado Community College's culinary arts program. From there he went to work at one of the Brennan family restaurants, Mr. B's Bistro in New Orleans's French Quarter, where he prepared such popular local dishes as barbeque shrimp, jambalaya, and gumbos.

From Mr. B's, Wolfe headed to Emeril's Restaurant, mastering all of the line positions, including pastry, saucier, and butcher, culminating in being named sous-chef, where he worked alongside Emeril himself.

Despite his increasing responsibility and media exposure, such as appearing with Emeril on *Good Morning America*, Wolfe still had his eye on being his own boss and continued to work on building his catering business on his days off. After eight years at Emeril's, Wolfe and his wife opened their own restaurant, Wolfe's of New Orleans, which has caught the eye of a number of critics and was named Best New Formal Dining Restaurant in New Orleans by *Bon Appetit*. Instead of begrudging his success, Emeril has fanned the flames, recommending the restaurant to others.

Although Wolfe may have been the first former employee who rose through the ranks to set up shop locally, Anne Kearney is another Emeril's alum who also left to run her own restaurant after spending time mainly behind the scenes of Emeril's TV show and publishing efforts. Kearney worked with Emeril from 1992 to 1995, researching and writing recipes and scripts for *The Essence of Emeril* and developing and testing recipes for his second cookbook, *Louisiana Real and Rustic*. Whenever she could, she also worked at any of the food stations at Emeril's Restaurant, keeping her connection to the kitchen and to customers, with her favorite station being the chef's table up front.

Kearney had arrived at Emeril's with training from the Greater Cincinnati Culinary Art Academy, but her initial exposure to cooking began at age 14 when her mother went back to work and Kearney began helping prepare nightly meals.[16] Armed with a love of cooking and culinary training, Kearney headed to New Orleans for Mardi Gras in 1991 and ended up staying for good. She landed a position working for John Neal at the Bistro at the Maison de Ville and went with him as his sous-chef when he left to open Peristyle. It was Neal who helped develop her palate and tutored her in classic French cooking techniques. So when Neal passed away in 1995, Kearney returned to Peristyle as chef and owner.

On her own, she has earned numerous awards, from being named the Gallo of Sonoma Rising Star Chef in 1997 to American Express's Best Chef in the Southeast in 2002. Although Neal may have helped develop her style, Emeril has helped build her clientele, referring patrons to his former employee for a good meal.

Isidore Kharasch, president of Hospitality Works, Inc., maintains that it says a lot about a restaurateur's confidence in his own operations if he is comfortable referring his own clientele elsewhere. In fact, it is good for business. "They won't lose a customer and the customers appreciate the recommendation and become an even bigger supporter," explains Kharasch.[17]

Emeril also supports fellow chefs, referring business their way and recommending their establishments to his own clientele. That unselfishness and friendly support reflects very positively on Emeril's image as restaurateur and business owner.

The Visionary

Ask industry observers what Emeril's biggest talent is and if the answer is not his cooking, it is his vision for his business. Able to visualize what he wants and develop a plan to achieve each aspect, few other CEOs rival his abilities. Shortly after graduating from Johnson & Wales, Emeril began deciding where he ultimately wanted to go. Although he recognized the need to spend time as a restaurant chef, learning the ropes, he also knew that he wanted to own his own restaurant eventually.

". . . I think that if you go through life worrying about small things and thinking small then that's exactly what happens," says Emeril.[18] Thinking big has meant developing the dream and then putting in place the resources to make it happen, rather than expecting to have to personally oversee each detail.

Once his list of restaurants surged past two, Emeril began to rely more heavily on his staff and management team inside each eatery. Although he checks in regularly and spends time in each site every few months, the day-to-day decisions are left to the on-site managers and chefs.

Add to that his television responsibilities, and Emeril recognized the need to bring on test kitchen chefs tasked specifically with developing recipes and scripts for use on his two shows; his protégé Anne Kearney held one of these positions for three years.

What's in a Name? Recognition and Reputation

Having a celebrity chef's name over the door does help bring in guests initially, agree the experts. The instant name recognition attracts attention and interest from consumers that can last months, but unless a celebrity restaurant can compete on quality food and service, diners will not come back a second time. So says restaurant industry analyst Bob Derrington of Morgan Keegan: "Celebrity chefs are good for the kickoff of a restaurant. . . . Emeril's name recognition in a market like New Orleans is higher than, for example, a market like Memphis. But once you get past the celebrity side of the business, it comes down to quality of the occasion and the consumer's enjoyment of that."[19] Which is to say, living up to the reputation that precedes his name becomes the true test of Emeril's abilities.

Part of the challenge of managing an image is knowing when to expand and when to pull back. When to exploit the power and cachet that goes with a hot brand name, and when to backpedal. Emeril is clearly still in expansion mode, using his name to gain entrée to popular tourist and business destinations in the South. However, the fawning praise is more subdued these days, as food critics in Atlanta and Miami Beach question whether, once the initial curiosity wears off, guests will continue to frequent Emeril's.

Emeril's Atlanta, which opened in 2003, is the chef's eighth restaurant but his first location in Georgia. Like his other restaurant locations, Atlanta features a warm climate, a strong convention and tourist trade, and a comparatively strong metro economy. It also boasts a local crowd that prefers to dine out—Atlantans average six casual dinners and two special dinners in restaurants each month, according to a 2003 survey by the *Atlanta Journal-Constitution*.[20] That is definitely a plus from a restaurateur's perspective, but it places added pressure on Emeril's staff to get it right from the beginning. And they did not.

Although the menu lists many of the same dishes served at Emeril's in New Orleans, the décor is decidedly different. Restaurant critic John Kessler, of the *Atlanta Journal-Constitution*, compares the two in his October 2003 review of the then just-opened eatery. "In New Orleans, you have a corner restaurant in a funky neighborhood that became a sensation and continues serving the excessive, yummy, feel-good food that made it famous. In Atlanta, you have a shiny new food palace in a city that likes high-gloss dining."[21]

That high-gloss element includes a glassed-in tower of wine bottles reachable only by ladder, serpentine stairs leading to a dining room above the chef's table, huge chandeliers, and wood woven along the long walls to soften them. Too over-the-top for New Orleans, perhaps, but in keeping with Atlantans' preference for glitz.

Unfortunately, Atlantans are not as impressed with the cooking as with the décor. Kessler skewered Emeril for the quality of the cooking, rating the restaurant as "fair." Ouch.

In truth, the menu at Emeril's Atlanta differs little from that of its New Orleans sister, although the key is in the preparation. Case in point is the Roasted American Rack of Lamb with Creole Mustard Crust, Rosemary Creamed Potatoes, Apple Mint Relish, and Rosemary Lamb Jus, which is available at either restaurant. Other common entrées include the Sauté of Gulf Shrimp with homemade pasta, Niman Ranch Double Cut Pork Chop or Andouille Crusted Redfish. The dishes vary subtly, although the main difference is in the menu description.

Desserts provide more variation, although J.K.'s Chocolate Soufflé appears on both. Atlanta guests can also choose Red Velvet Layer Cake with Amaretto-Almond Cream Cheese Frosting, Warm Double Chocolate Praline Tart with Candied Louisiana Pecans, or Chocolate Peanut Butter Pie, among others.

Similar menu variations can be found at Emeril's Miami Beach, the company's newest restaurant, which opened just a few months after Emeril's Atlanta and is the newest addition to Emeril's portfolio of restaurants. It likewise sports a razzle-dazzle interior, with a large lobby and bar, chef's table, and floor-to-ceiling chandelier. It's also another partnership—Emeril's is located within the Loews Miami Beach Hotel, just one block off the beach.

As in his other restaurants, Emeril includes menu favorites from the original Emeril's as well as additions with a local flare. In Miami Beach, that means Crispy Yucca, Coconut Rice Pilaf, or mango salsa on the side. Here Emeril has wisely tweaked his standard menu to reflect local cultural influences. Just as he carefully modified some of the recipes at Commander's Palace on his arrival, making minor alterations to add his own touch without making the dishes unrecognizable to the regulars, here Emeril has adapted some of his popular menu entrées to try and match the preferences of his local clientele.

He knows his name will be a major draw, but it also seems that Emeril is becoming wiser about catering to his local customers.

Handling Image Problems

Although the words "Emeril" and "controversy" are rarely heard in the same sentence, events in Atlanta and Las Vegas in the last few years brought unwanted negative attention to Emeril's restaurants, slightly tarnishing his crystal-clean image.

Back in 1999, Emeril was forced to go before the Clark County Commission in Nevada to apologize for the embarrassing and lewd behavior of one of his guests at the Delmonico Steakhouse, located within the Venetian Resort/Hotel/Casino in Las Vegas. Apparently *Lifestyles of the Rich and Famous* host Robin Leach, who was a consultant with the Venetian, and about five female companions were enjoying more than the food while seated in the Delmonico's private dining room atop the kitchen.

Emeril was not a witness, but he had to appear before the commission to plead his case to avoid formal disciplinary action, which could have included losing the restaurant's liquor license. Fortunately, the commission recognized the unusual and difficult situation his employees were forced to deal with and agreed to issue an "administrative reprimand" that required a manager to be on-site at all times and that employees work with a crisis management team for two years.[22]

Given his distance from the situation, it is unlikely that Emeril's reputation was battered at all by the incident. The Atlanta Q100 situation, four years later, is another story.

Shortly after Emeril's Atlanta opened in August 2003, Emeril began making the rounds of the local media, doing interviews about the new restaurant. When radio station Q100, which plays predominantly pop music, contacted the Food Network about interviewing Emeril on the *Bert Show*, the producer, Jeff Dauler, was told that Emeril would not be doing any radio interviews to promote the restaurant. So imagine Dauler's surprise when he turned on the radio and heard Emeril's voice.

To find out what had happened, Dauler called Emeril's Atlanta and was told that Q100 listeners "aren't the clientele that dines at Emeril's." Oh, *really*, thought Dauler. So he and *Bert Show* host Bert Weiss took the slap public. Listeners responded, expressing disappointment and dismay. The general reaction was, as one listener put it, "Don't make generalizations about me because of the kind of music I choose to listen to."[23]

Of course, Emeril apologized to Weiss and Q100 listeners, by mail, writing: "This is not the way we conduct business. Not only is this comment not true, but it in no way reflects the way our company views Q100 or your listeners. The person who made this comment was not authorized or qualified to speak on behalf of myself or the restaurant."[24] But it still does not answer the question of why he would have appeared on so many other local radio stations, including one of Q100's sister channels, but not the "All the Hits" station. He may have tried to make amends, but his man-of-the-people image took a hit here. Fortunately, the situation was localized and few folks outside of Atlanta ever knew about the flack.

10

MAXIMIZING MERCHANDISE

There's a cap on restaurants and success. Consumer products are where [Emeril] can expand.

—Samantha Ettus, brand expert, Ettus Media Management[1]

The Emerilware launch sales exceeded projections and was [sic] responsible for one-half of the company's 42% growth in 2000. In 2002, a year that saw economic downturn and flat profits for most cookware companies, All-Clad's sales grew 31% and Emerilware posted an impressive 65% increase in sales."[2] So reads the marketing case study, underscoring the power of licensing to both manufacturer, in this case All-Clad cookware, and celebrity endorser, in this case Emeril.

Moving beyond cookbooks and seasonings, the obvious brand extensions, Emeril's association with All-Clad boosted both brands, in terms of sales as well as exposure. The partnership with Emeril enabled All-Clad to move down market from its high-end brand position without damaging its reputation and provided Emeril a means of developing cookware with a professional-quality name that was less expensive. It was a win-win situation.

Few would argue that Emeril Lagasse is one of the best-known chefs of all time. By virtue of his talent and charisma, he has built an impressive personal brand that fuels his career and business enterprise. But a personal brand only goes so far, says Samantha Ettus, president of Ettus Media Management. "You want your brand to outlast you," she says. But most personal brands do not.

Ettus cites Suze Orman as one example of a brand that should outlast its originator, Suze herself, and perhaps fashion designer Ralph Lauren would be another, but the examples are few and far between because of the difficulty of separating a person from an entity. Ettus says, "Building a successful brand out of a personal brand is the epitome of success."

And yet, Emeril has done so.

Beyond talent and charisma, two rare attributes that Emeril has in spades, observes Ettus, the chef has also learned to use the media to his advantage. "If you look at all successful personal brands—those that have been converted to brand names—there are a multitude of mediums through which the brand has been developed." On the foundation of talent and charisma is involvement in book publishing, television, film, magazines, radio, charity work, and consumer products. Those are the pieces of the successful brand puzzle. In order to sustain itself beyond the life of the individual on which the reputation has been built, a brand must be active in multiple media.

Emeril is currently evident, or actively involved, in all of the media avenues except radio and film. Then again, he is only 44—give him time.

The bulk of Emeril's acclaim is based on his restaurants, however, and Ettus believes there is a limit to how far he can expand his brand through his eateries. "There's a cap on restaurants and success. Consumer products are where he can expand," she says.

So far, the consumer products in his marketing arsenal include cookware, cutlery, wine, apparel, spices and seasonings, and cookbooks. His most recent introductions target the younger chef, with apparel, a cookbook, a sous-chef kit, and video. And his line of tableware and linens is due out shortly. But there is certainly more that he could do.

The Martha Model

Emeril is most frequently compared to his culinary peers—stars like Paul Prudhomme, Wolfgang Puck, and Julia Child—although, in many ways, his business approach is more similar to Martha Stewart's. Like the dethroned diva of domesticity, Lagasse has worked tirelessly to transfer his name and reputation—his personal brand— to a variety of forums, including his restaurants, television, publishing, the Web, and several culinary-related product lines.

Although her image, her brand, and her respectability have clearly been tarnished, perhaps irrevocably, due to her felony conviction related to her personal stock sale, the strategy she used to extend her name across multiple channels worked for years. Whereas Martha made her mark with her catering business, Emeril has built his culinary empire on a solid base of upscale eateries. Martha has 14 cookbooks, Emeril has 9, the first 7 of which sold nearly four million copies.[3] At the height of her career Martha had a TV show and guest spots on shows like *Good Morning America*, and so, too, does Emeril. Martha associated her name with virtually anything related to home décor, and Emeril has positioned himself as the culinary equivalent.

Although Emeril has made great headway in the past decade in terms of heightening awareness of his name, one of the few places where Martha has a leg up is her own magazine, *Martha Stewart Living*, which, until recently, had done well with readers and advertisers. Emeril's image has graced a number of magazine covers, from *Woman's World* to *South*, but so far he has shied away from owning his own publication.

Martha was also the master of repurposing, or reusing, material she created, and Emeril shows signs that he may do likewise. Recipes from his restaurant have been packaged and sold as a cookbook, *From Emeril's Kitchens*. Some of the recipes from his TV shows are now featured as content at his web site, Emerils.com. And if he wanted to, he could easily sell videotapes of past TV episodes, perhaps as a series on preparing certain types of foods, or pursue a syndicated newspaper column that makes use of material he has already developed for his shows or books. Right now, virtually anything associated with his name is of interest to his fans.

Leveraging Assets

It is clear that Emeril understands that his brand name is his company's most significant asset—an asset that, when properly exploited, can lead to new avenues for revenue creation and growth and new vehicles for reaching potential customers. One of the most effective tools to achieve these objectives is licensing and new product development contracts. Although the agreement may take different forms, the result is the same: the creation of a product line that bears the Emeril brand that is produced and sold by someone else.

Proof of his understanding of the importance of consumer product development is that he has established a separate entity to manage all of his licensing deals, called Food of Love Productions, LLC. Already, Food of Love contributes a large portion of his company's total revenues; the restaurants, organized under the Emeril's Homebase moniker, bring in an estimated 40%,[4] with licensing partnerships and his television show comprising the remaining 60%. Tony Cruz, director of finance and business manager for Emeril's Homebase, says that each licensing deal is unique, based on a percentage of sales, "depending on what we're trying to accomplish."[5] That could range from entering a new market to growing an existing market, generating short-term revenue, or investing for a longer-term payoff, among many possible scenarios.

Although most celebrities use an agent to broker licensing deals for them, Emeril has apparently decided he can handle his own deals and is believed to negotiate his own agreements without the help of an outside agent. While unusual in the industry, the move to retain complete control of his business dealings is typical Emeril.

By working as his own agent, through his Food of Love division, Emeril saves the 30 to 50% fee paid to agents for their services. Marty Broxteen, executive editor of *Licensing Letter*, explains that an agent can provide market knowledge and contacts useful for negotiating a profitable licensing deal, in addition to managing the time-consuming aspects of such a contract.[6] But since Emeril finalizes few deals each year and has market knowledge and the administrative resources to manage the paperwork, he must have decided to forgo an agent's services and keep the standard fee for himself. When millions of dollars are involved, pocketing the agent's commission can make a big difference.

Licensed properties, as Emeril's brand name is, typically involve some form of an advance from the licensee, which is an up-front payment credited against projected sales, a royalty of somewhere between 5 and 12% of the wholesale price of the product, and a guarantee, which is an amount the manufacturer agrees to pay to the licensor even if no product is ever sold. Lower-priced food items, such as Emeril's seasonings and spices, probably yield royalties on the lower end of the scale, at around 5 to 6%, say industry experts, while higher-end merchandise would command a higher percentage.

In addition to tightly controlling the licensing of his brand, Emeril has also kept his options open when it comes to distribution, choosing to partner with specialty suppliers—companies that are tops in their field of expertise—rather than handing everything off to one or two major distributors. Emeril has gotten far by retaining strict control over every aspect of his career, image, and reputation. So it comes as no shock that this is how he would approach brand extensions. "I'm too used to being in control of my own destiny," he says, explaining why he is now limiting his focus to business pursuits, rather than new TV deals. "I'm too used to being a businessperson."[7]

Of course, there are always critics eager to weigh in on each business decision. And some question the soundness of such an entry into product development and licensing. Admits Emeril, "They're like, 'He's selling out. What's he trying to do to the business?' "[8] But like most successful business leaders, Emeril refuses to let such criticism or discouragement sway his own plans and vision for his company. He keeps moving ahead, undeterred.

One savvy decision that Emeril made was to attach his name to culinary and food products—from spices to sauces, wine, cookware, and cutlery. And why not? In addition to generating tens of millions of dollars in revenue for his company, the branded products provide one more way to keep the chef's name in the public eye and ensure his continued prominence.

Although outsiders may chastise Emeril for selling out, he is in the majority when it comes to commercializing his name. Chefs Wolfgang Puck, Paul Prudhomme, Daniel Boulud, and Bobby Flay, among many others, have all licensed their names or developed their own product lines to appeal to demand from their fan base. Puck has several sets of serving dishes he has recently rolled out, Prudhomme has his own cookware, Boulud custom knives, and Flay his own seasonings and marinades. Additionally, Jacques Pepin has been known for his copper cookware, and Joyce Chen, until recently, owned the company that manufactured and marketed her line of Asian cookware. If Emeril had not sold out in this way, he would clearly be missing out.

In fact, say branding experts, there is nothing wrong with brand extensions. Rather than weakening the brand, such spin-offs can actually strengthen it, when done well. According to William Arruda, president of Reach, Inc., the international branding consultancy, "a line extension is OK as long as it is consistent with the brand's attributes." That is, Emeril-branded products need to match consumers' perceptions of the man behind the name.

Strong brands, such as Emeril's, have three Cs, says Arruda: clarity, consistency, and constancy. Emeril is clear about what he is and what he is not. And his fans are as well. He is a talented chef, restaurateur, and TV host whose work and life revolve around food. Everything associated with his personal brand is food or kitchen related.

He is also consistent in his actions and words. Whether consumers see him in person at one of his restaurants or at a public event, such as a book signing, or watch him on TV, Emeril is always Emeril. He is sincere, friendly, sometimes funny, and passionate about cooking. What he says is exactly what you would expect him to say, and how he acts is how you would expect him to act.

Finally, Emeril is everywhere. He maintains a constant presence in the public eye, whether through television, newspaper articles, or products sitting on consumers' kitchen shelves. "Even in a fairly crowded market," [Emeril] stands out," remarks Arruda.

Brand Extension Opportunities

Leveraging his cachet and brand strength, Emeril successfully negotiated the development of entirely new product lines under the umbrella of some of the best culinary brands in the world—All-Clad, Wüsthof-Trident, and Fetzer Vineyards. He also is regularly expanding those existing lines at every opportunity.

Given his popularity, recognizability, and charisma, Emeril has presumably been presented with countless product licensing opportunities; he reportedly receives 300 offers a year just to open new restaurants. But through careful analysis, he has culled the list of licensing opportunities to focus only on those that relate to food and cooking and are with companies marketing upscale, higher-end consumer products—essentially, companies marketing to the same market segment Emeril is attempting to reach.

Of course, Emeril is by no means the first chef to jump on the merchandise development bandwagon. Chefs promoting particular culinary tools started more than 30 years ago, in 1973, with the introduction of the Cuisinart food processor. Consumers were unconvinced that the expensive Cuisinart was a kitchen necessity until Julia Child and James Beard raved about it, triggering a buying stampede among gourmands.

Child and Beard were not compensated for their endorsement, as today's chefs routinely are, but manufacturers witnessed the power of the celebrity mouthpiece. Partnering a product with a popular chef meant sales.

Crossing Over into Cookware: All-Clad Emerilware

Although buying a chef endorsement does not cost much, says Hugh Rushing, executive vice president of the Cookware Manufacturers Association, "if a chef is well-known, well-liked, and owns a popular restaurant, his name gives [the cookware line] instant credibility. . . . The wider the exposure the chef has, the bigger the value of his endorsement." So why would a company like All-Clad, a subsidiary of Waterford Wedgewood, well known for professional-grade cookware, need Emeril Lagasse's name on its pans? Most chefs would agree that All-Clad is considered one of the best lines in the business, even without Emeril's endorsement.

The answer, perhaps, is market growth. For years, All-Clad's expensive cookware has been embraced by professional and amateur chefs, who have been willing to pay about $150 for a 12-inch fry pan—nearly four times the price of a standard steel or cast-iron pan—to get an All-Clad product. In the 1990s, gourmet cooking moved into home kitchens, which were upgraded to allow for better-quality meal preparation and entertaining. Along with kitchen renovation came cookware replacement, boosting All-Clad's sales from $5 million in 1988 to more than $110 million in 2003.[9]

"Cookware [went] from a chore to a social activity, and there are people who want to use the best tools possible," says Peter Cameron, All-Clad Metalcrafters' president and CEO. "It's like wanting to have

Tiger Woods's golf clubs. People want the pan Emeril uses," explains Cameron.[10] (He knows that for a fact, since sales of Emerilware were up 30 to 40% from 2002 to 2003.)

However, the All-Clad/Emeril relationship started out on a very small scale. In 1999, All-Clad packaged Lagasse's *Emeril's TV Dinners* cookbook with a 2½ quart stainless steel saucier pan and called it the Emeril Everyday Pan, which sold for $89.99. Although it was launched late in the year, sales of the pan-cookbook combo were so strong that it was the single best-selling stainless steel cookware item of the year.[11] If it was a test, the results were a resounding success.

Strong sales of the Emeril Everyday Pan and Lagasse's impressive popularity are probably why All-Clad was willing to let him drive the Emerilware product development process to a great degree. Much more than a product endorsement, Emeril is staking his reputation on his line of pots and pans, which is presumably why he invested so much time verifying its quality. Reports Emeril, "I did everything I could to that bakeware: I dropped it, I baked with it, I tried to let it rust. I tested it for six months." Manufactured of heavy-gauge aluminum with a patented diamond-patterned baking surface, Emeril seems proud of the 100-odd pans[12] that bear his name. Underscoring the lengthy product development cycle, Emeril explains that quality was most important: "It's not just 'let's get it out.' It's 'let's get it right.'"[13]

The benefit to consumers? Claims Emeril, "You can be a bad cook and really look like you're a good cook with Emerilware."

But why would he want to align his brand with All-Clad's? The arrangement is a classic cobranding deal in which both brand names appear on the product packaging, combining the strengths (and weaknesses) of each brand. In this particular case, Emeril's brand is more prominent, indicating that the line is primarily targeted at his established customer base rather than All-Clad's. The Emerilware line of pots and pans is emblazoned with *his* name first and foremost rather than All-Clad's. All-Clad can use its involvement to gain entrée into the middle market, from its position in the upscale segment. Observing this, Rushing applauds that approach. "It was a good idea to hook up with Emeril and an even better idea to develop a line that was Emeril's. All-Clad's name isn't first—Emeril's name is. Smart."

What he means is, All-Clad does not jeopardize its prestigious brand name by directly linking it with another's, while at the same time moving down market to increase its customer base. Even All-Clad's president admits, "It's good, honest cookware, but it's not All-Clad." Company officials have described Emerilware as "middle strata" gourmet cookware.[14] So is that good for Emeril?

The answer is "yes." Yes, because part of Emeril's appeal is demystifying gourmet cooking, bringing it to the level of the average consumer. While most chefs at home might balk at paying $150 for an All-Clad pan, paying $69.99 for a similar Emerilware item sounds more palatable.

An association between the top-of-the-line All-Clad and the mass-market Emeril is an excellent means of attracting serious and would-be chefs at home to try the products, as sales of the products can attest. With a price tag less than All-Clad's professional grade, Emerilware brings in roughly $40 million a year to Food of Love Productions.[15]

But bakeware is just the tip of the iceberg for the Emeril/Waterford Wedgewood partnership (as mentioned, All-Clad is a subsidiary of Waterford Wedgewood). According to CEO Cameron, the company intends to roll out textiles and tabletop products in addition to the existing bakeware, stainless steel, and nonstick cookware lines. And a new line of electrical appliances will soon debut. "We will continue to expand the Emerilware brand beyond the kitchen with an aggressive textile program," says Cameron. "You'll see other items this year, including a focus on tabletop and entertaining as opposed to food prep,"[16] including flatware and glassware. Such an expansion, for the Emeril brand at least, suggests a strategy to broaden the scope of the brand from pure meal preparation to entertaining.

Whether he meant to or not, Emeril has also inspired some of his colleagues in the direction of new product development. Jamie Oliver, Nigella Lawson, and Daniel Boulud, among others, are all designing their own lines of cookware,[17] while other colleagues are branching out into tableware and accessories.

Cobranding with Fetzer Wines

Just as Emerilware was designed to entice average cooks to upgrade to better cookware, Lagasse's Emeril's Classics is a line of "affordable, food-friendly wines targeted to novice wine buyers."[18] Acknowledging that many consumers find wine selection intimidating, Emeril says, "I hope that any influence I have will be to make wine more fun and more approachable."[19] Just as he has helped educate novice chefs about food preparation, his line of wines aims to improve the public's appreciation of the product as a meal accompaniment. But he fully admits that his celebrity may be the main reason buyers give it a try.

Introduced in 2002 through Brown-Forman Corporation subsidiary Fetzer Vineyards, Emeril was involved in every step of winemaking, "from visiting vineyards to tasting trial blends."[20] Two Emeril's Classics wines were released in select markets in 2002—the Red Table Wine 2000 and the White Table Wine 2001, both with a $9 price point at the Fetzer web site. In late 2003, two more wines were to be released, including a Mendocino Chardonnay and a California Cabernet Sauvignon, priced around the same. The wines are available mainly through supermarket chains and at the Fetzer web site, as well as at Emerils.com.

Like Emeril's cooking style, which involves blending and enhancing food flavors, his line of wines consists of grape blends. The Red Table Wine, for example, is a blend of cabernet sauvignon, syrah, and zinfandel that provides a taste that combines currant, blackberry, herb, and tar essences.

This move to brand his own line of wines comes as part of a three-year marketing contract with Fetzer to promote the company through point-of-sale materials and radio spots.[21] Part of those initial negotiations included an agreement to develop and produce an Emeril-branded line of wines.

Brown-Forman senior vice president of marketing, Doug Rogers, said of the partnership, "Emeril is one of the true superstars and most recognizable figures in the culinary world today. The affiliation of Emeril with Fetzer will add a lot of excitement to our marketing mix and leverage our efforts to reposition the brand."[22]

Just as Emeril relies solely on the finest organically grown produce in his cooking,[23] keeping close ties with local ranchers, farmers, and fishermen to ensure a steady supply, Fetzer has played a leading role in organic farming of vineyards.[24] In that sense, too, the relationship between the companies is complementary.

The new wine product line is a natural for Emeril, mainly because of his restaurants' reputation for stocking and serving a vast selection of fine wines. Part of the Emeril's dining experience consists of enjoying a carefully selected bottle of wine, perhaps at the suggestion of the sommelier. The restaurants have won a series of awards, for both cuisine and wine, including the Grand Award from *Wine Spectator* magazine for Emeril's wine list, the Ivy Award from *Restaurants and Institutions*, and Best Restaurant of the Year from *Esquire.* Each of his New Orleans restaurants keeps around 17,000 bottles of wine at any given time to meet its patrons' sizeable demand for the drink.[25]

Most important, the new line of wines is generating results. "We partnered with those guys to release a line of red and white wine a little over a year ago—in late 2002. We've sold 40,000 cases of our first wine," says Cruz.[26] At $8.99 a bottle, that amounts to more than $4.3 million in sales in just a few months. Obviously, demand is there for the Emeril brand.

45 Spices and Sauces

One of Emeril's first forays into product development was the development of a line of seasonings, salad dressings, marinades, and pepper sauces, named Emeril's, which is produced by B&G Foods.[27]

Marvin Schwinder, director of marketing for B&G, says that four years ago "I initiated the discussion with Emeril. He has so many fans, we thought there was a marketing opportunity there."[28] Translation: Fan base equals virtually guaranteed sales.

Today, the company produces 45 different food products for Emeril and is a major contributor to Food of Love's bottom line, generating $50 million a year in retail sales. Here, too, Lagasse is personally involved with developing the recipes for the products, which B&G then produces en masse. Emeril's spices and sauces sport the zesty names that incorporate the Emeril lexicon: Emeril's Chicken Rub, Steak Rub, Fish Rub, and Rib Rub; Bayou Blast ("spices up dishes with ingredients that reflect the richness of Creole cooking" along with other international flavorings); Emeril's pasta sauces, including Kicked Up Tomato™ and Roasted Gaaahlic™; Kick It Up Red and Kick It Up Green pepper sauces; Kicked Up French salad dressing (and other flavors); and BAM! BQ sauce and Baby BAM! Essence (a mellower flavor, for kids). All of these—and more—are available at the company's web site, Emerils.com.

Although sales are hot today, in the beginning, the brand was positioned as a specialty line. "The product line itself couldn't be mass-marketed, so we started it off as a gourmet line that is now becoming a mainstream item," says Cruz. "We got the product distributed to 85 percent of the marketplace without having to invest a tremendous amount in advertising."[29] Recently, however, B&G did invest $5 million on a television campaign to build sales of the brand.[30]

As Emeril's brand has become better known, both companies have benefited, with sales of his seasonings rising. Other products have also become more popular, such as his line of knives.

Cutlery

"To have a great time in the kitchen, it's essential to start with good knives," says Emeril. "They'll be your best friend, the tools you can rely on to complete a multitude of tasks in preparing food."[31]

Consequently, Lagasse turned to one of the top names in cutlery, Wüsthof-Trident, to manufacture his own line of Emerilware knives.

Like All-Clad, Wüsthof-Trident is considered a premium cutlery brand. And perhaps for the same reasons as All-Clad had for going down market, Wüsthof worked with Emeril to develop a branded line of knives—another staple of a true chef's kitchen.

Whereas Wüsthof's Classic five-inch cook's knife sells for $59.99 on Amazon.com, Emeril's equivalent, the Emerilware five-inch cook's knife, is just $24.99. The Wüsthof Classic 10-piece block set runs $399.99, while the Emerilware 12-piece block set is $199.99. Other Wüsthof knife sets have similar pricing differentials versus Emerilware, which provides a vehicle for targeting middle-market gourmands.

Cookbooks

Even more important than pots and pans or knives are the recipes that a chef creates—recipes that are uniquely theirs and reflect their special talents. In that regard, Emeril is also a standout. His eight cookbooks—a ninth is forthcoming—provide a significant portion of his company's revenue, with more than four million copies sold, at a cover price of between $25 and $35 each. At standard royalty rates of 10%, those cookbooks have yielded between $10 million and $14 million for the Food of Love coffers. And given Emeril's strong track record, it is likely that those figures are on the low end of what he actually received.

Publishers typically pay an advance against royalties that represents what the book will likely generate in sales, with royalties of 6 to 12% paid for each book sold. But the stronger the sales for a chef's or author's last book, the better the advance on the next one.

On top of that, books sold through Emeril's web site earn him significantly more than the standard royalty since he can buy the books at wholesale and sell them at retail, earning closer to $12 to $13 per book. And when you are selling millions of copies, those dollars quickly add up.

Wearables

In addition to all of his cobranded products, Emeril also offers Emeril "wearables" to his fans. These include baseball caps, T-shirts, and golf shirts, as well as white long-sleeved chef coats (all with the "Emeril's" name/logo), bright-green "BAM!" aprons, and the same black clogs that Emeril is famous for always wearing on his TV show. These are also available on his web site.

Products That Appeal to Children

In addition to marketing to adult chefs, Emeril has also recently begun developing products for the younger set—children. In the last few years, he has published a children's cookbook, put out a children's cooking video, and created a junior sous-chef training kit, with all the major (albeit plastic) tools necessary to whip something up in the kitchen. Youth chef coats, T-shirts, and even Kid's Essence seasoning are now available at the Emerils.com web site, and a family cookbook is due out shortly.

His devotion to children-related charitable causes is evidence that his interest in this market is not just self-serving. He seems to really enjoy connecting with younger fans and encouraging them to pursue their dreams. But the availability of kid-sized products dovetails nicely with his core business and helps him form buying relationships with consumers at a very young age.

In many ways, Emeril's entrance into the youth market is much like Apple's strategy for gaining acceptance of its Macintosh computers back in the 1980s. By pushing the computers onto college campuses with discounted pricing, Apple built a loyal following of users who brought their devotion to the product to work with them after graduation. Those college students quickly grew up to be corporate and institutional decision makers and influencers when it came to computer purchases, driving sales of Apple Macintosh computers through the roof in short order. Apple penetrated the market quickly with its new product because it started by influencing young buyers.

Already, children constitute a sizeable portion of Emeril's television fan base, providing a significant revenue-generating opportunity. Harris Interactive estimates the purchasing power of the 8- to 21-year-old age group to be $172 billion, on top of the strong influence they have on the products and brands their household buys.[32] By targeting this market segment early on, Emeril may have an easier time convincing his young chefs to buy his cookbooks so they can cook like him or pester Mom or Dad to pick up some of Emeril's seasonings at the grocery store. Leveraging his role model status could result in a profitable lifelong association with his young fans.

Brand Personality

What is it about the Emeril brand name that has manufacturers and distributors clamoring for the chance to work with him? To a large degree, it has less to do with the Emeril brand name and more to do with the personality.

Perceived as a nice, very talented chef, Emeril enjoys the respect and admiration of much of the buying public. In stark contrast to controversial figures, inconsistent celebrities, or haughty business leaders, Emeril comes across as a man, and a brand, that is moving up market quickly. Through his many personal appearances nationwide and his intermittent presence at his restaurants, in addition to his daily television shows, consumers have the sense that they know Emeril personally—and they like him. That is a rare combination.

The fact that this well-loved celebrity is part of a multi-billion-dollar industry is a bonus; the U.S. restaurant industry alone is valued at approximately $280 billion, according to CIBC World Markets, which accounts for a percentage of the total culinary industry.

In addition to his charming personality and sincerity, Emeril also has a reputation for excellence in all that he does. Whether he is selecting fresh fish and produce from local growers, informing the waitstaff at one of his restaurants about the day's guests, or taking the time to chat with the throngs of fans who show up at one of his book signings, he aims to exceed his customers' expectations.

Even if he does not always hit the mark—perhaps the food served was a bit bland, or the day's episode of *Emeril Live* not quite as lively—Emeril devotees are generally very forgiving because they know his extremely high standards.

Those characteristics are all highly desirable to any consumer products manufacturer looking to increase its market share. The Emeril brand name has significant value. Or, as Samantha Ettus says, "The key for him is to make sure that whatever he does, he has to make sure he is not compromising the quality."

Future Business Opportunities

Moving forward, the number of new business opportunities Emeril will have to field will rise and fall with his brand strength. The better his existing branded products sell, the more new opportunities will surface. Conversely, if sales begin to decline, new opportunities may as well. Right now, Emeril's prestige factor is high, as are his prospects, says Ettus.

In addition to building on his solid base of restaurants, media outlets, and consumer products, Ettus sees a number of possible avenues for growth. First, exploring opportunities on radio would round out his broadcast and print publicity channels. Second, expanding his online presence to focus less on his restaurants and more on his products would yield significant business benefits. Third, going public seems like an obvious way to expand his brand and increase opportunities for consumers to have a buying relationship with Emeril. Finally, breaking out of his high-end restaurant mold and considering an upscale fast-food format restaurant chain would introduce other consumers who do not travel to the four cities in which his restaurants are located, giving them a chance to do business with him and sample his cooking.

The main threat to Emeril's continued success is overexposure. At some point, being seen everywhere becomes a liability rather than an asset, and Emeril may eventually approach saturation in this respect.

However, any activity that cheapens the Emeril mystique is a threat—which is why his appearance in a 2003 Crest toothpaste commercial is so puzzling.

Collaborating with Crest

Of all Emeril's forays into the consumer products arena, the one that has raised the most eyebrows is his decision to star in a Crest toothpaste commercial. Although he is never identified other than through his car's personalized license plate, Emeril's well-known visage is seen using Crest Whitening Expressions toothpaste and stating his trademark phrases "BAM!" and "kick it up a notch."

This marketing campaign to introduce the new line of flavored toothpastes cost Procter & Gamble an estimated $80 million. However, given that the U.S. toothpaste market is valued at $1.5 billion,[33] there is significant upside potential from a new product introduction that appeals to a new, or underserved, demographic group.

Celebrity spokesperson Emeril may have appealed to Crest's parent, Procter & Gamble, because of his ethnic background. Part Portuguese, Emeril's Latin looks could be a plus in courting Hispanic customers, who were expected to appreciate the toothpaste's stronger bite. Explains Bryan McCleary, associate director for oral care, "[Hispanics are] more discerning in terms of flavors." Positioned as gourmet toothpastes with a strong cinnamon, citrus, or herbal mint flavor, Crest's link with Emeril is based more on philosophy, says Crest, than anything else. "Emeril's not so much about food as about kicking it up a notch," says McCleary. "He uses spices to enhance food; we wanted to make the brushing experience more exciting."[34]

As Emeril explained the link, "I'm all about surprising people's palates and exceeding their sensory expectations. I wanted to work with Crest Whitening Expressions because the line of pastes shares my view on flavor."[35]

But is Emeril's brand definition truly associated with flavor or with cooking? Despite's Crest insistence that "Emeril's not so much about food," isn't food at the core of the Emeril brand? And if so, does an association with toothpaste really enhance Emeril's image? Or is it just another revenue stream?

"I don't know that that was a wise decision for him [to appear in the commercial]," says Samantha Ettus. Emeril's leveraging of his brand and his trademarked phrases and applying them to someone else's product leaves Ettus wondering why. "He's leveraging this brand he built for someone else's products [Crest's], for someone else to make money off of him," she points out. Although the short-term benefits may be huge, such as in the form of a fee, there may be long-term damage to his brand.

According to Ettus, "Those phrases are indigenous to who he is. Why wouldn't [he] want to apply those to products that [he's] endorsing, believing in, and selling? Or at least products that are in [his] category, [his] industry. Toothpaste is not even close to his industry."

"If [he's] going to put [his] own phrases behind something, put it behind All-Clad or another premium brand," she counsels.[36] A brand that is clearly upscale, quality, and—most important—food-oriented. Cuisinart would have made sense, as would KitchenAid or Jenn-Air, for example—brands associated with making delicious food, rather than cleaning it away.

Other than money, there are few reasons that it would make

sense for Emeril to align his brand with a product that is distanced from his core focus.

The good news for Crest is that following the debut of Emeril's commercial for the company, and the rollout of the product, Whitening Expressions moved Crest past Colgate for market leadership for the first time since 1998.[37] He really did help them kick it up a notch.

11

CHANGING THE IMAGE OF COOKING

I've been criticized by a lot of "foodies" that maybe I don't take it serious enough, or that I am bastardizing a craft that has been a culinary history—religion for hundreds of years.

—Emeril Lagasse[1]

"Oh him? He's rarely here," was the reply restaurant reviewer Sara Roahen got when she asked about Emeril's whereabouts one night at NOLA back in 2001. Although not surprising, it was still disappointing to hear that Emeril was nowhere in sight. Instead, chef de cuisine Joel Morgan was on duty, focusing his attention mainly on expediting orders to waiting guests, reports Roahen.[2]

Noting that his absence was "why busy chefs—even ones without sitcoms—hire chefs de cuisine," Roahen was stating a fact more and more evident in the era of celebrity chefs too busy to run their own restaurants. Not content to remain solely restaurateurs, some of the biggest names in the business are finding new applications for their culinary talents—everything from licensing agreements to TV shows to publishing and beyond. Many have Emeril to thank for some of those opportunities. The groundswell of interest in culinary arts, in part due to Emeril's omnipresence, has led to new career paths and projects for many of America's chefs.

Making Cooking a More Popular Career

Emeril has also opened the door to new opportunities in the culinary arts through his popularity and notoriety. Considering a career in fine dining and food service is now acceptable, even trendy, thanks to Emeril, rather than being unusual or rare as it once was. "Television chefs are almost like rock stars now," says David Finnie, who teaches in the Vancouver School District.[3] While more than two out of five adults have worked in the restaurant industry at some time during their lives, reports the National Restaurant Association,[4] the profession has not always been held in such high esteem as it is today, thanks to Emeril. Degrees from schools such as Johnson & Wales and the Culinary Institute of America are now viewed with more respect. In fact, many culinary programs are growing just to keep up with the demand from students of all ages, since cooking degrees are now perceived as a viable stepping-stone to a satisfying and rich career.

"Students who come here are valedictorians in high school," says Michael Moskwa, director of culinary education at Johnson & Wales University in North Miami, Florida. "I can't imagine the valedictorian of my high school in the '60s saying, 'I'm going to cooking school.' "[5] But today, thanks in part to Emeril, culinary schools represent a professional option not considered a decade or two ago. According to Moskwa, Emeril was the first to bridge the gap between professional chefs and cooks at home.

As of 2004, the restaurant industry is the largest private-sector employer, providing jobs for 12 million workers, or almost 9% of the

U.S. workforce.[6] Those jobs are in more than 878,000 restaurants nationwide, generating sales of an estimated $440 billion in 2004.[7] Sales at full-service restaurants were expected to reach $153.2 billion in 2003, nearly a 5% increase over 2002, with restaurants overall expected to serve more than 70 billion meals and snacks in 2004.[8]

Although the median annual salary for culinary positions is not huge, there is the potential to make it big like Emeril did, which appeals to many students. The annual pay for a sous-chef averages around $30,000 says the National Restaurant Association, with executive chefs making around $48,000. Of course, those chefs who go out on their own have potentially unlimited earning potential; Emeril makes more than $7 million, according to Forbes,[9] and Wolfgang Puck pulls in more than $15 million.

Opening the Kitchen to Men

Although men have historically dominated the culinary profession, holding head positions at the world's greatest hotels and restaurants, women have traditionally controlled the less respected home kitchen. This schism has kept women from rising to the position of executive chef at most top restaurants—including Emeril's, incidentally, where only one chef de cuisine is female—and restricted men from participating in meal preparation at home. Until recently.

"Cooking is cool now," said Emeril in a Playboy interview. "Now men can cook anything."[10]

Emeril has been instrumental in transforming the kitchen at home from a woman's domain to the family's domain, in which the man of the house is more than welcome to partake—even take over—cooking for family and guests. In part because of a cultural change and in part because of Emeril Live, through which Emeril has become a role model for men, it is now acceptable for men to cook at home.

Emeril explains, "In the mid-Seventies, the Department of Labor changed its classification of cooking from a blue-collar to a white-collar profession. Cooking became more respected . . . suddenly men were cooking."[11] Removing the stigma of being women's work allowed men to cultivate their culinary creativity.

James Beard's Influence

But even before that, renowned chef James Beard, the father of American cooking, showed men that it was acceptable to be in the kitchen. Observes Emeril, "Beard influenced a lot of people, particularly men. He was the first man to show that it was OK to be a guy and to cook."[12] Appearing on his own television show, *I Love to Cook*, from 1946 to 1947, Beard, like Emeril, broke new ground.

Growing up in the early 1900s in Portland, Oregon, Beard briefly attended Reed College and then headed abroad to try his hand at acting, touring with a theatrical troupe. Although he kept trying to land theater and movie roles when he returned to the United States in 1927, he eventually accepted that he needed a part-time career to supplement his meager acting wages. So he opened a small food shop called Hors d'Oeuvre, Inc., in 1937, which helped to drive the cocktail party as a respected form of socializing and entertaining. His subsequent book, which was the first major book on cocktail food, *Hors d'Oeuvre and Canapés*, led to a second book, on outdoor cooking, another groundbreaker in terms of its subject matter.

After returning to New York following service in the war, Beard penned several more books, appeared in his own cooking segment on NBC as well as on other networks, and contributed articles and columns to major magazines such as *Woman's Day* and *Gourmet*. He also found time to run his own restaurant on Nantucket while serving as a consultant to other restaurateurs and food producers.

In 1955 he formed the James Beard Cooking School, where he personally taught women and men to cook until his death in 1985. Emphasizing fresh, American ingredients, Beard traveled around the country, teaching. At the same time, he continued to write cook-books that would become American classics, reflecting the era in which they were created.

Although Beard certainly furthered the cause of letting men in the kitchen, Emeril was the tipping point; before him, the kitchen was still somewhat off-limits to men. But after him, having seen someone like them doing what was formerly considered women's work, men are more confident, or less self-conscious, about their culinary interests.

Julia Child's Influence

Interestingly, although most proprietors of haute cuisine were men, one of the best-known chefs before Emeril happened to be a woman. Many Americans relied on Julia Child's cooking tips and guidance for years through her television program, *The French Chef*, which debuted back in 1963. Her on-air persona was authoritative but friendly and, like Emeril, she provided encouragement to women, mainly, who were interested in trying to prepare new dishes.

Fast-forward 40 years and the most popular chef on TV is now a man, whose fan base consists primarily of men age 30 and up. That demographic accounts for 42% of his viewing audience for *Emeril Live*.[13] Not bad for a vocation previously considered appropriate only for women. His second-biggest group of fans is children ages 5 to 15, followed by housewives, who were formerly thought to encom-pass the core fan base.

Emeril echoes this assessment: "The biggest audience for *Emeril Live* is men—college kids to guys 50 and older. And they're not the kinds of guys you might expect to find in aprons. These are regular Joes who come from regular backgrounds. Because it's OK now. You don't have to stay in the closet if you like to cook dinner. You don't have to worry that the guy across the street is going to laugh at you—because he's probably doing the same thing."[14]

Transforming the Mundane into Entertainment

One of the main differences between Julia Child and Emeril Lagasse is that she approached her program as a teacher, which she was, and he approached his as an entertainer, which he was. His years spent touring as a musician in his youth surely shaped how he perceives, and plays to, the audience. The two different approaches reflect their individual backgrounds and in some ways defined how consumers of their time perceived the activity.

"He brought fun to cooking," observes Samantha Ettus, brand expert and president of Ettus Media Management. "Cooking is an industry that is based on precision; on exact measurement. There's something inherently unsexy about such precision. But if you look at what Emeril does, he makes cooking accessible to men and women. He makes it look like something you can do. You don't need to be obsessively precise about it. You can have fun with it."

Anyone who has ever followed a recipe knows how methodical and boring the process can be. Add two teaspoons of this to a cup of that, mix it up, and throw it in the oven. Considered drudgery by some, cooking was certainly not a type of entertainment. It might be a necessary evil, such as in preparation for a shindig at home, but the act of cooking was not generally considered fun. And traditional cooking shows did nothing to dispel that perception.

Although amusing, Child's TV shows were primarily instructive and educational—her videos are even categorized as such—not exciting and fun. She was straightforward, and that is how the American public was trained to view cooking. She is also well loved and can be credited with moving American cuisine beyond mere meat and potatoes. Under her tutelage, women across the country learned about beef bourguignonne and vichyssoise, about selecting the freshest fish and using the best knives. Her approach was practical and informative, because that was her primary goal, informing.

But along came Emeril, a highly respected chef who combined

instruction with entertainment. Instead of plodding through a recipe, ingredient after ingredient, Emeril mixes cooking with comedy, guest appearances, and music. Yes, you have a completed dish at the end, but the whole cooking process is entirely different. It is eatertainment with audience participation. There is laughing, there is joking, and no one is being nitpicky about the exact amount of anything being thrown in the pot.

No longer considered an everyday chore to be avoided, everyone is getting into the act of cooking. More men and children are muscling in on the meal preparation activity, eager to demonstrate a particular recipe or technique they saw Emeril use on his show. Others enjoy simply relaxing and watching someone else cook, rather than doing it themselves. Just as some people enjoy drifting off to sleep watching David Letterman or Jay Leno, others take the same degree of pleasure catching Emeril Lagasse bamming it up on his show.

The concept of blending cooking and entertainment spills over into his restaurants as well, with Emeril's use of the chef's table, or counter. This is the spot where 10 guests can sit on tall chairs inside the restaurant and watch the chef prepare their meal right in front of them, with the kitchen team bustling about in full view behind them. Bowing to demand for visual stimulation during mealtime, Emeril's restaurants provide just that.

In contrast, traditional high-end restaurants keep the kitchen activity tucked away in back, far from the eyes and ears of guests seated at tables in the dining room. Expert chefs toil away, preparing the perfect dish, only to hand it off to the waitperson who promptly delivers it to the customer at the table. As if by magic, the plate appears before the diner, adding to the air of mystery that surrounds haute cuisine. Emeril seems determined to strip away that mystery and let guests in on all the work that goes on in the background, showing patrons of his restaurants that it is not really magic responsible for the delicious creations. After all, he says, "it's not rocket science," which helps the average consumer to understand that good cooking does not have to be mysterious.

The perception of cooking has changed dramatically, thanks to Emeril.

Changing Highbrow Cuisine into Mainstream Eating

Gourmet food has the reputation of being restricted to members of the upper class who can afford to enjoy it, but Emeril has turned that impression on its ear. He has redefined haute cuisine as a level of quality just about anyone can enjoy and appreciate, mainly by educating the American public.

Emphasizing the simplicity and beauty of fresh, local ingredients, Emeril won converts who had been scared off by the perceived complexity and snobbery of gourmet cuisine. Emeril's message is that haute cuisine does not have to be difficult; it just needs to be fresh. "I always tell people that to have great cuisine you just have to have great ingredients prepared honestly. Nothing has to be expensive. Preparations don't have to be complicated," says Emeril.[15]

He had the same effect on Creole cuisine, broadening appreciation for it by introducing it to the masses. Originally a type of food that was appreciated mainly by Louisianans and foodies, Emeril brought it into the mainstream. Through education, demonstration, and appreciation, he taught Americans what Creole cooking was all about and why they should love it, just as he did with what were formerly considered gourmet dishes.

One of his main vehicles for this evolution was his cooking shows, where he could reach millions of people in one broadcast. The content of and approach to *The Essence of Emeril* and *Emeril Live* seek the lowest common denominator among the viewers, keeping the dishes manageable and the ingredients easy to find. "You feel that you could be there with him or you could do this at home after you see what he does," concurs Michael Batterberry, editor in chief of *Food Arts* magazine.[16]

Unlike cooking shows of decades ago, Emeril's energy level on his shows suggests he understands the frenetic pace at which we all live. Rather than showing viewers how to prepare a dish in an hour or two, Emeril is more likely to demonstrate how to get two or three dishes completed in an hour or less. Although gourmet cooking is not known for the speed with which it can be prepared, Emeril has managed to pick up the pace of instruction to help fans make the most of the limited time they have available to cook.

He also has tweaked standard recipes to make them family friendly. Although you will not find Emeril's Spaghetti Pie at any of his restaurants, you will find it in his cookbook and at his web site. Recognizing the struggles parents often face convincing children to eat food that is good for them, Emeril offers ideas for meals that are entertaining *and* feature green vegetables.

Even his restaurants have made gourmet cuisine approachable. Located in more casual, nonthreatening places such as Universal Studios and the MGM Grand Hotel and Casino, several Emeril-owned eateries serve upscale entrées without the formality typical of white-tablecloth bistros. Virtually all his restaurants advertise a business-casual dress code, for instance, and NOLA even allows casual attire, although tank tops and cutoffs are prohibited.

A Sociological Shift: A New Food Culture

Ironically, the rising interest in gourmet cooking—actually, in all things cooking related—contrasts with the number of hours adults (mainly women) have been spending slaving over a hot stove. Two generations ago, mothers spent all day planning, purchasing, cleaning, and preparing the evening's meal. Cooking consumed much of their day. One generation ago, mothers spent a few hours on cooking for the family, though other activities and responsibilities had crept in, too. And today's generation of women spends as little time as possible in the kitchen; hence, the growing number of prepared foods and packaged complete meals lining the supermarket shelves.

Contrasted with the rapidly declining amount of time spent on cooking is a newfound fascination with the activity. Instead of being viewed as a necessary evil, it has evolved into a weekend form of entertainment.

Part of the credit for rejuvenating interest in the skill can be given to television cooking shows, such as Emeril's, which have picked up where Mom may have left off. In fact, members of Generations X and Y may not have learned the basics of cooking from their mothers, who were heading back out into the workforce. Without a solid foundation to build on, consumers are gravitating toward TV chefs who make it look easy. Lacking the basics, pros like Emeril, Martha Stewart, and Lidia Bastianich demonstrate for us, encourage us, and entice us into the somewhat unfamiliar kitchen.

For some, the pull is due to increased home entertaining. With a rise in dining at home with friends, more time, energy, and money is being spent on preparing food for evening get-togethers.

Although Emeril may have fueled consumer interest in gourmet cooking, Martha Stewart can be blamed for kicking entertaining up a notch—placing added emphasis on every aspect of a gathering. In some ways, Emeril and Martha are at odds. Emeril tells us to "have fun" with cooking and loosen up a bit about following the rules, while Martha counsels us on the litany of proper serving utensils needed for the meal to accompany the starched linens, place cards, centerpiece, wineglasses and water goblets, candles—you get the picture.

Both Emeril and Martha, however, happened to recognize growing consumer interest in home-related activities. While Emeril focused on cooking and Martha on entertaining and homekeeping, consumers were nesting or, as Faith Popcorn termed it years ago, *cocooning*. The process of nesting resulted in consumers paying to surround themselves with beauty and convenience, so that they would not need or want to leave their homes to enjoy themselves. Instead of heading out to expensive bistros or bars, as they had during the 1980s, consumers stayed in, inviting friends and family to join them.

As demand for new housing continued to climb in the late 1990s and early 2000s, fueled by lower mortgage interest rates and a rising stock market, consumers remained focused on their homes. Even after September 11, 2001, and the subsequent stock market collapse, housing starts remained strong. Despite higher unemployment figures in late 2003, new home construction accelerated to its fastest pace in 18 years, according to the Department of Commerce.[17] New home construction spurred new home design books and television programs to help Americans feather their nests in style.

Never before had Americans poured so much money into their homes—paying more to own larger spaces and to furnish them properly. Furniture manufacturers thrived, television's Home & Garden Network debuted and flourished, and common household items, such as bedsheets and tableware, moved up market in response to consumer demand for high-end beauty and comfort. Fascination with the kitchen was a natural evolution.

Americans were also becoming more interested in good food, due in part to the increasingly global nature of travel. As more consumers traveled abroad, tasting the cuisine of other countries, they began to appreciate regional styles of cooking, such as Mario Batali's take on Italian, reports the *New York Times*.[18] Well-known chefs became chic and glamorous as yuppies became enamored with fine dining and entertaining. That fascination with everything culinary likewise boosted interest in books such as Anthony Bourdain's *Kitchen Confidential: Adventures in the Culinary Underbelly*.

Increased interest in cooking spawned a new food culture that called for professional-quality appliances, such as a Viking stove, warming drawer, and Subzero freezer in the kitchen. Where one oven was plenty for our parents, two is now the norm in upscale new homes. Granite is the preferred countertop material, with tile or hardwoods on the floor. Cast iron has given way to Calphalon cookware—or Emerilware—and KitchenAid is the mixer must-have. Cooking has morphed from task to lifestyle, as families have rearranged how they live in order to be able to participate more fully.

Rising interest in ethnic cooking, furthered by Emeril's own exploration of lesser-known cuisine, has also pushed the addition of built-in grills and woks, providing flexibility and stylishness. Emeril's respect for and use of ethnic ingredients, recipes, and techniques has boosted interest in preparing a wider range of dishes at home, rather than just going out to eat. In addition to Chinese, Italian, and French cuisine, which have been mainstays in the American diet for decades, consumers can now find Eritrean, Turkish, and Cuban eateries, for example. Sparking curiosity and interest in other cultures, Emeril has expanded our horizons and our palates.

Creating New Choices to Build a Culinary Empire

Emeril has certainly shown Americans how to have fun with food and how to make simple dishes that taste exquisite, as well as more complex ones that are well worth the effort. He is a role model for people of all ages, spurning a new interest in gourmet cooking that has revitalized the culinary industry. The restaurant industry alone is expected to grow 30% by 2005, according to the Bureau of Labor Statistics, adding chef and management positions within organizations to keep pace with consumer demand for dining experiences outside the home.

In addition to impacting consumers, Emeril has also blazed new trails for his colleagues. Karen Page, coauthor, with her husband Andrew Dornenburg, of *Becoming a Chef* (Wiley, 1995), points out that chefs now have opportunities that did not previously exist. "Everybody's got a different place they want to go as a chef. And it's not everybody's dream to have multiple restaurants because it takes the focus away from the cooking. There are going to be chefs who have very personal, single restaurants. But for the first time in history, it's a matter of choice."[19] Where Wolfgang Puck and his chain of Wolfgang Puck Express restaurants are at one end of the continuum, Paul Prudhomme and his stand-alone K-Paul's Louisiana Kitchen are at the other, with Emeril and his nine restaurants somewhere in between. And that is acceptable.

Emeril may also have inspired some colleagues to dream bigger. Previously, it might have been inconceivable to own a restaurant and host a cooking show simultaneously, but now talented chefs know that it is a possibility. Some chefs may have been satisfied with developing and selling a single line of seasonings or sauces, but now they have seen that it is possible to do more—why limit yourself to only one or two products if there are others out there that you admire or that you would like to improve upon? And if traveling is not a problem, Emeril has also proven that geographically dispersed restaurants can be managed from afar if you have the right staff in place.

Well known for developing and pursuing a wide range of business opportunities, Emeril has also shown uncharacteristic restraint in some respects. Although known for his larger-than-life personality and passion for cooking, Emeril has deliberately reined in the number and pace of new restaurants he has opened, choosing to stick to warmer cities where the opportunity is good for everyone. He has also turned down lucrative offers that would impede the functioning of his existing franchise. And he has suggested that he will not be a TV star forever.

Emeril has also demonstrated that marketing is a key factor when it comes to brand building. Investing time and money to promote his restaurants, books, show, and products is required on a regular basis in order to remain a strong brand. Some chefs may not have understood that before, but Emeril has stepped up to the plate to give it a shot. He has shown them that being good at what you do is not enough to make it big, although it certainly helps. Getting the word out starts the whole process of becoming a *celebrity* chef.

The Downside of Entertaining Cooking

With the positives of increasing involvement in cooking come the negatives, say observers, which include diminishing the exclusivity of the field. By making cooking appear simpler, Emeril unintentionally belittles the intensive training and years of service that the country's leading chefs endured to reach their current posts. Most do not appreciate it.

"The programmers have somehow altered the format of Emeril's program so that it's more entertainment than instruction. Not to say that he's not trying to teach. . . . But a lot of people in the business are concerned that it's dumbing down food," observes *Food Arts* magazine's Batterberry.[20]

That potentially translates into lower-quality experiences inside fine dining establishments, where chefs aim to please a wider variety of palates and preferences than ever before. Without a high level of expectation, a restaurant's quality of product and service can easily fall, warn food critics. So far, that has not happened to Emeril, however.

EPILOGUE

There's no denying that television had a great impact in helping us get to where we are today. But, first and foremost, Emeril is a great restaurateur.
—Eric Linquest, Vice President, Emeril's Homebase[1]

Some of Emeril's success can be attributed to being in the right place at the right time: His first restaurant is established in a rundown section of town slated for redevelopment. After Emeril's is named Best Restaurant in the Nation, he meets an acquisitions editor at an industry convention. His first book debuts just as a new television show about cooking is looking for a host. The show, *The Essence of Emeril*, becomes popular as cable networks are catching on nationwide and overworked Americans tune in to be entertained rather than taught. Major hotels begin looking for a new restaurant concept to boost lackluster food and beverage revenues, and branded merchandise takes off as a merchandise concept. Yes, he has been fortunate, but he also knows how to distinguish between synergistic opportunities and wastes of time.

He also understands the value of hiring the best and keeping them. Surrounding himself with the best talent he can find, despite how clichéd that sounds, has been one of his secrets of success. As Emeril's empire has grown—beyond a size that he can personally manage—he has had to put into place individuals who are now responsible for maintaining the same quality levels he set and that guests now expect. He recruits locally, relies on graduates of culinary programs for kitchen positions, and looks for waitstaff who aim to remain waitstaff, and then immerses his candidates in Emerilization for several weeks before introducing them to live customers. It is a formula that has worked in nine restaurants and has resulted in continuing profitability despite a down economy.

As his responsibilities and projects have grown, Emeril has had to rely increasingly on others to help get the work done. New recipes and TV show topics are left primarily to his test kitchen staff to develop, and licensing deals are handled by his in-house counselors and negotiators. Collaborators and ghostwriters are hired to help pull together his best-selling cookbooks, and suppliers are relied on for their expertise in creating quality products Emeril's fans can afford. Although Emeril himself is not involved in every last detail, he does have the final say.

It's All about Control, Baby

Above all else, Emeril's smartest business strategy has been retaining control over virtually every aspect of his company. Although he may not personally be behind the counter in each restaurant, he keeps close tabs on who is doing what and how things are going. He is still involved in recipe development to a large extent, relying more on chefs in the test kitchens than before, but certainly still playing a role. It is also said that he is the ultimate decision maker regarding any aspect of brand management—any decision regarding the use of his name on products is Emeril's alone. *That* he does not delegate.

Not wanting to lose his best employees to the competition or to anywhere else, for that matter, Emeril developed employee retention tools to entice his top workers to stay. These tools have worked.

Beyond above-average earnings—some waiters are said to make over $100,000—staff members are given the opportunity to pursue a career in food service at Emeril's Homebase. Those employees who aspire to be more than a waiter or a sous-chef can work their way up through the organization, potentially earning the opportunity to buy into a restaurant. Once locked into the corporation through part ownership, it becomes costly to leave Emeril's employ.

He is also patient. Rather than giving up financial control in order to open his restaurant more quickly, Emeril doggedly pursued bank financing in the form of a loan. With his reputation and following at Commander's, it is very likely that he had offers of financial backing—private investors—even before he tendered his resignation. But instead of selling off part ownership in order to immediately open the restaurant, he took the more difficult and time-consuming route of debt financing. And that made all the difference.

Emeril's Vision for the Future

While his days and nights are typically filled with work-related activities, his family may ultimately determine the course his company takes. Emeril's third wife, Alden Lovelace Lagasse, and his one-year-old son, E.J., travel with him almost everywhere he goes, providing the stability and support he needs to avoid professional burnout. But there may come a time when he returns to life as a celebrity restaurateur. In 2008, when his Food Network contract expires, Emeril's son will be ready to enter kindergarten and he may be ready to stay closer to home. He has even hinted that his career in television may be coming to a close once his five-year contract is up.

So where can the country's best-known, most popular chef go from here? Some would argue, anywhere. With charm, sincerity, and friendliness going for him, minus any major faux pas, there is little he cannot do. As long as his restaurants continue to maintain the high-quality standards his guests expect, his cooking show remains entertaining, and his products reflect the upscale-but-within-reach positioning he has staked out, the only reason business opportunities would slow would be fickle trendiness. Even then, the company's strong financial position make it an attractive business partner in spite of any minor drop in demand.

One option is obviously to continue expanding the business as before, by adding new restaurants at a pace of about two a year and supplementing the existing line of Emeril-branded products with new merchandise; his upcoming tableware and accessories products suggest this is one road he will take. Cookbooks will continue to be published annually, with regular TV specials, public appearances, and a hefty dose of charity event participation thrown in—as well as the occasional golf game.

Another option is to realign the company's profit centers to allow Emeril to focus on the activity he is enjoying most at the time, whether that is managing his restaurants, supporting charitable causes—including his own foundation—or beefing up the Emeril product line with more kitchen-related merchandise. He has suggested that his TV show will not go on forever, although it will be on the air at least into 2008. During that time, he will have plenty of time to visualize where he wants to go from here. Given his track record, it is very likely he will get there.

ENDNOTES

Introduction

1. *Emeril Lagasse*, VHS (A&E Home Video, 2000).
2. Ibid.
3. David Sheff, "Emeril Lagasse," *Playboy*, February 1999.
4. *Emeril Lagasse* (A&E Home Video).
5. Bonnie Warren, "The Emeril Empire," *New Orleans Magazine*, December 2001.

Chapter 1

1. Victor a Forrest, "BAM. It's Emeril Lagasse," Fabulous Foods.com.
2. John Grossmann, "Recipe for Success," *Cigar Aficionado*, January/February 1998.
3. Ibid.
4. *Emeril Lagasse* (A&E Home Video).
5. "Emeril Lagasse," Parenting.com, July 2002.
6. *Emeril Lagasse* (A&E Home Video).
7. Biography Resource Center, Gale Group, 2003.
8. Ric Oliveira, "Emeril's Food Fans Eat It Up," Fall River, Massachusetts, *Standard-Times*, December 12, 1997.
9. Grossmann, "Recipe for Success."
10. Emeril Lagasse biography, Gale Resource Group, 2001.
11. Emeril Lagasse, *Emeril's New New Orleans Cooking* (New York: William Morrow, 1993), 309.
12. Linda Richards, "Emeril Lagasse," *January*, November 2000.
13. *Emeril Lagasse* (A&E Home Video).
14. Oliveira, "Emeril's Food Fans Eat It Up."
15. *Emeril Lagasse* (A&E Home Video).
16. Grossmann, "Recipe for Success."
17. *Emeril Lagasse* (A&E Home Video).
18. "Celeb Chef Stirs Up a Passion for Food," CNN.com, 2001.
19. Grossmann, "Recipe for Success."
20. Sheff, "Emeril Lagasse."
21. Ibid.

22. "Celeb Chef Stirs Up," CNN.com.
23. Sheff, "Emeril Lagasse."
24. "Celeb Chef Stirs Up," CNN.com.
25. Richards, "Emeril Lagasse."
26. Andrew Dornenburg and Karen Page, *Becoming a Chef* (New York: Wiley, 1995), 182.
27. Sheff, "Emeril Lagasse."
28. Grossmann, "Recipe for Success."
29. Sheff, "Emeril Lagasse."
30. Sandra Berger, "Mentor Relationships and Gifted Learners," ERIC Clearinghouse on Disabilities and Gifted Education, 1990.
31. Grossmann, "Recipe for Success."
32. *Emeril Lagasse* (A&E Home Video).
33. Ibid.
34. "Celeb Chef Stirs Up," CNN.com.
35. Grossmann, "Recipe for Success."
36. Sheff, "Emeril Lagasse."
37. *Emeril Lagasse* (A&E Home Video).
38. Grossmann, "Recipe for Success."
39. Ibid.
40. *Emeril Lagasse* (A&E Home Video).
41. Phone interview with Rene Petrin, January 27, 2004.

Chapter 2

1. Laura Yee, "Ella Brennan on a Half Century in the Family Business," *Restaurants and Institutions,* May 15, 2000.
2. Mary Beth Romig-Price, "Chef of the Year: Emeril Lagasse, Makin' Music in the Kitchen," *New Orleans Magazine,* September 1993.
3. *Emeril Lagasse* (A&E Home Video).
4. Ibid.
5. Grossmann, "Recipe for Success."
6. Phone interview with Tom Fitzmorris, December 2003.
7. Donna Balancia, " 'Wunderchef' Cooks Up a Fortune," TCPalm.com, December 8, 2003.
8. *Emeril Lagasse* (A&E Home Video).
9. Sheff, "Emeril Lagasse."
10. Lagasse, *Emeril's New New Orleans Cooking.*
11. Thomas Matthews, "Emeril Live," *Wine Spectator,* August 31, 1999.
12. Ibid.
13. Ibid.
14. *Emeril Lagasse* (A&E Home Video).
15. Dornenburg and Page, *Becoming a Chef.*
16. Jane Alexander, "Emeril's Favorite Dish," *South,* September/October 2003.

17. Robert Sullivan, "The Golfing Gourmet," *Travel & Leisure Golf,* November 1998.

18. "Ella Brennan," *Louisiana Legends,* May 17, 1998.

Chapter 3

1. Dennis Love, "Ready for Prime Time," (cookbook review), www.ireadpages.com, November/December 2001.

2. Richards, "Emeril Lagasse."

3. *Emeril Lagasse* (A&E Home Video).

4. Sheff, "Emeril Lagasse."

5. *Marquis Who's Who.*

6. Romig-Price, "Chef of the Year."

7. John Tanasychuk, "Despite His TV Shows, Millions of Cookbooks and Celebrity Status, America's Most Famous Chef Is Still Just Emeril," *Sun-Sentinel,* November 6, 2003.

8. Emeril interview with Patty Gay, February 9, 2004.

9. Liz Scott, "The Emeril Aisle!," *New Orleans Magazine,* March 1997.

10. Ibid.

11. Grossmann, "Recipe for Success."

12. Ibid.

13. Pamela Parseghian, "The New New Orleans," *Nation's Restaurant News,* February 1, 1993.

14. Sheff, "Emeril Lagasse."

15. Parseghian, "The New New Orleans."

16. Carolyn Walkup, "Emeril Lagasse: The Essence of the Big Easy's TV-Star Chef Is That Food Is His Life, His Love and His Passion," *Nation's Restaurant News,* January 1997.

17. Ibid.

18. Walkup, "Emeril Lagasse."

19. "Chef Larry Forgione," Travel Channel profile, travel.discovery.com.

20. "Chef Larry Forgione," CuisineNet.com.

21. Leslie Crawford, "Brilliant Careers: Alice Waters," Salon.com, November 16, 1999.

22. Kathy Finn, "When Chefs Open a Second Restaurant," *New Orleans Magazine,* September 1993.

23. Phone interview with Marty Kotis, January 28, 2004.

24. Tanasychuk, "Despite His TV Shows."

25. Walkup, "Emeril Lagasse."

26. Finn, "When Chefs Open a Second Restaurant."

27. Phone interview with John Mariani, January 19, 2004.

28. Mariani phone interview, January 19, 2004.

29. Phone interview with Lisa Ekus, November 25, 2003.

30. Ibid.

31. Ibid.

32. Scott, "The Emeril Aisle."

33. Ibid.

34. Romig-Price, "Chef of the Year."
35. "Chefs Shake Up the Cookbook Market," *Publishing Trends*, August 2000.
36. Ibid.
37. Ibid.

Chapter 4

1. *Emeril Lagasse* (A&E Home Video).
2. Robert Rastelli, "Food Network Spices Up Its Lineup," *Seattle Times*, January 14, 2004.
3. 2002 E.W. Scripps Annual Report.
4. Kristin Eddy, "Chefs Right at Home," *Chicago Tribune*, October 29, 2003.
5. Associated Press, "Food Network Steaming Hot Channel Serves Surprise Success," *Cincinnati Post*, September 9, 2001.
6. Rastelli, "Food Network Spices Up Its Lineup."
7. Food Network web site, February 2, 2004.
8. 2002 E.W. Scripps Annual Report.
9. Phone interview with Samantha Ettus, October 12, 2003.
10. Emeril Lagasse, *Emeril's TV Dinners* (New York: William Morrow, 1998).
11. Ibid.
12. Phone interview with Tom Fitzsimmons, December 15, 2003.
13. Sheff, "Emeril Lagasse."
14. *Emeril Lagasse* (A&E Home Video).
15. Lagasse, *Emeril's TV Dinners*.
16. Sheff, "Emeril Lagasse."
17. Ibid.
18. *Emeril Lagasse* (A&E Home Video).
19. Malcolm Gladwell, *The Tipping Point* (Boston: Little, Brown, 2000).
20. *Emeril Lagasse* (A&E Home Video).
21. Lagasse, *Emeril's TV Dinners*.
22. *Emeril Lagasse* (A&E Home Video).
23. Barbara Durbin, "Network Staff Cook the Book," *The Oregonian*, December 23, 2003.
24. Sheff, "Emeril Lagasse."
25. Lagasse, *Emeril's TV Dinners*.
26. Sullivan, "The Golfing Gourmet."
27. *Emeril Lagasse* (A&E Home Video).
28. Matthews, "Emeril Live."
29. Phone interview with H.G. Parsa, January 23, 2004.
30. Mariani phone interview, January 19, 2004.
31. Eddy, "Chefs Right at Home."
32. Sheff, "Emeril Lagasse."
33. http://tv.zap2it.com/tveditorial/tve_main/1,1002,271%7C85126%7C1%7C,00.html.
34. "Emeril Lagasse," Biography Resource Center, Gale Group, 2003.

35. Kimberley McGee, "Cooking Up Comedy," *Las Vegas Sun*, October 11, 2001.
36. McGee, "Cooking Up Comedy."
37. "Celeb Chef Stirs Up," CNN.com.
38. Ibid.
39. Parsa phone interview, January 23, 2004.
40. Gladwell, *The Tipping Point*.
41. Ekus phone interview, November 25, 2003.
42. Phone interview with Robert Manasier, January 26, 2004.
43. Sheff, "Emeril Lagasse."
44. Ibid.
45. "Julia Child," Starchefs.com.
46. "Julia Child Biography," Chef2Chef.com.

Chapter 5

1. Ray Richmond, "An Epicure All," *Hollywood Reporter*, November 18, 2003.
2. Phone interview with Stephen Perry, November 17, 2003.
3. Phone interview with Brett Anderson, February 6, 2004.
4. Backgrounder provided by Sabrina Written of New Orleans Public Facility Management, February 9, 2004.
5. New Orleans Metropolitan Convention and Visitors Bureau web site.
6. Ibid.
7. Ibid.
8. Ibid.
9. S. Written, February 9, 2004.
10. E-mail information supplied by Arleen Kropf of New York City Visitors Bureau, February 9, 2004.
11. Jennifer Shubinski, "UNLV Economists See Modest Local Growth in 2003," *Las Vegas Sun*, December 18, 2002.
12. E-mail interview with Michael Hughes, March 5, 2004.
13. Perry phone interview, November 17, 2003.
14. Anderson phone interview, March 6, 2004.
15. A. Lee Levert, "The Emeril Touch," *Horizon Magazine*, 2000.
16. E-mail interview with Patty Gay, Preservation Resource Center, February 9, 2004.
17. Richards, "Emeril Lagasse."
18. Ibid.
19. Levert, "The Emeril Touch."
20. Ibid.
21. "Meet the Chef," chefpaul.com.
22. Grossmann, "Recipe for Success."
23. Fitzmorris, phone interview, December 15, 2003.
24. E-mail interview with Tom Fitzmorris, February 9, 2004.

25. Ibid.
26. Ibid.
27. Warren, "The Emeril Empire."
28. Ibid.
29. Ibid.
30. Tanasychuk, "Despite His TV Shows."
31. Ibid.
32. Anderson phone interview, February 6, 2004.
33. Tanasychuk, "Despite His TV Shows."
34. "Chef Profile," Travel Channel.

Chapter 6

1. J.T. Harris, "3,000 Fans Wait Hours to See Emeril . . . BAM!," Treasure Coast Palm.com, December 10, 2003.
2. R.W. Apple Jr., "In Las Vegas, Top Restaurants Are the Hot New Game," *New York Times*, February 18, 1998.
3. Ibid.
4. Ibid.
5. E-mail interview with Marty Kotis, February 22, 2004.
6. "Lagasse Opens Las Vegas Eatery," *Nation's Restaurant News*, November 27, 1995.
7. Apple, "In Las Vegas, Top Restaurants."
8. "Lagasse Opens Las Vegas Eatery."
9. Dawn Iacobucci (ed.), *Kellogg on Marketing* (New York: John Wiley, 2001), 122.
10. *Emeril Lagasse* (A&E Home Video).
11. Ibid.
12. Ibid.
13. Jeff Wuorio, "How Business Failure Paves the Way to Success," bCentral.com.
14. Ibid.
15. Ben McConnell and Jackie Huba, *Creating Customer Evangelists* (Chicago: Dearborn Trade Publishing, 2003), 8.
16. *Emeril Lagasse* (A&E Home Video).
17. Walkup, "Emeril Lagasse."
18. Ibid.
19. *Emeril Lagasse* (A&E Home Video).
20. J.J. Miller, "Anthony Bourdain's Braises and Praises," *O Magazine*, March 2004.

Chapter 7

1. James Gordon, "Emeril Lagasse," *Nation's Restaurant News*, January 27, 2003.
2. Richards, "Emeril Lagasse."

3. 2003 *Restaurant Industry Operations Report*, National Restaurant Association.

4. Reagan Walker, "Recipes for Success," *Atlanta Journal-Constitution*, August 25, 2003.

5. Tanasychuk, "Despite His TV Shows."

6. E-mail interview with Les McKeown, February 19, 2004.

7. Ibid.

8. Jeffrey Pfeffer, *The Human Equation* (Boston: Harvard Business School Press, 1998), 16.

9. Culinary Institute of America, *Remarkable Service* (New York: John Wiley, 2001), x.

10. Phone interview with Hugh Rushing, January 5, 2004.

11. Ben Rand, "Massive Layoffs," Rochester, New York, *Democrat and Chronicle*, January 22, 2004.

12. Pfeffer, *The Human Equation*, 66.

13. Ibid., 69.

14. Harvard University web site, undergraduate admissions statistics, February 13, 2004.

15. Pfeffer, *The Human Equation*, 74.

16. Warren, "The Emeril Empire."

17. Jane Clover Alexander, "Inside Emeril's Empire," *South*, September/October 2003.

18. Ibid.

19. Ibid.

20. 2003 *Restaurant Industry Operations Report*, National Restaurant Association and Deloitte and Touche, 2003, 79.

21. Warren, "The Emeril Empire."

22. Bob Mervine, "Tchoup Chop! The Bam Man Is Back in Town," *Orlando Business Journal*, January 31, 2003.

23. Tanasychuk, "Despite His TV Shows."

24. Phone interview with Isidore Kharasch, February 10, 2004.

25. Gordon, "Emeril Lagasse."

26. Tanasychuk, "Despite His TV Shows."

27. Tim Schooley, "Cranberry Franchisee Brings Wolfgang Puck Express Here," *Pittsburgh Business Times*, April 11, 2003.

28. Piper Jaffray industry note, January 8, 2004.

29. Ibid.

30. H.G. Parsa, "Restaurant Failure Rate Much Lower Than Commonly Assumed, Study Finds," study presented at the International Council on Hotel, Restaurant and Institutional Education, Palm Springs, 2003.

31. Gordon, "Emeril Lagasse."

32. E-mail interview with Marty Kotis, February 11, 2004.

33. Ibid.

34. 2003 *Restaurant Industry Operations Report*.

35. "A Food Empire's Key Ingredient," Business Week Online, February 21, 2002.

36. Ibid.

37. Janie Ginocchio, "Tigers in the Kitchen," *Arkansas Times*, January 30, 2004.

38. Phone interview with Art Brief, January 15, 2004.

39. Dornenburg and Page, *Becoming a Chef.*
40. Ibid.
41. Gordon, "Emeril Lagasse."
42. Ibid.
43. Dun & Bradstreet credit report.
44. 2003 *Restaurant Industry Operations Report.*
45. Iacobucci, *Kellogg on Marketing,* 6.

Chapter 8

1. Scott Allmendinger, "Emeril Lagasse, Emeril's," *Restaurant Business,* June 10, 1990.
2. Mervine, "Tchoup Chop!"
3. Ibid.
4. Warren, "The Emeril Empire."
5. Gordon, "Emeril Lagasse."
6. Todd Pack, "Growing Number of High-End Hotels Bringing in Name Chefs," *Orlando Sentinel,* February 10, 2003.
7. Rebecca Oliva, "Taking Control," *Hotels,* May 2001.
8. Pack, "Growing Number of High-End Hotels."
9. Ibid.
10. Ibid.
11. "How to Find Strategic Alliance Partners," Corporate Partnering Institute web site, February 15, 2004.
12. Thomas Matthews, "Gambling Gourmets," *Wine Spectator,* September 15, 1999.
13. Ibid.
14. "How to Find Strategic Alliance Partners."
15. "Emeril Brings Home Bacon to Sister Lillian," New Orleans *Clarion Herald,* May 11, 2000.
16. Grossmann, "Recipe for Success."
17. Heather McPherson,, "Passion Flavors His Creations," *Orlando Sentinel,* October 12, 2000.
18. Ibid.

Chapter 9

1. Parsa phone interview, January 23, 2004.
2. Rushing phone interview, January 5, 2004.
3. Parsa phone interview, January 23, 2004.
4. Warren, "The Emeril Empire."
5. Ibid.
6. Ibid.
7. Walkup, "Emeril Lagasse."
8. Parsa phone interview, January 23, 2004.

9. Walker, "Recipes for Success."
10. E-mail interview with Donna Jo Napoli, February 17, 2004.
11. Ibid.
12. Scott, "The Emeril Aisle!"
13. Mariani phone interview, January 19, 2004.
14. Scott, "The Emeril Aisle!"
15. Tanasychuk, "Despite His TV Shows."
16. "Chef Profiles: Anne Kearney," Countrycook.com, 2001.
17. E-mail interview with Isidore Kharasch, February 27, 2004.
18. McGee, "Cooking Up Comedy."
19. Balancia, " 'Wunderchef' Cooks Up a Fortune."
20. Walker, "Recipes for Success."
21. John Kessler, "Eat: Lost in Translation," *Atlanta Journal-Constitution*, October 23, 2003.
22. Adrienne Packer, "Chef Apologizes for Table-Top Antics of Television Host at Strip Restaurant," *Las Vegas Sun*, August 4, 1999.
23. Richard Eldredge, "Emeril Embroiled in Q100 Brouhaha," *Atlanta Journal-Constitution*, October 17, 2003.
24. Ibid.

Chapter 10

1. Ettus phone interview, October 12, 2003.
2. "All-Clad Metalcrafters' Multi-Year Brand-Building Marketing PR Program," Ptanaka .com.
3. Patricia Talorico, "Emeril Keeps Focus on Reality, Not Television," Wilmington, Delaware, *News Journal*, October 15, 2003.
4. Balancia, " 'Wunderchef' Cooks Up a Fortune."
5. Ibid.
6. Phone interview with Marty Broxteen, March 1, 2004.
7. Talorico, "Emeril Keeps Focus on Reality."
8. Ibid.
9. Peter Jensen, "Heavy Metal," Baltimore *Sun*, November 5, 2003.
10. Ibid.
11. Elizabeth Large, "Flash in the Pan," Baltimore *Sun*, December 10, 2003.
12. Jensen, "Heavy Metal."
13. Thyra Porter, "All-Clad: Extra Plans in Store for Emerilware," *HFN*, January 20, 2003.
14. Jensen, "Heavy Metal."
15. Balancia, " 'Wunderchef' Cooks Up a Fortune."
16. Porter, "All-Clad."
17. Large, "Flash in the Pan."
18. MaryAnn Worobiec, "Emeril Kicks It Up a Notch," *Wine Spectator*, March 31, 2003.

19. Ibid.
20. Ibid.
21. Jessica Materna, "Emeril Will Promote Fetzer," *San Francisco Business Times*, September 1, 2000.
22. Business Wire, Fetzer Vineyards, July 27, 2000.
23. Emeril Lagasse biography, Gale Group, July 2001.
24. Business Wire, Fetzer Vineyards, July 27, 2000.
25. Darren O'Donoghue, "The Essence of Emeril," *TV Guide*, August 18, 2001.
26. Balancia, " 'Wunderchef' Cooks Up a Fortune."
27. "B&G Kicks It Up a Notch," *Supermarket Business*, September 15, 2000.
28. Balancia, " 'Wunderchef' Cooks Up a Fortune."
29. Ibid.
30. Ibid.
31. "Emeril's New Edge," *HFN*, September 16, 2002.
32. "YouthPulse 2003," Harris Interactive.
33. Associated Press, "Consumers Help Companies Develop Products," *Lancaster Eagle-Gazette*, November 29, 2003.
34. Aude Lagorce, "Spice for Your Smile," Forbes.com, October 27, 2003.
35. Food editor, "Tired of Mint? Emeril Kicks Up Toothpaste," Arlington Heights, Illinois, *Daily Herald*, September 24, 2003.
36. Ettus phone interview, October 12, 2003.
37. Jack Neff, "The Man Who Turned P&G Around," AdAge.com, February 23, 2004.

Chapter 11

1. *Emeril Lagasse* (A&E Home Video).
2. Sara Roahen, "Bam It!," *Gambit Weekly*, July 10, 2001.
3. Tan Vinh, "High Schools Whipping Up New Interest in Cooking," *Seattle Times*, January 22, 2004.
4. National Restaurant Association, FAQs, www.restaurant.org, February 13, 2004.
5. Tanaschuk, "Despite His TV Show."
6. 2003 *Restaurant Industry Operations Report*, 6.
7. National Restaurant Association, FAQs, February 13, 2004.
8. Ibid.
9. "The Celebrity 100," *Forbes*, June 19, 2003.
10. Scheff, "Emeril Lagasse."
11. Ibid.
12. Ibid.
13. Scott, "The Emeril Aisle!"
14. Scheff, "Emeril Lagasse."
15. Ibid.
16. *Emeril Lagasse* (A&E Home Video).

17. Mark Gongloff, "Starts Swell, but No Bubble," CNN.com, November 19, 2003.

18. William Grimes, "From Emeril to Dweezil, It's Not Just about Arugula Anymore," *New York Times*, January 11, 2004.

19. Tanaschuk, "Despite His TV Show."

20. *Emeril Lagasse* (A&E Home Video).

Epilogue

1. Gordon, "Emeril Lagasse."

ACKNOWLEDGMENTS

Foodies and nonfoodies alike helped make this book possible, giving me a behind-the-scenes look at what it's really like to manage a multi-faceted culinary empire like Emeril's Homebase. Thank you to everyone who invested their time to help me, including Brett Anderson, William Arruda, Art Brief, Marty Broxteen, Lisa Ekus, Samantha Ettus, Todd Finkle, Tom Fitzmorris, Randy Herz, Isidore Kharasch, Marty Kotis, Gregg Lederman, Robert Manasier, John Mariani, Donna Jo Napoli, H.G. Parsa, Stephen Perry, Rene Petrin, Hugh Rushing, Curt Sahakian, and Michael Sands, as well as those who chose to remain anonymous.

This book would never have happened if not for my agent, Susan Barry, of the Barry-Swayne Literary Agency, who suggested it.

Jeanne Glasser and Pamela van Giessen shepherded the book through the editorial process at Wiley, with the help of Ruth Mills, Melissa Scuereb, Lara Murphy, Alexia Meyers, and Jennifer Mac-Donald.

Thanks, too, to my writing colleagues at ASJA and FLX, who are so generous with their knowledge and experience.

My family, Charlie, Grant, and Amanda, also deserve thanks for keeping me smiling throughout the project, and my friend Sandy Beckwith has my deepest appreciation for her help with writing-related questions.

INDEX